W9-BLL-840

# HEMINGWAY AND THE MOVIES

# Hemingway and the Movies

Frank M. Laurence

UNIVERSITY PRESS OF MISSISSIPPI
Jackson

THIS BOOK IS AUTHORIZED
AND SPONSORED BY
MISSISSIPPI UNIVERSITY FOR WOMEN



**Library of Congress Cataloging in Publication Data**

Laurence, Frank M.
Hemingway and the movies.
Originally presented as the author's thesis, University of Pennsylvania.
Bibliography: p.
Includes index.
1. Hemingway, Ernest, 1899–1961—Film. adaptations. 2. Film adaptations. I. Title.
PS3515.E37Z689 1980 813'.52 79–56697
ISBN 0–87805–115–5

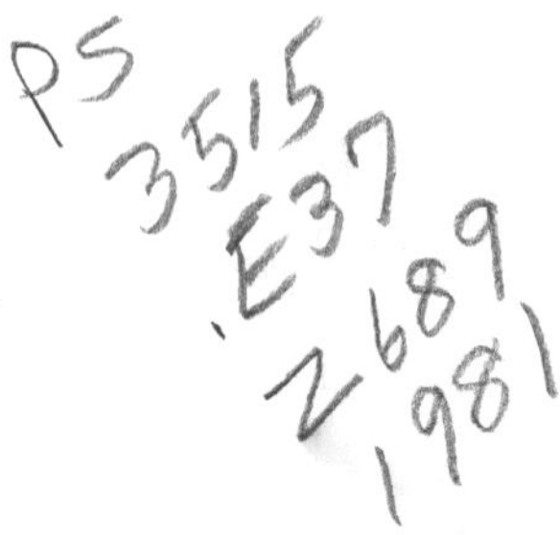

*In memory of my grandfather,*
*Daniel Laurence,*
*and for my parents,*
*Daniel C. and Myrl L. Laurence*

# Contents

# Acknowledgments

In my first semester as a graduate student at the University of Pennsylvania I took a very fine, very intense seminar in Fitzgerald and Hemingway with Professor Robert F. Lucid. Dr. Lucid gave me his interest in the subject of the writer as public figure, he helped me develop a dissertation topic on the Hemingway movies, and he persuaded the graduate faculty to accept it as a field of research for a Ph.D. in English. After I had the degree, he continued to recommend the research as having some further purpose, and he helped with extensive revisions. I am grateful that his interest has continued so long. Ten years after graduate school I still wish there could be a Lucid seminar for me to take.

When living in Philadelphia, I used to watch film classics on a television program called "The Movie Buff." The host for the series was David Mallery, Director of Studies of the National Association of Independent Schools and a member of the Board of Trustees of the American Film Institute. David Mallery answered various short questions for me when I would write to him at the TV station. Years later, when I began to do the dissertation over again as a book, he offered me more elaborate judgments and excellent stories. He did this for me in many long, encouraging letters, for actually we never have met. I cannot imagine a better reader for a book about movies, for he is endlessly interested in the subject.

Carlos Baker allowed me to use the files of letters and interview notes from which he wrote *Ernest Hemingway: A Life Story*. He was very helpful to me during the several days I visited with him at Princeton.

The movie studios have helped me find scripts and allowed me to use them; also to use frames. I am grateful to Paramount, Twentieth Century-Fox, United Artists, Universal-MCA, and Warner Communications.

I have done research for this book at a number of libraries: the American Academy of Motion Picture Arts and Sciences, the American Film Institute, the Theatre Collection of the New York City Library, the Museum of Modern Art, the University of California at Los Angeles, the University of Southern California, and Washington University. I am grateful for all the courtesies extended to me.

I spent many, many hours viewing film prints at the Motion Picture Section of the Library of Congress, where the staff gave me every assistance, even with the complicated directions down to the cafeteria. I would particularly like to thank Pat Sheehan for all the miscellaneous information he has found out for me since this project began. He has been my best reference source.

Many of the good stories about the making of the Hemingway movies came directly from the movie people, as Hemingway called them. I sent out a file drawer full of letters. Most of them were answered, if only by a note in the margin, but often at length. I hope that I remembered to thank everyone for any point of information. The people cited here sent pages and pages of letters, or they gave me interviews when I could get to New York or out to Los Angeles. They were generous in many ways—by letting me use their scripts, for example, and always by giving their interest and cooperation. It has been so long since I wrote or talked to some of them that I guess they have assumed the project never was finished. Some of them will see the book, and I hope that they approve.

I will remain grateful to Leland Hayward and Peter Viertel for information about *The Old Man and the Sea*; to Helen Hayes for her recollections about *A Farewell to Arms*; to Howard Hawks, Ranald MacDougall, Daniel Mainwaring, and Donald Siegel, regarding the several movies made from *To Have and Have Not*; to Ingrid Bergman and Mrs. Goddard Lieberson (Vera Zorina) for sharing with me stories about the casting of *For Whom the Bell Tolls*; to A. E. Hotchner, for explaining to me the history of the writing of his script for *Hemingway's Adventures of a Young Man* and his other Hemingway adaptations; to Peter Bart, Franklin Schaffner, George C. Scott, and Ken Wales for talking to me about *Islands in the Stream* even before it was finished; to Jay Weston, for sharing with me his plans for the biographical picture.

Mrs. Mary Hemingway has helped by both letters and conversations, especially with the material in the chapter about *The Old Man and the Sea*. I hope that the book seems to her to have integrity.

Many student assistants have been involved with the tedious typing of this manuscript. At least it did not have to be done on the mimeograph contraption. I would like to thank them collectively for their careful work.

J. Barney McKee, Director of the University Press of Mississippi, has been very patient during the editing. I would like to thank him for his enthusiasm for the production of a movie book.

Friends have been very encouraging, of course: among them, John Davis (who spotted production details about *For Whom the Bell Tolls*), Joe Durfee, John Garvick, and Walter Merrill.

My wife and children have kept awfully good temperaments about "the book" year after year. Michael (eleven) and Valérie (six) are getting to be old enough to help me with the research if there is a next book, and then it won't take so much time away from family.

In this last paragraph I would like to thank my faculty colleagues on the Research Committee for the travel allowances and research grants summer after summer. I am grateful to three Directors of Research, Harvey Cromwell, Ellie Mae Sowder, and James Murrell, for having presented my proposals to the Committee with their favorable recommendations. I also appreciate the strong support for my work from the administration: my chairman, Ralph Hitt, two Deans of Arts and Sciences, Don King and Charles Lucht, especially the Vice President for Academic Affairs, Harvey M. Craft, and two MUW Presidents, Charles P. Hogarth and James W. Strobel.

Frank M. Laurence
Mississippi University for Women
Columbus, Mississippi

# Preface: Main Titles

Over the years Hollywood has produced fifteen movies from Ernest Hemingway's stories and novels, sometimes adapting the same work two or even three times.

1. *A Farewell to Arms*, Paramount, 1932; produced and directed by Frank Borzage; screenplay by Benjamin Glazer and Oliver H. P. Garrett; starring Gary Cooper and Helen Hayes.
2. *For Whom the Bell Tolls*, Paramount, 1943; produced and directed by Sam Wood; screenplay by Dudley Nichols; starring Gary Cooper and Ingrid Bergman.
3. *To Have and Have Not*, Warner Brothers—First National, 1944; produced and directed by Howard Hawks; screenplay by Jules Furthman and William Faulkner; starring Humphrey Bogart and Lauren Bacall.
4. *The Killers*, Universal, 1946; produced by Mark Hellinger; directed by Robert Siodmak; screenplay by Anthony Veiller; starring Burt Lancaster and Ava Gardner.
5. *The Macomber Affair* (based on "The Short Happy Life of Francis Macomber"), United Artists, 1947; produced by Benedict Bogeaus; directed by Zoltan Korda; screenplay by Casey Robinson and Seymour Bennett; starring Gregory Peck and Joan Bennett.
6. *Under My Skin* (based on "My Old Man"), Twentieth Century-Fox, 1950; produced by Casey Robinson; directed by Jean Negulesco; screenplay by Casey Robinson; starring John Garfield and Micheline Prelle.
7. *The Breaking Point* (based on *To Have and Have Not*), Warner Brothers—First National, 1950; produced by Jerry Wald; directed by Michael Curtiz; screenplay by Ranald MacDougall; starring John Garfield and Patricia Neal.
8. *The Snows of Kilimanjaro*, Twentieth Century-Fox, 1952; pro-

duced by Darryl F. Zanuck; directed by Henry King; screenplay by Casey Robinson; starring Gregory Peck, Susan Hayward, and Ava Gardner.

9. *The Sun Also Rises*, Twentieth Century-Fox, 1957; produced by Darryl F. Zanuck; directed by Henry King; screenplay by Peter Viertel; starring Tyrone Power and Ava Gardner.

10. *A Farewell to Arms*, The Selznick Studio/Twentieth Century-Fox, 1958; produced by David O. Selznick; directed by Charles Vidor; screenplay by Ben Hecht; starring Rock Hudson and Jennifer Jones.

11. *The Gun Runners* (based on *To Have and Have Not*) Seven Arts/United Artists, 1958; produced by Clarence Greene; directed by Don Siegel; screenplay by Daniel Mainwaring and Paul Monash; starring Audie Murphy and Patricia Owens.

12. *The Old Man and the Sea*, Warner Brothers, 1958; produced by Leland Hayward; directed by John Sturges; screenplay by Peter Viertel; starring Spencer Tracy.

13. *Hemingway's Adventures of a Young Man* (based on selected Nick Adams stories), Twentieth Century-Fox, 1962; produced by Jerry Wald; directed by Martin Ritt; screenplay by A. E. Hotchner; starring Richard Beymer and Susan Strasberg.

14. *The Killers*, Universal, 1964; produced and directed by Donald Siegel; screenplay by Gene L. Coon; starring Lee Marvin, Angie Dickinson, John Cassavetes, and Ronald Reagan.

15. *Islands in the Stream*, Paramount, 1977; produced by Peter Bart and Max Palevsky; directed by Franklin J. Schaffner; screenplay by Denne Bart Petitclerc; starring George C. Scott.

This is not a very detailed list. Complete production credits and cast lists are given in the Appendix.

One cannot depend on a title to identify a Hemingway movie, because producers were free to change Hemingway's titles. Also, there have been movies with Hemingway titles only by coincidence, movies having nothing to do with his stories. *After the Storm* (Columbia, 1928), *In Our Time* (Warner Brothers, 1944), and *The Undefeated* (Twentieth Century-Fox, 1970) are instances of this. In 1930 Fox Film Corporation paid Hemingway for the use of the title *Men Without Women* for a movie about the rescue of a trapped submarine crew. (The studio did not have to settle with Hemingway, for titles of themselves are not protected by copyright law.) In 1941 Soundies Corporation made a cartoon called "For Whom the Bell Tolls," and a few years later the Disney studio made a Goofy cartoon called "For Whom the Bull Toils." Feeble comic play on that Hemingway title turns up now and again, as in a newspaper ad for an employment agency, "For Whom the Belles Toil."

On the other hand, a number of movies without Hemingway titles have a more or less obvious similarity to his material. *The Last Flight* (First National, 1931) is about four wounded aviators in Paris after the war, recalling Jake Barnes, the wounded aviator of *The Sun Also Rises*. One of them falls in love with a liberated woman of Brett Ashley's style, and they all go to Lisbon for the bullfights. *The Last Flight* was adapted from John Monk Saunder's novel *Single Lady*, which seems to have been an imitation of the Hemingway book.

*Force of Arms* (Warner Brothers, 1951) seems like a very faint imitation of *A Farewell to Arms*, now with a World War II background. An American soldier is wounded, then falls in love with a WAC officer before going back to the front. Warner Brothers did own the rights to *A Farewell to Arms* at the time, and of course the studio knew the extent of the similarity. However, Hemingway's name was not listed in the credits. Story credit was given to Richard Tregaskis, author of *Guadalcanal Diary*.

*Fighter Attack* (Allied Artists, 1953) was a blatant copy of *For Whom the Bell Tolls*. *Fighter Attack* is the saga of an American pilot (played by Sterling Hayden) shot down in Italy who helps a band of mountain fighters blow a Nazi tunnel. "Roberto," that is, Robert Jordan of *For Whom the Bell Tolls*, is "Steffano" in *Fighter Attack*, Maria is Nina (played by Joy Page). Nina, like Maria, has had bad experiences with the enemy. Also, Miss Page styles her hair the same way Ingrid Bergman did hers as Maria. Pablo of *For Whom the Bell Tolls* has lost some of his keenness for the fighting, it seems to the others. He was once the much feared leader of the guerrillas, but now he has too much wealth in his horses, perhaps, and too much comfort, and he does not wish to be driven out of the mountains after they blow up the bridge. Bruno of *Fighter Attack*, who is a brute of Pablo's kind, is also a little too cautious in fighting—because his poor aged mother lives in the village near the tunnel they have to destroy. *Fighter Attack* has an ending that is fairer and happier for a movie of its class than that of *For Whom the Bell Tolls*. It is Bruno who is killed in the attack. Steven survives to come back after the war to marry the girl.

*Rampage* (Warner Brothers, 1963) seems a revamping of "The Short Happy Life of Francis Macomber." One reviewer remarked, "Hemingway got there first. This is the old jungle [now Malayan jungle] triangle jazz."[1]

These are just a few of the movies whose plots turn more or less like the pages of Hemingway books. A list of movies vaguely "Hemingwayesque"—by character, theme, or scene—would be very much longer.

Aside from the Hollywood features, there has been at least one Hemingway movie, *My Old Man*, made specifically for use in the classroom. Also, there have been amateur film adaptations of some of the stories.

Film has not been the only medium for Hemingway adaptations. The very first adaptation was a stage play, Laurence Stallings's 1930 dramatization for Broadway of *A Farewell to Arms*. When Paramount bought the rights for the first Hemingway movie, they bought the Stallings play as well. Never published, it seems to be a lost play, and it is impossible to determine whether or not it was actually used in the writing of the screenplay. Both the 1932 *Farewell to Arms* and the 1957 remake acknowledged Stallings in the credits, but that may have been merely a legal safeguard.

Perhaps there has not been a theater performance of a Hemingway novel since 1930 (though an A. E. Hotchner play based on five stories is noted below). In 1955 Orson Welles considered staging a dramatic reading of *The Sun Also Rises*. Nothing came of the plan, but Hemingway would have appreciated his idea for the casting, for Marlene Dietrich, one of Hemingway's favorites, was to have read the part of Lady Brett.

In the era of radio drama there were some fine Hemingway broadcasts. The first of five different radio productions of *A Farewell to Arms* was in December, 1938, for "The Campbell Playhouse" over CBS. Orson Welles supervised the production and read the part of Frederic Henry. Katharine Hepburn played Catherine Barkley. For the second radio version, Frederic March and Florence Eldridge played Frederic and Catherine for the "Star Theatre" production over NBC. In the third production, John Lund and Lurene Tuttle played the leads for the "NBC University Theatre," in August, 1948. (If one is familiar with the book, this version sounds a little funny for the informal way Frederic is always called Fred.) In the next remake, Fletcher Markle and Helen Hayes, in the role she played for the original Paramount movie, acted *A Farewell to Arms* for the "Ford Theatre" in June, 1949, over CBS. The last radio version was produced by the "Theatre Guild on the Air" in October, 1950. Perhaps several million people heard each one of these broadcasts. That was an enormous audience for *A Farewell to Arms* during those years.

There were two radio versions of *For Whom the Bell Tolls*. The popular "Lux Radio Theater" produced one-hour reductions of popular movies. Gary Cooper and Ingrid Bergman recreated their movie roles of Robert Jordan and Maria for a broadcast in February, 1945. *For Whom the Bell Tolls* was produced again for the "NBC Theater" in November, 1949.

Humphrey Bogart and Lauren Bacall starred in the "Lux Radio Theater" production of *To Have and Have Not* in October, 1946. The only other Hemingway radio title was "The Short Happy Life of Francis Macomber," originally broadcast on the "NBC University Theater" in November, 1948.[2]

In 1971 a French national radio network presented adaptations of five Hemingway novels across seven weeks of daily programs, each episode ninety minutes long. *For Whom the Bell Tolls* ran to fifteen hours in ten parts. These must have been the most complete Hemingway adaptations ever presented.

About as many television adaptations have been produced. The first was "Fifty Grand," for the CBS "Schlitz Playhouse of Stars" in July, 1952. Still another version of *A Farewell to Arms*, this one starring Guy Madison and Diana Lynn, with script by Gore Vidal, was presented on the CBS "Chrysler Climax Theatre" in May, 1955. "The Battler," starring Paul Newman, the first of several television adaptations by Hemingway's friend A. E. Hotchner, was presented on the CBS "Playwrights '56" in October, 1955. *To Have and Have Not*, starring Edmond O'Brien and Beverly Garland, was shown on the NBC "Lux Video Theatre" in January, 1957. "The World of Nick Adams," based on five of the stories, was originally written by Hotchner as a stage play, then was adapted again for the "7 Lively Arts Theatre" in November, 1957. Hotchner's version of "Fifty Grand" appeared on the NBC "Kraft Television Theatre" in April, 1958. Hotchner's *For Whom the Bell Tolls*, with Jason Robards and Maria Schell, appeared in two parts in March, 1959, and his "Killers" appeared on the CBS "Buick Electra Playhouse" in November, 1959. Robert Geller's television play of "Soldier's Home" was one of the series "The American Short Story" for the PBS channels in 1977.

The most recent television production of a Hemingway story was "My Old Man," for CBS on December 7, 1979, with script by Jerome Kass, directed by John Erman, starring Warren Oates and Kristy McNichol. The boy Joe of the story is Jo (for Joanna) in the television play. The adaptation makes Hemingway's writing into the kind of horse story that so many early-teen-age girls are crazy about.[3]

Finally, there have been adaptations of Hemingway's life, various biographical dramas, such as Trevor Reese's 1968 off-Broadway play *Before I Wake*, about the relationship between Hemingway and Fitzgerald, or Frederic Hunter's *Hemingway Play* for PBS in 1976. Wilford Leach wrote the text and Ben Johnston wrote the music for a musical play about Gertrude Stein, "Gertrude," produced by La Mama company of New York in 1970. One of the major characters in the comedy is Gertrude's dog, a pointer, called Ernest.[4]

Not in his lifetime but soon afterwards there were documentary films about Hemingway and Hemingway's places. Fausto Canel produced his *Hemingway* in 1962 in Cuba. CBS produced Hemingway's *Spain: A Love Affair*, a travelogue of Spanish scenery with dramatic readings by Rod Steiger and Jason Robards. A film of greater historical importance about Hemingway's Spain dates from 1937—*The Spanish Earth*, a documentary about the Civil

War which, with Joris Ivens and John Ferno, Hemingway himself helped to film.

Except for passing references, this book is about Hemingway's fiction on the movie screen, his stories and novels in their Hollywood versions.

Notes to Preface

1. Howard Thompson, "From the Jungle," *New York Times* October 17, 1963, p. 39.

2. See Frank M. Laurence, "The Hemingway Radio Broadcasts: 'The Short Happy Life of Francis Macomber,'" *Hemingway notes*, V (Spring, 1980), 22–25.

3. Two other stories—"Hills Like White Elephants" and "The Capital of the World"—were announced as adaptations for a three-hour special "ABC Theatre" in the 1974–1975 season. The script by James Costigan was also to include a romantic event in Hemingway's life in Paris in the 1920s. Apparently nothing final ever came of the plans. See "Hemingway Story Planned as ABC Special," *Variety*, June 4, 1974, p. 1.

4. Actually, Gertrude never had a dog called Ernest, but she did play Hemingway games with her poodle named Basket. "Be fierce! Play Hemingway!"

# HEMINGWAY AND THE MOVIES

"We know all that, bright boy," Max said. "Talk about something else. Ever go to the movies?"

"Once in a while."

"You ought to go to the movies more. The movies are fine for a bright boy like you."

Ernest Hemingway, "The Killers"

CHAPTER I

# Introduction

In the comic strip "Apartment 3-G," Professor Papagoras suffers with a sad love. On the "Today" show, Candice Bergen presents a picture tour through Hemingway's home in Cuba as she photographed it on a recent visit. In its travel section, the *Cincinnati Enquirer* runs a feature story about Key West and the tourists who come from all over the country to claim an eight-toed cat, one of the descendants (remote) of Hemingway's pets. From the cover of *Redbook* smiles Margaux, the granddaughter: "Can They Make This Woman a Superstar?" For a fashion spread on the *Esquire* look in sportswear, Jack, the son, stands in as a model: "In front of the Sun Valley Lodge, Hemingway displays the proper tweedy look of a sportsman. It's Country Britches' wool-and-nylon Donegal-tweed unconstructed suit with bellows pockets and adjustable side tabs (about $165)." During an episode of the continuing daytime drama "Somerset," the lawyer character tries to persuade a girlfriend to spend the weekend with him in the Michigan lake country. He knows a nice place—"Hemingway used to go there." At a restaurant and lounge in Memphis called the Mississippi River Company, cocktails are advertised: "Our drinks have as much character as a hero in a Hemmingway novel." Hemingway's name is misspelled. In its "Lusty Guide" series of travel articles, *Penthouse* reviews the live sex-shows of Paris and also recommends that the tourist find the famous bookstore Shakespeare and Company, because "Hemingway would have gone there to pick up girls." Over the AP newswire comes the dateline St. Simon's Island: "President Carter and his family took a Hemingway voyage to the edge of the Gulf Stream Sunday and cast their lines into the sapphire sea for hard-fighting fish that hide in the deep." Inside the country and western magazine *Country Style* is a "Free Color Poster" of singer Jimmy Buffet; the caption for the cover calls Buffet "A Damn Genius . . . Hemingway of the Caribbean." From a suggestion in a *Ladies' Home Journal* article "What You Should Call Your Pet," some cute "literary" dog gets named Hemingway. The name means, one learns, "Road belonging to the well-dressed-one." This is all trivial, out-of-date Hemingway clutter accumulated during the drafting of this book. Nineteen years after his death the mass media still print and broadcast the Hemingway name and the Hemingway image (Professor "Papa"-goras is Hemingway's image) all through the culture.

Hemingway had the popularity and recognition long before he died, of course. He was one of the kind for whom Gertrude Stein used the term "publicity saint," or celebrity, as we say more prosaically. Certain other important American writers have been made major celebrities by the media, too, such as Norman Mailer and Truman Capote among the next generation of authors and, conspicuously, Scott Fitzgerald among Hemingway's own generation.

How does one become a literary celebrity? It does not seem that it happens simply because of the importance of one's books. Of course it was very important for Hemingway's celebrity status that he won the Nobel Prize. But by that time the public knew about his other accomplishments and recognized him in his much publicized roles as soldier, war correspondent, adventurer, sportsman, and connoisseur. About fifty years earlier, in 1900, the *New York Times* had used the expression "the Hero as Man of Letters" to identify Mark Twain, who was by far the greatest literary celebrity of the previous century.[1] "Hero as Man of Letters" is what Hemingway became, too.

Impressive accomplishment has something to do with becoming a literary celebrity, and so does one's public personality. In this regard the public did not know Hemingway very well. Because he was not seen and heard talking informally very often, there was not a general sense of his temperament. Hemingway never established, as did Twain and Robert Frost, the familiar, compelling, completely attractive presence on a stage of public awareness.

One remembers that Hemingway was not even there at the ceremony when the Nobel Prize was awarded, and someone else read his acceptance remarks.

On the other hand, like Twain and Frost, Hemingway had the marvelous image. Something that all writer-celebrities have in common is that their images develop on film in wonderfully interesting ways. (Walt Whitman was the first writer to appreciate the importance of his camera image.) The last ten years of Hemingway's life were not his most significantly creative. They were, however, his greatest years as a celebrity, when he became his most photogenic. A very good-looking young man, Hemingway became magnificently handsome again after fifty. His image then was recognized almost everywhere—the massive head, the splendid beard. It is this image that almost inevitably will be used when finally a commemorative stamp is engraved.

*Parade,* the Sunday supplement magazine for scores of American newspapers, featured a color cover of Hemingway for its issue of July 27, 1957: the famous Karsh portrait of the writer wearing the high-necked Nordic sweater knitted as heavy as woven armor. Typically *Parade* covers picture dogs, cats, or babies, sometimes a government figure, often an athlete, many times a movie star. In the decade before Hemingway's death there were covers for dozens of movie stars.[2] Of all the *Parade* covers in those ten years, only two featured artists who were not entertainers—on the occasion of her one hundredth birthday, Grandma Moses (May 1, 1960), and Ernest Hemingway. The caption for the Hemingway cover read, "At 58, he's Hollywood's favorite author."

Accompanying the *Parade* story were more pictures of Hemingway, some of them old news photos from the files: "FOURTH WIFE Mary smiles with 'Papa' after their safe return from an air crash in East Africa three years ago." Another shot showed Hemingway stripped to the waist, wearing boxing gloves, admiring himself in a full-length mirror: "RUGGED TORSO and flat stomach are a source of pride to Hemingway. Though his hair has whitened since this photo was taken, he still retains his strength and stamina." He was still a "demi-god of American manhood." The latest photo showed Hemingway and Spencer Tracy together: "STAR AND AUTHOR," the caption read; "Spencer Tracy and Ernest Hemingway confer during the recently completed filming of *The Old Man and the Sea*."

From time to time in other magazines the public had seen pictures of Hemingway fraternizing with the stars: with Ingrid Bergman, having salad and white wine for lunch; with Ava Gardner, watching the bullfights; with Gary Cooper, hunting ducks. Hemingway was about as much of a celebrity as Spencer Tracy or Gary Cooper. Scott Fitzgerald, writing about himself, doubted that quite this much fame could come to a writer: "It seemed a romantic business to be a successful literary man—you were not ever going to be as famous as a movie star but what note you had was probably longer-lived."[3] But there were movie people who believed that there was no such limit on Hemingway's fame. Producer Jerry Wald once said, "Hemingway is as big a name as any Hollywood star."[4] *Parade* magazine quoted David O. Selznick saying the same thing: "Hemingway is himself a star. He has box-office."[5]

A celebrity has to have the familiarity that comes through the mass media. For many reasons on many occasions Hemingway was good news and good news photo. In addition to all the rest of his news coverage, during the twenty-five years when Hollywood was making all the Hemingway movies, he also had a very strong Hollywood press.

The main interest of the Hollywood press is with actors and movies. But while promoting the Hemingway features, the press also promoted Hemingway's own reputation and that of his books. The *Parade* cover story, titled "Hollywood Goes Hemingway," noted that several new Hemingway movies were being made all at once; Hemingway had become "filmdom's favorite story source." Hollywood columnist Lloyd Shearer felt that this was a fitting distinction for the winner of the Nobel and Pulitzer prizes, who could now take the "further satisfaction" that *The Sun Also Rises, A Farewell to Arms* (in remake), and *The Old Man and the Sea* would soon come to the screen.[6] Shearer was highly respectful of Hemingway's novels, and was therefore disappointed that *The Sun Also Rises* and *A Farewell to Arms* had been "seriously altered in adaption to the screen." They would not be "pure Hemingway." Shearer did feel that both movies would do well at the box office, whereas he did not feel so confident of the commercial success of *The Old Man and the Sea*. (Shearer was expressing the conventional Hollywood wisdom that close adaptations are high risk. It turned out, in fact, that *The Old Man and the Sea* was a financial ruin.) On the other hand, *The Old Man and the Sea* was a more accurate adaptation than the other two (really, more accurate than any other Hollywood version of a Hemingway book). *The Old Man and the Sea* would be "the only pure Hemingway distilled in the Hollywood laboratories in 1957."[7]

Shearer was talking about just the sort of thing that most people want to know when they think of movies made from books. Is the movie as good as the book? What did they change? One of Hemingway's friends, Harvey Breit, said such questions made up "a parlor game" for "book-club matrons."[8]

Serious critics who work between literature and film feel that many questions of the general category "What did they change?" are somewhat naive, for a book must change when it is made into a film. Literature is one thing and film is something else, with different aesthetic conditions. Literature and film are not in *every* way different; some of the more interesting theoretical and practical problems in translation come up because the media do work in some of the same ways. Still, one has to account always for the separate exigencies of the media.

A novelist named Albert McKisco is a character in Scott Fitzgerald's *Tender is the Night*. "You don't like me," he says, "but that can't be helped. I'm primarily a literary man." When McKisco feels insecure, he pleases himself by making "withering remarks about the movies." This book about the Hemingway movies is written by someone who is primarily a literary man. That can't be helped, though one hopes not to be McKisco's kind of a fool.

Still, even with the best attitude, it is not enough to consider adaptation only as an aesthetic question between two media. Some of the most conspicuous (one may even say egregious) changes that can happen between a novel and its movie really have nothing to do with the differences between the media as such. These other changes should be understood as having to do with a difference between art and entertainment.

It is somewhat more difficult to discuss the differences between art and entertainment than between book and film. With book and film one always knows which is which; one does not confuse the experience of watching a movie with that of reading a book. Usually between art and entertainment such a separate sense does not exist. Certainly there is entertainment that is not artistic at all, and there is art that is totally boring. But much entertainment is very artistic, and much art is highly entertaining. This is true whether one is speaking of experiences within the film medium, or the book medium, or any medium at all. Whether one is talking about a good novel or a good motion picture, the concepts of art and entertainment blur with each other.

If one has an adequate cross-media theory, one can explain without deprecation why the film adaptation is bound to be different from the literary form. Sometimes it is very difficult for critics, especially literary critics, to be without bias in this. Of the countless interesting films worthy of study, only a very limited number are adaptations of significant literary works. Those who choose such adaptations to work with tend to be critics or teachers of literature in the first instance, who might not understand the other medium as well as film critics or film teachers do.

An article in the American Film Institute's "Education Newsletter" discusses this problem. Many film classes—comparative courses with such titles as "Novels into Films"—are being taught out of English departments, and most of the teachers hold English degrees.

> There is concern on the part of some film educators regarding this situation. Fears abound that English teachers are not properly trained to teach film, that they are merely exploiting the subject matter in order to beef up lagging enrollments in more traditional courses, that they are only teaching literature and film courses in order to enable them to sneer at the failure of cinematic adaptors to live up to the original literary masterpeices.[9]

The article goes on to affirm that there are sound, valuable reasons for looking at film from the perspective of literature, but some of the anxiety of the film people is very fair.

To simplify this, we might assign discriminated meanings to

some of the terms we have to use over and over. Let us say that the words "film" and "book" denote the two media, that is, the celluloid and the paper versions. The word "movie," especially by its connotation, means the kind of popular entertainment that Hollywood is in the business to make, whereas "literature" connotes such writing as may be appreciated for its art value, beyond whatever may be its popularity as an entertainment. The Hemingway adaptations represent films made from books. The Hollywood versions of his novels and stories also represent movies made from literature. By that sense of what the process of adaptation entails, certain art values of Hemingway's writing were diminished, if not cancelled—the reason being that the mass audience for whom the movies were made had a great liking for certain low and common values in entertainment and not much appreciation for the relatively sophisticated art of Hemingway's writing.

When one starts talking about audiences in such a relative way, one encounters yet another touchy problem—attitude. There are the English teachers, the book people, who might resent film for the changes it has to make in a book. Then the film people do not like the literary folk for their resentment, and become defensive themselves. So it happens when an elitist critic begins to describe popular culture as "vulgar." A certain professor at the University of Pennsylvania (in the Department of Sociology, not English, by the way) has said that he never watches television because "if that many people like it, it can't possibly be any good." If a literary critic were continually to use that tone about movie adaptations, movie critics naturally would find his attitude insufferable.

It is not true that the Hemingway movies could not possibly be any good because that many people liked them. Quite apart from whether or not they are good adaptations (and a few *are*), some of them are very good movies, in any or all of the ways that movies ever are good, as entertainments. Some, too, are impressive as "cinema," if one needs a word with a connotation like "literature" to express the art potential of movies.

But this is still explaining the matter from the tolerant point of view of someone who goes to the movies perfectly sure of the value of literature and already highly respectful of Hemingway as artist.

The interest of this book, however, has more to do with Hemingway's reputation from a quite different perspective. For very many people among Hemingway's audience at the movies do not read much of anything, certainly not literature as sophisticated as his. And many people, though they do read, clearly prefer movies to books. A television commercial for the Evelyn Wood speed-reading program presents this testimonial to the success of the system: "Now I enjoy reading a good deal, for now it's more like going to a movie than reading a book!" Movies are so much easier for some people that they automatically think about movies when they are speaking of books. The dean's secretary has been attending my lectures on *The Sun Also Rises,* which at first she found very difficult to follow (unlike *Sister Carrie,* which we did two weeks ago). Finally she thinks she feels less confused about all the conversation apparently without any point to it, and I recommend that she read another Hemingway book, *A Farewell to Arms,* which she will probably enjoy. "Oh, I saw that movie," she tells me, "but it's been *years* ago." If one wants to understand how Hemingway related to all of the American culture, the dean's secretary's impression is as important as a teacher's or critic's.

In his book *Notes from a Sea Diary: Hemingway All the Way,* Nelson Algren predicted what could happen to an artist or intellectual who could not relate to all of his culture. Some vitality would go out of his art or his thought:

> For the painter no longer in touch with people who don't look at pictures begins to die as a painter. The actor whose life has moved away from the market-place to the studio begins to act falsely. The novelist, grown remote from people who don't read, becomes untrue to those who do read. The thinker who loses contact with those who never think at all, no longer thinks justly.[10]

From the point of view of people who went to the movies—though most of them did not read at Hemingway's level—Hemingway did not seem remote. For all his eminence as an author, he was not irrelevant to the mass culture of Americans at the movies, who were his fans.

CHAPTER II

# Hemingway on Movies: *The Old Man and the Sea*

Hemingway was certainly entitled to an opinion. What did he think about Hollywood, and how did he see the movies made from his books? What did he think that a film adaptation could be?

The last of the movie adaptations released during Hemingway's lifetime was the Warner Brothers production of *The Old Man and the Sea*. It was six slow, interrupted years in the planning and production before its release in 1958, and during the waiting there was strong expectation in the press that *The Old Man and the Sea* would be, as expressed in *Life*, "the first successful effort to get Hemingway's flavor on film."[1] Of course that had been said about earlier Hemingway movies, too. This advance publicity sounded nearly credible, however, because studio publicists for Warner Brothers did everything possible to give the impression that the movie had Hemingway's personal sanction. As never before, Hemingway had been directly involved with the production. In press release articles he was identified as "sponsor" or "coproducer" of the movie.[2] The points were made that Hemingway had entrusted the movie to producer Leland Hayward because Hayward was his friend of many years standing, and that he was also the close friend of screenplay writer Peter Viertel, whose script he had personally approved. Hemingway was said to have concurred in the choice of John Sturges as director, and to have named Spencer Tracy as "his first choice for the solo role." The publicity emphasized that Hemingway spent long hours coaching Tracy about the part. One publicity photo showed Hemingway sighting through a movie camera, as if he had some actual charge over the camera operations.[3] As "marlin producer," he had gone to Peru "to fish the big one."[4] And, because he "wanted to be a part of *The Old Man and*

Hemingway took a genuine interest in the camera work during the location shooting of *The Old Man and the Sea*. This photo is a Warner Brothers publicity still, here courtesy of Mary Hemingway.

*the Sea*," Hemingway supposedly made his "acting debut" as a face in the crowd in the hand-wrestling scene.

Much of this publicity was either not true or highly exaggerated. Hemingway had had nothing to do with the naming of Sturges as director, nor, for that matter, the naming of Fred Zinnemann, the original director who left the production. He had not selected Tracy to play Santiago. It was true that he had gone to Peru to try to catch the giant marlin for the camera, but he had not been successful. (Hemingway wrote to a friend telling him to expect a lot of fake publicity from the studio about the fish).[5] If he had been one of the supernumeraries in the crowd scene where the old man hand-wrestles the Negro from Cienfuegos, his moment on film, like Alfred Hitchcock's appearance, seems to have been edited out of the release print of the picture, though Mary Hemingway does appear as a tourist very near the end of the movie.

All the activity about which the publicists wrote seemed to indicate, in the words of one press release, that "Ernest Hemingway, notably reluctant in identifying himself with motion pictures, took an opposite stand when Warner Bros. decided to film *The Old Man and the Sea*." There was little that Hemingway could do about the exploitation of his name. It was the consequence of his having realized far too late that his association with the production had been a serious mistake.

It was not a mistake he had ever made before. What had he been thinking in 1952 when the production was first planned? The answer to that question requires a careful account of the special circumstances surrounding the idea for this movie and, beyond that, a review of Hemingway's attitude towards movies in general and especially the earlier movies made from his books.

In the first place, he might not have become interested in filming *The Old Man and the Sea* except that the idea was suggested to him by Leland Hayward, who had been his friend for more than twenty years. It had been Hayward who had negotiated the sale of the rights to *A Farewell to Arms* for $80,000 for the first Hemingway movie, released in 1932. (This happened to have been a movie that Hemingway thoroughly disliked, but that had been no fault of Hayward's.) It had been Hayward who had read *The Old Man and the Sea* in manuscript, convinced Hemingway to publish it separately instead of saving it as the coda for a longer book (which would be published posthumously as *Islands in the Stream*), and, as agent, had sold the first publication rights to *Life* magazine in 1952. Hemingway was impressed with that business deal. Thanks to Hayward, he had money that he would have missed with the novel's first publication as a Scribner's book.

Leland Hayward was a highly successful Broadway producer—of *Oklahoma* and *South Pacific*, among many other plays. As soon as *The Old Man and the Sea* became a best-seller, Hayward began thinking that he could do something with it for the stage, like a dramatic reading in the style of recent productions of *John Brown's Body* and *Don Juan in Hell*. The reading would be a perfect vehicle for Spencer Tracy, with whom Hayward had been discussing all of his plans. *The Old Man and the Sea* would tour the country as a one-man show, or actually one man and one boy (Santiago's friend Manolin).

Hemingway felt unsure that a reading of the book would have much appeal, but it sounded like an attractive proposition if, as Hayward promised, the production could clear $3,500 to $5,000 a night, with 10 percent going to the author.[6] If the reading proved successful, then afterwards, Hayward suggested, they should think about making a movie.

Spencer Tracy was enthusiastic about the dramatic reading. Unfortunately, he had contract commitments in Hollywood that would block any other engagement for several years, until 1955 or 1956. So they all had to give up the idea of a stage version, though they kept the idea of a movie as a future possibility.

Hemingway was intending to be very shrewd about any picture deal. He thought that the movies offered a splendidly easy way for a novelist to make a lot of money. He also thought that he had usually been screwed by Hollywood. Agents and lawyers were partly to blame. But Hemingway thought it was his own failure, too, for not outsmarting Hollywood and making his old age secure.[7] There had been a few lucky contracts. He had earned $150,000 from Paramount for the rights to *For Whom the Bell Tolls*, which as of 1941 was the record price for the sale of a novel.[8] "The

Short Happy Life of Francis Macomber" and "The Snows of Kilimanjaro" had both brought $75,000, from United Artists and Twentieth Century-Fox, respectively. Less luckily, Universal had paid only $35,500 for "The Killers," though the 1946 picture had been enormously successful, eventually grossing several million dollars. In the year of *The Killers,* because of its profits, Hollywood was willing to bid heavily for Hemingway's new work-in-progress, the novel *The Garden of Eden* (to this day still unpublished). For some reason, perhaps because he was having difficulty with the writing, Hemingway declined an offer of $300,000 from Twentieth Century-Fox.

He had made a bad deal with *To Have and Have Not* when he sold the rights for $10,000—in Hemingway's opinion a "derisory" sum—to finance the writing of *For Whom the Bell Tolls.*[9] What was worse, *To Have and Have Not* had been remade in 1950 as *The Breaking Point,* and would be remade again in 1957 as *The Gun Runners,* with no more money coming to Hemingway since the film rights had been sold outright.[10]. Losing so much of his profits from Hollywood to his tax account had always hurt, too. Of the *For Whom the Bell Tolls* money, Hemingway claimed $87,500 of it had gone to the government.[11]

The financial arrangements he was talking over with Hayward were based on a different approach and sounded better than anything he had been offered before. The principle was that Hemingway, Hayward, and Tracy would be equal partners in the enterprise, each being paid $75,000 for "personal services" to the production (which payment Hemingway *imagined* would be nontaxable) and taking equal percentage of the picture's profits, which of course, they liked to believe might be enormously high, given the reception of the book.

As for Hemingway's personal services, as an expert game fisherman he would be in charge of a special production unit that would take the film of the fight with the marlin—the "combat shots," as he called them.[12] This filming would be finished early in the production and later edited into the footage of the old man in the boat.

Hemingway believed that his presence would help to guard the artistic integrity of the production, to keep it, in his words, honest and straight.[13] He was not getting involved because he especially liked or was interested in movies.

When Lillian Ross was visiting with him to write her wonderful "Profile" essay for the *New Yorker*, Hemingway listed for her all the things he would like to do during his stay in New York. "I'd like to see all the new fighters, horses, ballets, bike riders, dames, bull-fighters, painters, airplanes, sons of bitches, café characters, big international whores, restaurants, years of wine, newsreels, and never have to write a line about any of it."[14] He did not mention the movies. It was as if he would go for the newsreel and leave before the feature was shown. Actually, he did go to movies sometimes, and he preferred seeing a movie to seeing a play. He had favorite movies. *The Gun Fighter* (Twentieth Century-Fox, 1949) with Gregory Peck was his idea of a really good picture simply as entertainment. *Around the World in Eighty Days* (United Artists, 1956) was another movie he thoroughly enjoyed when he saw it in Cuba. He came back the second night to see the second half. He once claimed that as a boy, with his grandfather, he had seen *Birth of a Nation* (Epoch, 1915) thirty times.[15]

Nevertheless, he did not respect movies very much at all. It does not seem surprising to know that this was his attitude. Many literary people look down more or less steeply on the movies. (It is not surprising to learn that this was Hemingway's attitude towards the movies in the the way it is startling to know Frank Lloyd Wright thought painting was a trivial art, the most trivial of any, and the farthest from the true art of architecture.) Of course there were many writers of Hemingway's generation, like Fitzgerald and Farrell, who were fascinated with movies and believed in the possibilities of movies as art. With Hemingway, though, it sometimes almost seemed that he was careful to hold to what was nearly a pretense of a preference for elite art, as by saying that he wanted to see all the new ballets in New York (as well as the bicycle races). Possibly his upper-middle-class, Oak Park background had something to do with his set of mind towards the movies. Movies were not genteel.

It is less of a guess to say that Hemingway looked down on movies because they seemed fraudulent in a way. Nothing about writing seemed more important to him than that it should be true. Realism was continually being tested against his experience. Hemingway often complained that movies were not true enough to be art. Producer Mark Hellinger was Hemingway's very good friend, and since Hellinger had been a newspaper man he knew what was true. Still, Hemingway told Lillian Ross, "Cops are not like they are in the Hellinger movies. Only once in a while."[16] Of the prostitute in *Islands in the Stream* Hemingway wrote: "Honest Lil began to cry, real tears, bigger and wetter than any in the movies."

Hemingway's son Patrick once said that "pictures on the silver screen were nothing but pure illusion to Hemingway and not to be taken seriously."[17] Sometimes it seemed serious to him, though, when Hollywood took one of his books and ruined the honesty of it. He seems never to have understood why movie people could not hold to the standard of realism that he set in his books.

Thus he was furious when he read an early draft of Dudley Nichols's screenplay for *For Whom the Bell Tolls*. He went over the script slowly, then sent a series of letters to his Hollywood agent Donald Friede complaining that Nichols had botched everything up. He listed instance after instance of material that was ridiculous or incredible. He objected to some of the diction. The guerrilla fighters were given to using words like "assassin" and "treachery" that were much too high-sounding for their peasant speech. They said "adios" when any Republican would say "salud." Names of characters were wrong: Rinaldo (not a character in the book) was Italian, not Spanish. Costuming was bad, as if for a cheap production of *Carmen*. The script called for the guerrillas to wear bright bandanas, whereas in fact they would have worn only grays and blacks. And, as Hemingway knew, no real Spaniard had worn a long moustache in a hundred years. Situations were phony, too. It was inconceivable that, in the opening scene, Jordan and Kashkin would be blowing the Fascist train by themselves, without the cover of machine guns to mow down the enemy as they tried to escape. Jordan would kill his wounded comrade Kashkin with a single shot in the back of the head—not three, as Nichols imagined the scene. (In the finished movie, as if by compromise, Jordan *faces* Kashkin and shoots him twice.) Then for Jordan to confer with General Golz in the backroom of a cafe, where security could not conceivably be well-guarded, was as unrealistic, to paraphrase Hemingway's metaphor, as a rape during mass in St. Patrick's. Hemingway noticed technical flaws also. There was no slit in a tank turret to drop a grenade through. A tank machine gun did not load the way Nichols imagined, and so on and on. Hemingway urged Nichols to get the script back into the finest tradition of realism in American pictures. (Hemingway did not really believe there was such a tradition, but this was good rhetoric for persuading Nichols.) If Nichols was unable or unwilling to fix the script, Hemingway said he would have to arrange for a press interview in order to repudiate it.[18]

Hemingway really ought to have appreciated the very fine detail of authenticity in the finished movie of *For Whom the Bell Tolls*. For example, the planes used for the production, American A-T-6 trainers, were modified, marked, and camouflaged to appear almost perfectly matched with the German and Italian fighter-bombers of the Nationalist aviation. And Hemingway need not have worried about the tank as Nichols described it. The production staff would make such details correct. This was not always true of war movies, especially not those produced during the early war years. But the production people of *For Whom the Bell Tolls* gave the planes and armor the same studied attention that the meticulous hobby craftsman gives his 1/72 scale models in plastic. One cannot feel sure that Hemingway was satisfied, though, as particular as he was about details. Jordan's squirrel, for example. The dawn of the day that he blows up the bridge Jordan listens to a squirrel chatter in a pine tree. Although the movie did show the squirrel, one can almost believe that Hemingway would not have liked it had he realized that the animal was of a species of grey squirrel native to California (*Sciurus griseus*) and not found in Spain.

Ray Bradbury included in *The Martian Chronicles* a story called "Usher II," about a man who in the year 2005 has had to flee to Mars to find a secret place to indulge his craving for fantasy. All the libraries had been burned long ago by the authorities at the Bureau of Moral Climates. Movies were still allowed to be made, but only if they were remakes of Hemingway novels. "My God, how many different times have I seen *For Whom the Bell Tolls* done! cries the hero. "Thirty different versions. All realistic. Oh, realism!"

People and places always had to look true to Hemingway, and always the animals. *The Old Man and the Sea* would be a failure this way, as would other movies, like Darryl F. Zanuck's 1957 production of *The Sun also Rises*. Faces in the crowd scenes were Mexican rather than Spanish because some of the sequences had been shot in Mexico City. The bulls were too small, Hemingway said, and it looked like their horns had been glued on for the day.[19]

Five years earlier Zanuck had ruined *The Snows of Kilimanjaro*, for which deed Hemingway liked to think about going back to the African mountain, there to stalk Zanuck's soul.[20] The only thing that Hemingway liked about that movie was the animal footage, real because shot on African plains.[21] (However, the hyena's laugh, an important sound effect during the "death scene," was mimicked on the soundtrack by director Henry King. Hemingway must have been fooled.)

Hemingway generously granted when a movie was good, if it looked real. Producer Casey Robinson's 1950 version of "My Old Man" (the movie title was *Under My Skin*) was worth compliments because the outdoor shots were all right to Hemingway's eye. Paris really looked like Paris and the race horses were good horses. People in the movie were important as well. Hemingway especially liked one of the jockeys—aparently not an actor.[22]

Hemingway's reaction to A. E. Hotchner's 1959 dramatization of "The Killers" as a television play is an especially clear example of Hemingway's sense of what kind of detail made true adaptation.[23] In that production Ingemar Johansson, then world heavyweight champion, was cast as the "Swede," the prize-fighter in the story. (The role did not require him to act much; perhaps just as well.) This touch of authenticity pleased Hemingway extremely.

The production crew for *Islands in the Stream* tried to make Thomas Hudson's boat like Hemingway's own boat, the *Pilar.* Mrs.

Hemingway advised as to details of the cockpit interior. Hemingway would have been pleased to know it.

When the cameras were in the actual places where the stories were set and when the cameras were filming real people who were not actors, then you had what Hemingway thought adaptation ought to be. Stylistically, movie adaptation of a literary property should approach documentary film. If Hemingway's regard for Hollywood movies was generally low, his respect for the potential of documentary film was very high. Documentaries were true, like long newsreels. In the first year of the Spanish Civil War he had worked with the making of two documentaries, *Spain in Flames* and *The Spanish Earth*, both films having the force of propaganda that would raise funds for the Loyalist cause. They represented a higher ideological than artistic commitment, but in Hemingway's mind they were a standard for cinematic authenticity that any industry producer ought to be able to meet, too. That is why in listing his many objections to the script of *For Whom the Bell Tolls*, Hemingway suggested that producer-director Sam Wood should see a screening of *The Spanish Earth* so that he could tell what Spanish peasants and the Spanish war really looked like.

Of course a novel in film was narrative rather than reportorial. But when a story was filmed with the realism of a documentary, the result was such a film as Vittorio De Sica's *The Bicycle Thief*. Hemingway said that he imagined the film of *The Old Man and the Sea* in comparison with *The Bicycle Thief*, and his wish was that De Sica would direct. *The Bicycle Thief* is always remembered if ever one see it. The realism of it has nothing of a Hollywood tincture. Hemingway's comparison is very meaningful. If Hemingway wished for a realism that intense, then there is almost nothing else as important to be explained about why finally he was disappointed with *The Old Man and the Sea*.

Also by Hemingway's wish, *The Old Man and the Sea* would be shot entirely on location, using "local people on a local ocean with a local boat."[24] In fact, Hemingway first supposed that the old man would be represented by a real Cuban fisherman, someone like the Cojimar fisherman Anselmo Hernandez, who was a model for Santiago in some ways. By the original plan as Hemingway understood it, Spencer Tracy would read the narration on the soundtrack and speak the old man's lines but would not appear on camera himself. Hemingway seems to have been faintly surprised when he learned that Tracy intended to act the part, too.

He soon adapted to the idea when Tracy, along with Hayward, visited him in Cuba in April, 1953. This was Hemingway's first meeting with Tracy, and he liked him right away. They had had a rough flight over; Tracy had taken a bad bruise on the shin. Hemingway liked the way that Tracy paid no attention to the pain of it. He was also impressed with Tracy's modesty and sensitivity and the determined way he was overcoming an old drinking problem. Since Tracy was intelligently interested in learning about the book, Hemingway gave him a tour of the Cojimar village and showed him Anselmo Hernandez asleep in his cabin. Hemingway was thinking now that Tracy was probably going to be very good in the role; he was even beginning to look like the old man.[25]

During that April visit there also were serious matters to be discussed with Leland Hayward. Hemingway was becoming concerned that Hayward's sense of the style of the production was passing far beyond the boundaries of the documentary approach. Hayward by now had decided to shoot the picture in color, and to Hemingway that sounded very commercial. He was almost ready to believe Hayward would be talking about 3-D next![26] Also, Hemingway was getting somewhat impatient to have a $50,000 advance that Hayward had promised to close the deal.[27] Nevertheless, their good relationship was holding out. When Hayward flew back to the mainland, Hemingway gave him a fine shotgun from his collection as a token of the good feelings that prevailed.

The economics of the picture were still a long way from being settled, even after Hemingway had his advance money in hand. Hemingway, Hayward, and Tracy had an agreement among themselves, but there had to be a studio to finance the picture. Although in talking about it to friends Hemingway gave the impression that his arrangement with Hayward was only one of several he had considered, in fact no studio seemed very eager to have *The Old Man and the Sea* as a property.[28] Several successful Hemingway movies had recently been released, others were being planned, and Hemingway's reputation was very high. For all that, there was a general feeling among movie people (a feeling not shared by Hayward and Tracy) that this particular book would not have much mass appeal.

It should not have been difficult to tell that *The Old Man and the Sea* was Hemingway's least likely novel for the movies. (*For Whom the Bell Tolls* was his most likely book for the movies, but that is the subject of a different chapter.) There were several reasons for this, one of the important ones being the rather sensitive subject of class appeal.

George Humphrey, Eisenhower's Secretary of the Treasury, supposed that the novel would be irrelevant to the affluent class during the prosperous fifties. Humphrey wondered, "Why should anyone be interested in some old man who was a failure and never amounted to anything anyway?"[29] Humphrey could not imagine from his point of view why so many people, perhaps from liberal sympathy if not radical chic, were interested in the old man to the point of real tears. There was, in contrast to George Humphrey, a class of readers who found it profoundly satisfying to discover human dignity reaffirmed by a lowly Cuban fisherman.

Dwight MacDonald was correct in identifying *The Old Man and the Sea* as a Mid Cult novel.[30] To the middle-to-upper-middle class it was a fine little art book—the better for that for being quite thin. It represented the novel as art in approximately the same way that *The Complete Poems of Robert Frost* represented the best middlebrow poetry. They were books for the same shelves in the same households. Even without the nice drawings that came with the *Life* format or with the Scribner's illustrated edition, *The Old Man and the Sea* was a beautiful book to read through, as some of Frost's poems were like Christmas card art. The editors of *Life* assured their readers that the 27,000-word story on the twenty middle pages would be "one of the most *pictorial* experiences you've ever had" (italics theirs).[31] Also, the Hemingway story had new expressions of platitudes that were comfortable to read: about the brotherhood of man with all creatures; how a man is born to do what he does; "Pain does not matter to a man"; "Man is not made for defeat." This was wisdom in the manner of the more obvious Frost: "Earth's the right place for love"; "Nothing gold can stay"; "Good fences make good neighbors" (which is the exact opposite of what Frost tried to instruct in "Mending Wall" but which is what most readers hear as the poem's lesson).

Leland Hayward had had the right sense that the middlebrow readers of *Life* were the best readers for *The Old Man and the Sea*. In turn, the editors of *Life* were gratefully proud that the book was for them and not the highbrow intellectuals whose fancy interpretations were scoffed at by a *Life* editorial:

> It is often highbrow practice to find symbolism in Hemingway's work. *The Old Man and the Sea* seems perfect to us [middlebrows] as it stands. But for those [highbrows] who like a little symbolism, we have tried to deduce some. Perhaps the old man is Hemingway himself, the great fish is this great story and the sharks are the critics. Symbolism won't match up to real life here though; there is absolutely nothing the sharks can do to this marlin.[32]

Movie people, who also could be sharks, might freely adapt a Hemingway property for the purpose of entertainment; and critics, in their ways, might create their own versions of a book for the purposes of their lectures and articles. Criticism—the interpretation, the analysis, the evaluation, the history—is almost exclusively an intellectual activity of High Culture, but it is not always intelligently done. Chess and Brahms tend to be High Cult activities, too, and are not always well played.

Subscribers to *Life* might have supported a stage version of *The Old Man and the Sea*, enough of them buying tickets for the old theaters downtown and driving in from the suburbs to hear Spencer Tracy recite the old man. Leland Hayward knew the Mid Cult audience very well, but the Mass Cult audience not well enough, it would seem. He could not quite tell that *The Old Man and the Sea* was so solidly a middlebrow novel that you could not very well make a movie of it that would be vulgar enough for the lowbrows as well. "No sex, no love affair, no excitement," as another producer dismissed *The Old Man and the Sea*.[33]

In June, 1953, Metro-Goldwyn-Mayer, Tracy's studio, finally announced that it would take the picture as a vehicle for their major star. By this time Hayward was already under a three-picture contract with Warner Brothers. In order that *The Old Man and the Sea* could count as one of the three with *Mister Roberts* (1955) and *The Spirit of St. Louis* (1957), Warners arranged to "borrow" Tracy from MGM for one movie.

An effect of these negotiations was to change the original plan whereby the three partners would each take a relatively modest $75,000 advance plus a later share of the profits. The Warners contract still offered the same small percentage points. But a third of Hayward's long-term contract was $150,000. Tracy's agent insisted that Tracy must have a matching sum. Then Hemingway's lawyer said that he must have the same $150,000 for screen rights, including advisory work.

Warners must have thought that $150,000 was a very high price for a novel no one else was trying to buy. Of course they were gambling that Spencer Tracy would assure its box-office success. Also, they would make it a lavish production, with a two-million-dollar budget. The movie was now sure to be more Hollywood in its style than Hemingway had originally intended.

Then for two years there was no need for Hemingway to think about the adaptation at all, since the production had to be delayed in the wait for Tracy to finish other movies and for Leland Hayward to make *Mister Roberts.* Work on the script would not begin until the summer of 1955.

All along Hayward had simply assumed that Hemingway would prepare the script himself, and so it had been announced to the press when the first MGM contract had been negotiated in 1953.[34] Either Hayward had misunderstood Hemingway's intention or Hemingway had since changed his mind. Whichever, Hayward was not happy about how the matter stood. Hemingway declined to write the script and there was nothing Hayward could do about it.

It is not likely that Hemingway had doubts about his ability to write a screenplay. Of course there was a technical aspect to screenplay writing that Hemingway knew almost nothing about. (Neither had he known anything about writing for the stage when he wrote his Spanish Civil War play, *The Fifth Column,* which was why the Theatre Guild had had Benjamin Glazer do a rewrite of it before risking a New York production.) But it is doubtful that he thought the technique of screenwriting was very difficult. Howard Hawks, one of Hemingway's Sun Valley friends, once said, "Whenever I tried to persuade Hemingway to write for the movies, Hemingway insisted that he could be a good writer of books, but he didn't know whether he could be a good writer of movies."[35] The modest voice does not especially sound like Hemingway's, but perhaps it was one polite way to say that he did not want to write for the movies. (Or perhaps Hawks was confusing Hemingway with William Faulkner, who worked for Hawks and was given to admitting that he doubted that he was a good writer of movies.)[36]

Hemingway did sincerely lament it when an author like John Dos Passos wrote for the movies. He did not like it when the good writers went out to Hollywood for the thousand dollars a week the studios paid. Holden Caulfield in *Catcher in the Rye* had hated it that his talented brother D. B. was in Hollywood "being a prostitute" and therefore had a Jaguar that cost almost four thousand bucks. It was not that Hemingway thought that the writers he knew went to work as studio hacks because they wanted fast cars. They wanted to eat. Then the salaries ruined them from then on, and they never wrote well after that. He hoped that it would not happen to John O'Hara as it had to others.[37]

Furthermore, at that point in Hemingway's career—he was fully expecting the Nobel Prize—it would have been demeaning to take a scriptwriter's job. And Hollywood knew that Hemingway had too much prestige to accept such employment.

In years past Hemingway had come close to getting in with the movie people, as he called them, on some deals where they would go someplace with him to film something worthwhile. In 1933 Hemingway had considered going to Spain with producer Lewis Milestone to make a picture using amateur actors.[38] By Milestone's recollection, it was to have been an original story, political in theme, written with a sense of war approaching. Nothing came of the project, however. Then in 1939 Hemingway thought about going on safari with Howard Hawks to film "The Short Happy Life of Francis Macomber."[39] That plan did not go past discussion either, so it never had to be decided whether Hemingway would do the script. As recently as 1954 *Variety* had reported that Hemingway had closed on a deal to write an original script about big-game hunting, then go to Africa with the production to act in it himself.[40] Right away Hemingway denied the report. Quite apart from the question of visiting locations, one sees there was never any thought to go out to Hollywood itself to write a movie. Once Hemingway went out to Hollywood to *show* a movie, *The Spanish Earth*, and to make a speech soliciting funds to send ambulances to the Republican army in Spain. That was in July, 1937, and perhaps it was the only time he ever was there.[41]

Hayward was not suggesting that Hemingway would have to be in Hollywood to write the script for *The Old Man and the Sea*, for the entire production would be coming to him. Hemingway had an alternate plan. He would select the scriptwriter himself. All the other properties had been out of his protection once the screen rights were sold; he had no "right of approval" on any grounds. This time he would protect his interest by naming a writer who would be respectful and responsible directly to him.

Hemingway had known Peter Viertel for five or six years and had once thought Viertel's early fiction showed talent. (Viertel's most popular book, *Love Lies Bleeding*, a romantic bullfight novel, was not published until 1964, after Hemingway's death.) Hemingway had talked with Viertel about his plans for *Islands in the Stream*. In those days Hemingway had thought that he would construct part three of *Islands* so that scenes of Hudson and his crew searching for U-boats would be intercut with scenes aboard a German submarine. Not knowing much about submarines, Hemingway asked Viertel if he wanted to do the research for him, perhaps even do some of the writing of the German chapters. Viertel seems to have understood that this was generous conversation but perhaps not an offer that Hemingway seriously expected him to accept.

As for the current project, Viertel was an experienced screenwriter. His most recent script was for the fine World War II spy thriller *Decision Before Dawn* (Twentieth Century-Fox, 1951). Naturally Viertel was very pleased to have Hemingway recommend him as the screenplay writer for *The Old Man and the Sea*.

Although Hayward had some reservations about the nomination, Hemingway assured him that there could be no problems since the script was going to follow the book exactly. Hemingway would supervise everything, and Viertel would do as he was directed, in a role something like that of a secretary. Such was Hayward's impression of Hemingway's intention.

Viertel and Hayward went to Cuba in June, 1955, for script conferences. It was not enough that Viertel should get the tour of Cojimar to see Anselmo Hernandez. Hemingway had the notion that Viertel should have to experience the life of a poor Cuban fisherman in order to work on the script with due sympathy. It made no difference that Viertel was only going to be using material that Hemingway had already written. The script would be more true, Hemingway was convinced, if the experience were Viertel's own. Hemingway had Viertel spend a night in a dilapidated roadhouse with no screens in the windows for protection against the mosquitoes so that he would have some idea what life in the old man's shack must have been like. Afternoons he gave Viertel intensive instruction in marlin fishing, and, in a peculiar way, was very worried that Viertel had no luck catching anything, even though the fish were running. How could a man write a script about marlin fishing if he were unable to catch one himself? One time, while cruising several miles from shore, Hemingway had Viertel climb into the dinghy towed by the *Pilar*; he then cut the tow-line, and abandoned Viertel for several hours so he would learn the sensation of being alone in an open boat in ocean waves. Viertel was miserably sea-sick by the time he was picked up. Privately, and in all seriousness, Hemingway told Hayward that he was having doubts whether a man so prone to sea-sickness was really the right person to adapt *The Old Man and the Sea*. Thinking that Hemingway was acting beyond reason about all this, Hayward defended Viertel. And since Viertel was being a good sport about suffering these various indignities, work proceeded on the script with no bad feelings.

There was not much to be decided in those script conferences, as far as Hemingway was concerned. He wanted a strict transcript of the book that Tracy could memorize and the cameramen follow.

There was no question of writing a new screenplay only "based on" the book. The script and book would match. Adaptation had to be matching, in Hemingway's mind.

Viertel had some new ideas to offer. He suggested that there should be a long opening scene in which the old man, discouraged by his many weeks of bad luck, goes to Havana to find work only to find city life intolerably oppressive. Hemingway vetoed the idea on the grounds that the book stood perfectly well on its own and needed neither the new theme nor the Havana scenery. Hayward came up with an idea calculated to introduce more characters and thereby reduce some of the monotony of having the camera on Santiago almost all the time. He wanted two short scenes of the boy, Manolin, with his parents—near the beginning, the boy trying unsuccessfully to persuade them to let him go in the boat with the old man, and near the end of the movie, the parents admitting they were wrong in forbidding him to go because his faith in the old man was justified. Hayward thought that such an addition would appeal to the "family audience." But Hemingway would not allow it, even though the first of these scenes was implicit on the first page of the book. Because Hemingway held this attitude inflexibly, the final script—except for a few very brief shots (of some boys calling Manolin to join their baseball game, for example)—contained no material that had not originally been in the book.

Hemingway was almost as adamant about deletions. Though he understood that the novel was too long to be filmed in its entirety, he allowed cuts only grudgingly. He even wanted the movie to show a moment while the old man urinates outside his shack when he gets up in the morning. Hayward protested there was simply no way to show that tastefully, or without laughs. It seemed to Hayward that Hemingway was obviously being stubborn in order to be difficult.

It was in the scenes at sea that Hayward and Viertel knew the deepest cuts had to be made. In a conventional adaptation, most description would have been replaced by film images corresponding to word imagery in the book, for it is a basic principle of adaptation that film is able to show actually what a book shows imaginatively. But for this adaptation, Tracy would be reading from the book on the soundtrack, so some of the verbal description would be retained. Hemingway wanted it so, even though there would be a duplication of visual and verbal images—a kind of cinematic redundancy. On this point Viertel and Hayward agreed with Hemingway, since the book's significance was due largely to the reputation of the descriptive prose. On the other hand, they also worried that too much footage of water, water everywhere would become boring in the extreme.

The "voice-over" was the film's conventional way of representing the interior monologue of a character's thoughts. Unfortunately, the convention strained easily over a prolonged sequence of film. This would again be a concern for Hayward in the filming of *The Spirit of St. Louis,* also about a man alone many hours at sea. With that movie, however, there was a speeding glory to Lindbergh's plane and a desperate excitement even in his thoughts, while ordering confusion or fighting fatigue. The old man's ruminations while being slowly towed by the fish seemed tiresome to Hayward. He wanted to cut at least the repetitive parts, though from Hemingway's point of view the repetition was important to the stream-of-consciousness style.

Hayward also doubted that the movie needed all the routine action about the process of catching a fish—for example, how the lines were baited and set, how the marlin was lashed to the skiff. The movie did not have to be quite so authoritatively detailed as the novel. Of course the book's expertise was very important to Hemingway. To him it had thematic significance, for it is relevant to the characterization of typical Hemingway heroes that they know all there is to know about the essential subjects of their lives—military tactics, writing, painting, or big-game hunting. And, too, the fishing detail was part of the fabric of realism of the book.

Hemingway once joked that *Moby Dick* was a very great many words about a whale.[43] The *The Old Man and the Sea* was, in scale, very many words about a marlin, and Hayward worried that so thin a book would make what would seem a very long movie.

For the release print of eighty-six minutes, the screenplay retained only about half the material of the novel. More than half the deletions were made during the final editing—without Hemingway's supervision. The script as Hemingway last saw it satisfied him well enough, as well it should have. No earlier Hemingway movie had been so accurate.

A script was not really necessary for the first shooting. Fourteen cameramen came to Cuba at the beginning of August, 1955, to film the marlin sequences, and Hemingway took over the captaincy of a tough operation. There were three camera units. Several men were on the *Pilar* with Hemingway with hand-held newsreel cameras. The others were on two motor launches mounted with the heavier camera equipment. The camera boats cruised among four small fishing boats with two Cuban fishermen to each one, ready to film the action from different angles and ranges whenever a marlin was hooked.

Hemingway liked the men he was working with, and, though it was driving up his blood pressure, he liked the invigorating challenge of the hard work: being up before dawn each morning, staying on the flying bridge eight to ten hours at a stretch, playing the fish for the cameras. There were high seas left by hurricanes elsewhere in the Caribbean, and that made it a better adventure. It was an emotional experience, and Hemingway was sure the cameras were recording beautiful stuff.[43]

The first day out they caught two marlin over 400 pounds, but a 1000-pound fish was needed for the movie. One might think it hardly mattered, since at a distance a 400-pound marlin would look huge. But Hemingway had to be satisfied, and he knew a huge fish jumped and splashed with strength and weight of special magnificence. Unfortunately, the giant marlin seemed not to be running off the Cuban coast that season. The chief problem with the picture, Hemingway said, was that there was a contract for everybody except the fish, who was the star.[44] Since they were not getting footage they could use, after two weeks the operation was scrubbed until the following spring.

By spring, however, Hemingway had begun to have some hostile thoughts about the production. His bad feelings must have started in March, 1956, when the entire production crew and cast assembled in Cuba. Hemingway did not care for the casting of Felipe

Pazos as Manolin—perhaps because he was the son of a bank president and not a fisherman's boy. At least he looked authentically Cuban, whereas, Hemingway decided in contradiction to his earlier impression, Spencer Tracy did not. He looked like a "very fat, rich" actor, Hemingway thought.[45] Tracy had promised to lose weight before shooting began, but he did not seem very committed to that intention.

Hemingway began to find fault with Tracy for any number of other reasons, almost as if Hemingway was making a concerted effort to dislike the man. There was an issue about drinking and not drinking. Before, Hemingway had admired Tracy's abstinence. Now like Bogart, whom he very much admired but did not know, Hemingway was suspicious about a man who did not drink. And he thought Tracy talked too much about being off the stuff. Then Hemingway heard, whether it was true or not, that Tracy did get tanked up before boarding a plane. The fear of flying suggested to Hemingway that Tracy was lacking in the great courage he would have to project truly in the characterization of the old man.

There was an exaggerated rumor making the rounds of Hollywood that the two men were about to square off for a fist-fight. (Tracy would have been overmatched.) Tracy might not have been aware that Hemingway was feeling this strongly. The problem might have been that Hemingway was beginning to resent the preeminence that Tracy had assumed in the production. At least from Warner Brothers' point of view, this was going to be a major picture more because it featured Tracy than because it was based on Hemingway's book. If Hemingway did sense this attitude, he would not have liked it.

Hemingway was not alone against Tracy, though. Director Fred Zinneman was getting a little too much of the actor, also. There were petty quarrels between them, as when Zinneman found Tracy, despite his avowed diet, spooning himself ice cream from a quart container. Tension between Tracy and Zinneman was overt and disruptive, because Zinneman had to work continually with him, whereas Hemingway could stay away.

Tracy said some things about resigning, in the way stars sometimes will threaten. Instead it was Zinneman who quit, after a quarrel with Jack Warner, back in Hollywood, about the best way to edit the arm-wrestling scene. (Zinneman wanted to hold the camera mostly on their hands and arms, cutting, in about equal time, to the faces of both men. Warner wanted to know why they were paying Tracy that kind of salary if they were not going to keep him on camera, and so on.) John Sturges replaced Zinneman. Sturges got along very well with Tracy, having established a rapport with him in the earlier movie *Bad Day at Black Rock* (MGM, 1954). But Sturges was not so committed to the documentary approach as Zinneman had been, and Hemingway lost an ally.

In this phase of the production Hemingway had no real function to serve, and he spent most of his time with the technical people, fooling with the cameras and thinking about another try at filming what he called "the miracle fish."[46] From the beginning he had had it in mind that if they could not catch the giant marlin in Gulf Stream waters off Cuba, then he would head a camera expedition to Capo Blanco, Peru, where 1000-pound marlin were not uncommon. They tended to be sluggish fish there, from eating 40-pound squid, but he hoped to get some good leaps from one monster of a fish.[47] So in mid-April, Hemingway was in Peru with a camera unit, his enthusiam high again. "It was steady punishing work each day," he later remembered, "and it was fun, too, because the people were nice and it was a strange new sea to learn."[48] Nevertheless, there was not much greater success than there had been in Cuba the year before. They did catch giant marlin—one was 920 pounds. (Hemingway distrusted the scales; he thought it might be bigger.) Every time, however, the cameras were in the wrong position, or light conditions were poor for color film. Something kept going wrong.

If Hemingway was not discouraged, it might have been that in a sense he was acting out the drama of the novel, day after day going out for the big fish, waiting for his luck to change, determined not to be defeated. Now he was more than making a movie, such was the intensity of his commitment. The novel was now his own experience more than it had ever been before. Jean-Paul Sartre wrote in *Nausea*: "Man is always a teller of tales, he lives surrounded by his stories and the stories of others, he sees everything that happens to him through them; and he tries to live his own life as if he were telling a story."

Eventually Hayward had to stop listening to Hemingway's assurance that they could get the fish. After thirty-two days, Hayward sent notice that the expedition was cancelled. All along Hemingway had admitted the possibility of defeat, writing with some bombast that he wanted to make a wonderful picture, but that it would be hard to do, because the Sea could ruin them all, whore that she was.[49] He had not, however, expected to be defeated this way. Hayward's decision seemed an unforgivable personal betrayal, and it terminated their friendship. In after years Hemingway never spoke to Hayward again—except on one occasion when, visiting New York, he called Hayward's office, told him he had "lost" all his guns, and asked him to send back the shotgun he had given him when the production was planned.

From Hayward's point of view, the decision to cancel the expedition was purely financial. All the location shooting—not only the crews in Cuba and Peru, but also marine camera units in Mexico, Panama, Columbia, and the Galapagos Islands trying to film the shark sequences—was making him fearful the production would cost $6 million, three times the original budget.[50] Each day's shooting for Hemingway's unit seemed an exorbitant expenditure, to say nothing of the initial expense of transporting the equipment to Peru and outfitting the boats. Hayward had almost given up hope that the picture could clear a profit. Now he was trying to prevent a financial disaster for the studio.

Approval of the Peru venture had been a last, grand gesture toward Hemingway's ideal of a documentary film. Now Hayward was thinking that they did not really have to have Hemingway's marlin footage. The previous winter, on Hemingway's own advice, the studio bought film of a world's record marlin catch at Capo Blanco by Alfred Glassell, a Texas sport fisherman. The Glassell film was not perfect for their purposes because it was mostly long shots. Still, they could only *hope* to shoot better film themselves, and hope cost too much. It probably would prove cheaper simply to pay Glassell his exorbitant price—a quarter of a million dollars.

As for the one brief close shot of the marlin lashed to the old

Spencer Tracy with the plastic and foam rubber marlin that Hemingway hated. Warner Brothers publicity stills, courtesy of Mary Hemingway.

man's skiff, they would use a store dummy—a plastic and foam rubber marlin.

Hemingway had once said of the book, "I tried to make a real old man, a real boy, a real fish and a real shark."[51] Point by point he had seen this realism compromised. There would even be some fakery in the filming of the sharks, since in order to make them appear larger and more horrific than they really were, underwater cameras filmed them attacking a skiff constructed on a smaller scale than the skiff in other scenes.

Except for a few shots, not even the ocean would be authentic Cuban waters. After weeks of shooting in Cuba, the executive decision was made that the Caribbean heat and sunlight were making working conditions unreasonably severe and slow, especially for Spencer Tracy, but for the cameramen, too. Far behind schedule, the entire production was called back to Hollywood. What other exterior scenes were needed would be filmed on Hawaiian beaches. All the scenes of Tracy in the boat would be shot in a studio tank.

This tank would not be a satisfactory simulation of the ocean. In the finished movie, the shallow waves looked artificial, and the boat rocked mechanically. Backgrounds were filmed projections of real ocean. But the color of the water in the pool and in the background did not perfectly match, and there was a loss of dimensionality where the edge of the tank met the background screen. Director John Sturges later admitted that *The Old Man and the Sea* was "technically the sloppiest picture I ever made."[52] The tank was relatively economical, however. All the shooting on the studio lot—about 80 percent of the picture—cost only about $900,000. From the studio's point of view, this more than justified a loss of authenticity.

Hemingway was glad when the movie people were finally gone from Cuba. When he came back from Peru he was absolutely finished with the cursed picture.[53] All the months he had spent attempting to make a true picture seemed now only so much wasted time.[54] He wrote a line about his feelings into *Islands in the Stream.* Willie, one of Hudson's crew, is in a "black ass" mood: "After the war," Willie says, "I'm going to be in Hollywood and be a technical adviser on how to be a horse's ass at sea. . . . I've been studying it now for over a year to train me for my career."

Hemingway did not make public statements about his anger; and he did not repudiate the production. "I . . . lent a hand with *The Old Man and the Sea*," he once said in an interview, playing down his sorry involvement, "but . . . didn't make out so well."[55] Perhaps he was trying not to ruin his chance of making further money on the picture from the small percentage of the profits that would be his due.

The profits never came. The studio was never able to make up the millions of dollars of cost overrun. Sport fisherman would have liked the movie. High school English teachers certainly did. Many students must have seen it on their teachers' recommendations. (To promote the school interest, the studio distributed to teachers, librarians, and principals all over the country examination copies of a study guide they could buy for a few cents for their students to use. This pamphlet, in the series "Photoplay Studies," endorsed by the National Education Association, described *The Old Man and the Sea* as "one of the finest motion pictures ever made.")[56]

But the movie turned out not to be much of an entertainment for the mass audience. The studio tried to promote the title's reputation as a literary masterpiece, as in this press release:

> The distinguished Warnercolor film is viewed as making a contribution to motion pictures equal to that made to world literature by Hemingway's deeply moving story. . . . Hemingway's story . . . brought him the Nobel and Pulitzer Prizes and new world acclaim as an artist of remarkable compassion and insight into the human heart. The Warner Bros. film faithfully and beautifully transfers these elements to the screen.

Pulitzer and Nobel prizes could not sell this picture, though.

To a different segment of the public the studio tried to sell it as a thriller, with such slogans as "MAN AGAINST KILLER MONSTERS OF THE RAGING SEAS!" (meaning the sharks) or "THE MOST DRAMATIC MAN-AGAINST MONSTER BATTLE EVER SHOWN!" The movie was hardly thrilling at all.

The monotony of it was its ruination, Leland Hayward decided, even as his early worry had told him. Hemingway had a different

The one-sheet poster for *The Old Man and the Sea*. The sky is deep yellow, the glowering clouds in shades of brown. The inset photograph of Spencer Tracy is printed in red. This was one of the most striking of the Hemingway movie posters. From the author's collection.

torney about picture contracts, he expressed the opinion that his reputation was perfectly safe from Hollywood's harm. Only the writing mattered, only the writing would last, and his reputation would stand on his books alone.

Obviously, this was true in a sense. Literary critics and historians, teachers and students, and Hemingway's serious reading public would refer their judgments of his importance to his books. But in his lifetime and afterwards Hemingway was important to another audience, too. This was the mass audience not especially, not necessarily familiar with his books, though they knew Hemingway as a personality and accepted the fact of his importance as a literary celebrity. Perhaps because less sophisticated, this was a more impressionable audience. Hemingway seems scarcely to have comprehended the fact that Hollywood had enormous influence over this inestimably vast, other public. More than his publishers did, the Hollywood studios affected Hemingway's popular reputation among all those people who knew a book like *The Old Man and the Sea* only from their impressions of it on the screen.

CHAPTER III

# Screen Romance: *A Farewell to Arms*

Hemingway once asked his friend Harvey Breit why anyone would make a rotten movie deliberately. It was 1957, only about a year after Hemingway was finished with the bad experience of the movie of *The Old Man and the Sea*. Now reports were coming to him about the bad movie David O. Selznick was making of *A Farewell to Arms*. What made it worse was that Hollywood had already ruined this same book twenty-five years earlier. The first time Hollywood had done that to *A Farewell to Arms* Hemingway had not worried, he told Breit, because he had believed that eventually the public's taste would improve and eventually they would make wonderful pictures. Now he felt disabused of that old expectation. Movies were just getting worse and worse.[1]

Hemingway's initial disappointment with movie adaptation had been in 1932, when Frank Borzage filmed *A Farewell to Arms* for Paramount.[2] That was when Hemingway first learned that Hollywood only made the kind of pictures that people wanted to see, and the public had bad taste. Even before the movie premiered, its publicity campaign showed Hemingway something about how the taste of the movie-going public was different from the taste of his reading public. In appealing to the mass audience, Paramount's advertising made *A Farewell to Arms* sound like the most vulgar kind of melodramatic mush. It was a great embarrassment to the novel to call it "Ernest Hemingway's world famous story of two who began in passion's reckless abandon with a love that grew until it heeded neither shame, nor danger, nor death." It was "the most tumultuous, passionate romance yet written or screened! The mad mating of two souls lost for love's sake to the thunder of a world gone mad!" One line of dialogue was quoted again and again on the posters and newspaper ads: "Let's love tonight. There may be no tomorrow!" That silly line was not even in the script, let alone in the novel.

Only Hemingway's readers really knew what Hemingway wrote. But the easy deceit of movie publicity was to pretend that the movie was just like the book. It had always been so in selling movies from books. The earliest literary adaptation in film was Edwin S. Porter's *Uncle Tom's Cabin* in 1903. The publicity for that Tom show claimed, "The story has been carefully studied and every scene posed in accordance with the famous author's version."[3] Almost the identical thing was said about the famous author's version of *A Farewell to Arms*. "The film follows the Hemingway novel with remarkable fidelity," claimed one press release article. "To the thousands who have read *A Farewell to Arms*, the sensitive, intelligent film version cannot be other than a fulfillment," said another.

This idea also could be suggested by an illustration. Some of the display advertising showed a copy of the novel, or a page ripped from it, illustrating the cliché "torn from the pages of." Bookstores could be asked to cooperate in promoting the picture, stacking copies of the novel near movie posters—a common promotional "tie-in."

A recurrent slogan of the campaign ran, "As you read it in the novel, you'll see it on the screen." One elaborate publicity gimmick promoters called the "Rejected by censor" mailing piece. If a theater manager were willing to take the trouble, he could send a flyer to all the women on his mailing list. The envelope was to be addressed to Lt. Frederic Henry, 1st Hospital Corps, Piave, Italy. The address lines were to be crossed through, and the envelope was to be rubber-stamped REJECTED BY CENSOR. Inside the envelope was this form letter:

> Dear Madam:
>
> War-time! Suppose you were alone in a dark, drab, Swiss hotel room! In a few weeks you were to become a mother—and the man you loved was miles away—on the shell-torn Italian front. You write letter after letter to him—twenty-one of them—and they are all returned stamped REJECTED BY CENSOR.
>
> This is just one of the dramatic situations in Ernest Hemingway's *A Farewell to Arms*, which comes to the _______ Theater on ____ (date).

> As you read it in the novel, you'll see *A Farewell to Arms* on the screen!

Obviously the effectiveness of such a publicity piece depended on the recipient's *not* having read the book—else she would recognize that no such situation exists in the novel.

The publicity was quite unconscionable in its insistence that the movie-makers were respectful of Hemingway. Some of the more seemingly sincere press statements said that the adapters had respected the rights of Hemingway's readers as well. An advance article headlined "Hemingway Fans Spur Film Makers to Follow Novel" praised the accomplishment of screenplay writers Benjamin Glazer and Oliver H. P. Garrett. Glazer offered a statement: "The country is filled with avid Hemingway fans who would resent any great liberties being taken with this book or with the dialogue." Everyone liked to hear something like that, even those who were not "Hemingway fans." It was gratifying to believe that going to a movie was as good as reading a book. If the book was as important as his fans' enthusiasm implied, then going out to this movie was worthwhile. But the fact remained that however many "Hemingway fans" there were in the country, there was an enormously greater number of people who had not read the book and never would. Furthermore, it made little difference whether or not those who read the book resented the movie. By that time they would already have paid their money. For that matter, some readers of the book would think that the movie was an improvement.

One of Paramount's executives must have had the temerity to believe that Hemingway himself would support such claims of the movie's authenticity. What the studio wanted as a final touch to the publicity campaign was Hemingway's recommendation of the movie to coincide with its release. The premiere had been set for December 7, 1932, at the Criterion Theater in New York. Almost at the last minute the studio decided there was a good newspaper story to be had if Hemingway would attend an advance showing. A telegram was sent to him in Piggott, Arkansas, where he was visiting his wife's family, saying that a print—unexpectedly available—made possible "a private showing of *A Farewell to Arms* to your family and friends at Piggott on the night of the Broadway premiere or before."[4] The studio requested an immediate reply, but without waiting for it, postponed the New York opening a day—this because, as explained in a press release, "Ernest Hemingway wanted to invite the whole town of Piggott, Ark., to the world premiere of his *A Farewell to Arms*."[5]

Hemingway had his reply ready when an Associated Press reporter telephoned him for comment. He quoted his answering telegram, which advised Paramount executives to "use your imagination" as to "where to put" the print of *A Farewell to Arms*, adding, "but do not send here." Hemingway went on to say that, although Paramount had bought the movie rights, they did not "also get the right to my sanction of the picture version." If Paramount persisted in their intention to send the movie to Piggott, they would find he was gone.[6] So the movie premiered in New York after all, and Hemingway was on a duck-hunting trip when it played the Franklin Theater in Piggott. It must have been a long time afterwards that he saw the picture, with no attendant publicity, and, of course, no recommendation.

His reaction was more than a way of getting even with Paramount for the vulgar publicity campaign. Although he had not seen the movie script, he had heard reports that it drastically changed the ending of the novel. In the novel, after her baby is born dead, Catherine Barkley herself dies from severe hemorrhaging. Screenwriters Glazer and Garrett had adapted the ending so that Catherine survives.

This is the action across the last few minutes of the movie. The doctor has told Catherine (Helen Hayes) that she has "not long." Frederic (Gary Cooper) is waiting to see her. First Catherine powders her face a little because, she says, "He never liked me to be pale." The nurses help her brush her hair. Then they leave her so that Frederic may speak with her privately. He sits at the edge of the bed and leans close to her. They try to talk bravely, though Frederic is weeping, of plans for after the war. Catherine tells him she is going to die. They vow to each other that they will never be parted:

FREDERIC: Whatever happens you'll not be afraid?
CATHERINE: I'll not be afraid.

FREDERIC: We've never been apart, really; not since we met.
CATHERINE: Not since we met.
FREDERIC: And never can be.
CATHERINE: Never parted.
FREDERIC: In life and in death. Say it, Cat.
CATHERINE: In life and in death. We'll never be parted.
FREDERIC: You do believe that, don't you, Cat?
CATHERINE: I believe it, and I'm not afraid.

Then Catherine has a blank and stricken look; it seems that she is a moment away from dying. Suddenly the tragic music that underscores the scene, the "Leibestode" theme from Wagner's *Tristan und Isolde,* is cut by the blast of a factory steam whistle, and the film dissolves to exterior shots. Church bells are chiming; doves, or pigeons intended to represent doves, are fluttering from the steeple; leaflets scatter in the breeze as a cheering crowd, in silhouette, gathers to read a wall poster. The war is over! Peace is declared! The film cuts back to Frederic and Catherine, who immediately know what the jubilation must mean. As with an infusion of hope and joy at the glad tidings, Catherine revives. The expression of her eyes is bright, and she is able to smile. "Armistice!" Frederic tells her. "Peace," she answers. The camera holds the shot of the happy lovers, their faces touching, to the final dissolve.

Frank Borzage, the movie's producer, said that this happy ending represented a possible interpretation of Hemingway's intentions.[7] In truth, interpretation had nothing whatsoever to do with it. The real reason for the change was that Borzage thought a picture with a blissful ending might be a better commercial risk than one with a tragic ending. It was a prevalent belief in Hollywood that audiences tended to prefer movies with a cheerful outlook at the end and, conversely, tended to react against movies that were uncompromisingly tragic. Studio opinion samplings indicated as much, and experience tended to confirm the surveys. The year before Paramount released *A Farewell to Arms,* for example, Universal had released *Waterloo Bridge,* another World War I romance. That movie ended with the heroine, Myra, biding farewell to her lover as he returns to the front. Moments later Myra is killed by a Zeppelin bomb. It was already a very sad movie because Myra and

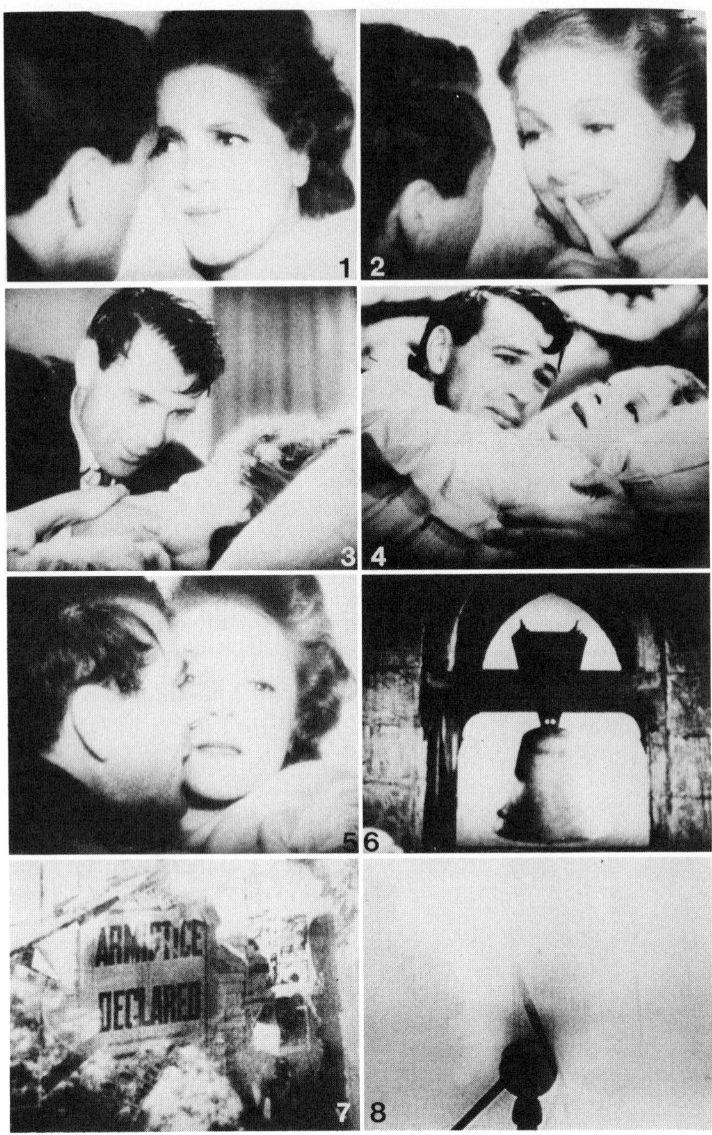


The death scene from *A Farewell to Arms* (1932), showing the alternate endings. Frederic and Catherine speak of happier things, how they will go back to America and be married again, this time in a real church. (This was the script's last chance to affirm the high morality of their love affair.) But they both know that this is the end, and at frames 4 and 5 Catherine is dying. In the street below bells are tolling, whistles are blowing, for the Armistice has been declared.

Frederic Henry, stricken with grief, hears the irony of the bells tolling for Catherine, and carries her body to the window, setting an elegantly pathetic tableau for the last shot of the picture. Frames 13–16 show the notorious "happy ending." The bells ring, and the whistle blows, and Frederic hears the jubilation in the streets. With the infusion of joy and life at frame 14, Catherine's eyes begin to flutter open, and at frame 15 she smiles. This version of the picture ends with Catherine happily alive and embracing with Frederic.

her lover had to be parted. Audiences at New York's Mayfair Theater were so distressed when, for all her misery, Myra is killed too that the management decided to cut the final minute or so of the movie lest audiences stay away. Borzage was concerned that *A Farewell to Arms* might have the same problem.

Actually, Borzage had been of two minds about the ending of *A Farewell to Arms*. He made the unusual decision to film *alternate* endings, to print both versions, and to make both sets of prints available for distribution. Theater managers could decide which version they would prefer to screen. *Variety* predicted that theaters would do better at the box office with the "sugar-coated compromise" at the end. *Variety* admitted that Hemingway's ending was more believable than Borzage's. On the other hand, "Caesarian operations are likewise more successful than fatal, actually."[8]

The other version is different only in the final seconds. Catherine does die in the moment before the bells chime. For its irony, it is the more powerful ending: the bells should be tolling for Catherine's death. Frederic lifts her in his arms (the bed linen trails in lavish folds), and turns towards the bright light now streaming through the window. "Peace—Peace," Frederic's voice throbs in ironic benediction. It is an elegantly pathetic tableau.

Even with Catherine gone, the movie ending was still distant from Hemingway's intentions and values. For one thing, the war has not ended in the book. Frederic has only seen a newspaper headline that there has been a breakthrough at the front. More important is the difference in tone. The book ends with Frederic's telling the nurses to get out of the room so that he can be alone with Catherine: "But after I had got them out and shut the door and turned off the light it wasn't any good. It was like saying goodby to a statue. After a while I went out and left the hospital and walked back to the hotel in the rain."

Frederic tells of Catherine's dying and his leave-taking with his emotion controlled. Perhaps that is the masculinity of his style, or perhaps it is the feeling of Emily Dickinson's line "After great pain a formal feeling comes." The *New York Times* reviewer had commented when the novel was first published: "A Victorian telling the story of Henry and Catherine would have waxed sentimental;

he would have sought the tears of his reader. And he would surely have shed tears as he wrote. We do not attempt to say how much Mr. Hemingway may have been affected by his narrative; but it is certain he has no desire to see his readers weep."[9] Though Borzage's intentions were ambivalent, by this pathethic version of the ending he certainly did desire his audience to weep. There is a romantic artiness to his direction of the scene, what with the Wagner and all. It is a "tear-jerker" ending in the extreme.

But the audience would cry at the "happy ending" too, during all the long minutes when it surely seemed that Catherine was dying. Perhaps there was not that much difference in the effect of the endings anyway. Borzage might have begun to think that what could ruin the effect of either ending was talking about it too much. That the press had publicized Hemingway's outrage was not good advance notice. It seems that Borzage decided, therefore, not to release the happy ending after all, at least not to major cities, where the critics just might take sides with Hemingway against him.

Suppressing the happy ending proved to be a good maneuver. The upshot of the affair was that critics tended to think badly of Hemingway for judging the movie without having seen it. "The reputation of the movies must be somethin' horrible," wrote the reviewer for the *Los Angeles Times*, "since Ernest Hemingway will not deign, according to all reports, to look at the production of his story!"[10] The reviewer for the *New York Evening Post* could see Hemingway's point of view but thought he ought really to be appreciative of the adaptation: "If Hemingway has any grievance against Paramount for the film version of his book I can assure him as a reverent admirer of the original and as one who has seen many novels and plays come desecrated to the screen, that the job represents one of the finer achievements of the cinema."[11]

The triumph was clearly Borzage's when reviewers said the emotionality of the movie was its greatest achievement. The review in the *New York American* was highly excited:

> Now you may believe that the cinema is an art rather than a racket, or even an industry! And as an art, it added cubits to its stature last night at the Criterion Theatre, where a personal tragedy of the great

war filled the hearts of the hard-boiled audience with emotions that welled to its throat and came from its eyes in hot scalding tears.[12]

The review in the *New York Daily News* was even more effusive in its praise:

> The picture is heart-rending and throat hurting. It moves you so deeply that it is often difficult to see the screen, for the haze which mists your tear-filled eyes. . . . There is no question about Borzage's genius. He tugs at your heartstrings until you positively can't stand it any more. . . . The final sequence is replete with pathos and tenderness, leading up to a gloriously climactic moment. *A Farewell to Arms* is terribly touching.

Then the *Daily News* reviewer turned on Hemingway. "And please, Mr. Hemingway, don't make yourself ridiculous by finding the slightest of faults with Paramount's production of your tale, for in Frank Borzage's picturization there lies a thousand times more than you, or any of you, will ever put into the sterile, colorless black and white of type and paper."[13]

Both these amazing opinions were written by women. It was the women in the audience, surely, who wildly liked this picture. Borzage had expected this to be so, and a considerable amount of the movie's promotion had been directed towards the women's market—the "rejected by censor" flyer, for example, or the recurrent slogan "If You're a Woman, You'll Live the Life of Helen Hayes in *A Farewell to Arms*—and Understand!"

*A Farewell to Arms* was what was called in those days a "woman's picture." *Waterloo Bridge* was another example of the type, and, going back to the silent era, *The Sheik* (UA, 1921) and *Seventh Heaven* (Fox, 1927), which was another Borzage picture. It was an enormously popular kind of entertainment during the Twenties and Thirties.[14] Women's pictures did not have audiences almost entirely female, in the way that women's novels or women's magazines have a readership of almost entirely the one sex. Still, such movies were plotted and styled for women's sensitivities. Hollywood believed it knew very well what most women wanted to see on the screen, which was why there was a considerable sameness to most of them.

The principles of composition of such movies were not rigid. By contrast with women's movies, women's soft romance novels with the Harlequin imprint always have "guaranteed happy endings that leave femme readers uplifted."[15] Romance movies could be slightly more sophisticated than Harlequin books. At least with respect to endings, the movies were at about the level of fiction in *Cosmopolitan* magazine, whose editorial policy (*Writer's Yearbook*, 1971) states that "a happy ending isn't mandatory, but the story shouldn't be too lugubrious or depressing." If one were writing for the movies, one had to have the right sense of what a story should and should not have in it, according to what women liked.

Of course, by the way Hemingway's reputation developed, he certainly did not come to be regarded as a woman's writer. Instead, one thinks of *A Farewell to Arms* as being one of his characteristically manly books. When Paramount bought the book, though, they looked upon it as wonderful material for a woman's movie. The war would have to be pushed farther into the background, some parts of the love story brought out more, and more things seen from Catherine's point of view. All considered, however, *A Farewell to Arms* lent itself rather easily to adaptation into a conventional screen romance of the times. Hemingway might have been mortified to know it.

Many things about the book could come to the screen without being changed. The title, for instance, was fine; women would like it. But when the novel did not match with the conventions of movie romance, then the adapters had some rewriting to do.

The following contrast in situation shows what is meant by a convention of movie romance. In the novel, Frederic Henry and Catherine Barkley meet in a very ordinary way. While Frederic has been on leave his friend Rinaldi has been seeing one of the English nurses at the British hospital. The evening that Frederic returns, he and Rinaldi go over to the hospital to see this Miss Barkley and one of her friends. Rinaldi had hoped that Frederic would like the other one, Miss Ferguson. But very soon after the introductions are made it is clear that Frederic and Catherine prefer each other. This scene was saved for the movie, but it is not the first meeting between Frederic and Catherine. There is a sequence in the movie before this that has no relation at all to the book, for it was a convention of movie romance that lovers ought to meet in some extraordinary way, thereby indicating at the outset that theirs will be an extraordinary love story.[16] Frederic has been at the front, not on leave, and he spends his first night back carousing at the officers' brothel. Air raid sirens warn that Austrian planes are starting a bombing run on the village. The officers and their girls run for the shelters. Nurses from the nearby hospital are running for cover as well. Frederic and Catherine find the same cellar. Catherine has lost a slipper while running. Frederic, as it happens, has a slipper in hand. A few minutes before he had been admiring a prostitute's arch (trying to explain to her in a drunken way his profession of architecture). He notices Catherine's bare foot and in the dim light mistakes her for the girl he was with. Catherine is shocked when a perfect stranger starts making advances towards her, saying something about his profession and how her profession is even older. She is glad to see him embarrass himself when the slipper won't fit. When the all-clear signal is sounded, Catherine calls him a lunatic and stalks off. Frederic is left standing speechless, staring after this lovely, haughty English girl.

This is an amusing scene, but not very good in the literary sense in which one thinks about books as real as *A Farewell to Arms*. It is highly contrived in the coincidence of the slipper. It is somewhat implausible with respect to Frederic's behavior, even allowing that he is drunk. And it is trite, in the way a matter of mistaken identity leads to the hero's finding the girl who, after all, will prove just right for him.

The movie audience never seemed to mind when a scene was exaggerated or familiar. (The lovers in *Waterloo Bridge* also met in a shelter while an air raid was on.) There is a kind of pleasure in easy understanding and recognition. And women especially would have found the scene quite delightful. It is a little risqué, looking in on the way depraved men abandon themselves to wicked women and drink. It has a funny reversal on the little girl's favorite story of Cinderella and Prince Charming—this boor with the slipper that won't fit. The scene offers some glee in the way it has a woman making a further fool of a man who is already making a fool of himself.

Everyone knows that these two are going to fall wonderfully in love with each other. (Someday they'll look back on this terrible beginning and laugh.) Readers of the book know this right away, too, one must say. But in the movie their love is predictable especially because Frederic is a conventional character type—the dashing rake of an officer who needs to be reformed through the redeeming love of a virtuous girl. In the movie Frederic and Catherine are both almost as simple as this.

In a woman's picture even a good girl can be swept off her feet. When she has surrendered herself, the audience may be absorbed with sympathy, wondering whether or not, or how soon, her seducer will marry her.

There is no seduction scene in the novel. During their evenings together before Frederic goes to the front, he plays at seducing Catherine, but he is not especially adept at managing her. She is an unusual girl—even odd. Perhaps because they are both self-conscious that it is a game they are playing, the seduction just does not come off. They do not actually become lovers until book 2, after Frederic is sent wounded to the hospital in Milan and Catherine is transferred to duty there. Their first intimacy is hardly a seduction, since they truly love each other by now. On his back in bed with his legs mutilated, Frederic cannot be an aggressor at all. Catherine must come to him.

In the movie there is a great rush of passion. The very next evening after their run-in during the bomb raid, Frederic and Catherine attend an officers' party at the hospital. Rinaldi introduces them, and they recognize each other right away. The awkward moment soon passes, and they start getting along very well. (Someone watching the movie should make a note of the time at this point, to see how fast the pace of this seduction is running.) Rinaldi goes off for a minute to return with drinks for them all. Then Catherine sends him off again to find Miss Ferguson. Frederic talks with her about what he is doing in the war. They wander away from the hospital grounds to walk in the village park. Catherine talks about her fiancé, who has already been killed in the war. They sit down cozily in the shadow of a rearing equestrian statue with the rider grasping his sword. (The sexual symbolism seems worth remarking.) Frederic gets slapped when he first tries to kiss her. They both apologize. Catherine tells him he's sweet; Frederic denies it. Catherine says that she would not mind if he kissed her now. (Most of their conversation is drawn from the book to this point, but what follows is certainly not.) Suddenly Frederic becomes very intense:

FREDERIC: Back home I'd have courted you and sent you flowers.
CATHERINE: Out here you crowd it all into one hour.
FREDERIC: Isn't that the way it's got to be out here? Look, tomorrow morning I've got to go up to the front again. And if a shell got me and you never saw me again, then we'd both be sorry we'd been so formal and waited. Besides, what's there so fine in putting it off, dragging it out, giving me your lips tonight . . .
CATHERINE: No.
FREDERIC: . . . your throat tomorrow?
CATHERINE: No! No, wait! Please! No.

As Catherine struggles, only half-heartedly, against his embrace, the film cuts away from the scene. They were introduced less than five minutes before. (The editing of this sequence gives the impression that more time has passed, for the film cuts away from Frederic and Catherine a few times. If the audience were actually keeping track of the time, the scene in the park would be unbelievable.)

When the camera comes back, Frederic is gently asking Catherine, "Why didn't you tell me?"—meaning, presumably, why didn't you tell me that you were an innocent girl? Catherine's feelings are all confused, but she is able to laugh distractedly at herself: "The lady sat in the public square and mourned her loss of innocence." She tells Frederic that she has no regrets. And Frederic says that he loves her.

Later that night Catherine confides to Ferguson what has happened. Ferguson is angry with her for letting herself become another "conquest"—one of a hundred. Ferguson doubts that Catherine will ever see him again. Catherine worries about that also.

Helen Hayes and Gary Cooper seated at base of equestrian statue for seduction scene in *A Farewell to Arms* (1932). Photograph shows the sound stage, with Frank Borzage on the camera platform. Courtesy of Paramount.

She believes that Frederic does love her, but as he had told her, a big offensive starts in the morning, and he might not come back.

Frederic comes to say good-by to her before his ambulance unit goes up to the mountains. In the novel the scene is not given with much emotion. Catherine wants Frederic to take a St. Anthony medal.

> "I'll take care of him for you. Good-by."
> "No," she said, "not good-by."
> "All right."
> "Be a good boy and be careful. No, you can't kiss me here. You can't."
> "All right."
> I looked back and saw her standing on the steps. She waved and I kissed my hand and held it out. She waved again and then I was out of the driveway and climbing up into the seat of the ambulance and we started.

With a few tears added, this was a good scene for the movies, for the woman's audience liked tearful partings. After Frederic takes the medal he tells Catherine that he wishes he could kiss her. Tears are coming, and she can only shake her head. To stay brave, she turns and walks away.

The war sequence that follows is considerably less important in the movie than in the book. Frederic's relation to the war is not an important subject of the movie. The action at the front is only the circumstance, an almost fortunate circumstance, whereby Frederic is wounded and reunited with Catherine at the hospital in Milan.

The camera effects as Frederic's stretcher is carried into the hospital are striking. The camera moves on a low truck, angled straight up, seeing, as Frederic sees from flat on his back, the high Byzantine vaulting of the hospital corridors, the faces leaning over to speak to him. (In the movie of *The Sun Also Rises*, again in the hospital sequence, the film works similar shots from Jake's point of view, but in a style not quite so extreme.) The moment she is alone with Frederic, Catherine's face blurs into the lens of the camera in what the publicity for the movie called the biggest close-up ever filmed.

That first evening in the hospital, though they hardly know each other and have been together almost no time at all, they are ready to marry. Frederic's friend the priest is with them, and he can tell from their faces that they are in love. Also, they talk about children. They explain to him it is only the technicality of army regulations that keeps them from being married. In a moment, they notice the priest is whispering in Latin. "Say, Father, are—is that the marriage service?" Frederic asks.

FREDERIC: Poor Cat! It's such a crazy marriage.
CATHERINE: At least I'm in white.
FREDERIC: No orange blossoms.
CATHERINE: I can smell them.
FREDERIC: No organ music.
CATHERINE: I can hear it plainly.
PRIEST: (Whispers in Latin; then . . . ) Amen. (He turns to the lovers.) It was a foolish notion, perhaps. I have not the right to say you are married, yet it has made me happy to do this. For now from my heart, I can say I bless you in His name.
FREDERIC: Thank you, Father.
PRIEST: Goodbye, and be happy, both of you.
CATHERINE: Thank you, Father.

In the novel Frederic and Catherine only *pretend* that they are married. These movie lovers, though, have had an extraordinary romance from the beginning. They have to have a "crazy marriage" so that the movie can be different from ordinary real life.

In the following weeks Frederic and Catherine have a lovely honeymoon in Milan. Frederic's legs seem not to bother him at all, though he is still at the hospital. Of course they keep their marriage secret from the hospital staff. What is more, Frederic does not even tell Rinaldi, and Catherine does not tell Fergy. That seems strange, but perhaps the audience does not wonder.

Months pass, and Catherine discovers that she is going to have a baby. In the novel Catherine tells Frederic she is pregnant, although she is afraid to tell him and wishes it were not true. The woman's movie audience loves secrets. Because Frederic is going off to war again, Catherine feels that he would worry terribly if he knew about the baby. The situation would be easier for her if he *did* know, but to the audience she seems a more wonderful character because she sacrifices her own happiness for the sake of her lover's.

When Frederic's troop train leaves, Catherine buys a ticket to Switzerland. Her pregnancy will soon be obvious, and there she will not have to suffer disgrace in the eyes of the hospital staff. Before she leaves she confesses to Ferguson that she is pregnant, though, quite implausibly—one would think even to the movie audience—she still does not tell her that she is legitimately married. Catherine explains that she intends to write to Frederic from Switzerland to let him know where she is.

At this point the movie version of *A Farewell to Arms* gives Rinaldi a function in the story not assigned to him in the book. The screenplay needs him as villain. In the novel, Frederic and Catherine's tragedy is caused (so Frederic believes) by an abstract, malevolent force—a dark design—that very purposefully kills Catherine. That is what the world does to all people who are good and brave:

> If [Frederic thinks] people bring so much courage to this world the world has to kill them to break them, so of course it kills them. The world breaks every one and afterward many are strong at the broken places. But those that will not break it kills. It kills the very good and the very gentle and the very brave impartially. If you are none of these you can be sure it will kill you too but there will be no special hurry.

The passage is characteristic of the very grim world view that governs *A Farewell to Arms*. It was all much too serious and difficult an idea for a screen romance. Such movies usually have no "idea" to them at all. Sad movies do not allow for abstract, impersonal forces to govern characters' lives, lest perhaps the audience experience the distress of wondering whether these forces affect their own lives. In movies, and in popular literature, the cause of tragedy is usually particularized in an individual, a villain, whom the audience can easily recognize and understand. In this adaptation Rinaldi is not a villain in the sense that he has out-and-out wicked motives. He is simply not a good egg. As he later admits to Frederic, "I am not a good egg." By his actions at this point in the screenplay Rinaldi causes all the unhappiness to follow.

The scene is the officers' quarters in a village near the front lines. Frederic is sitting at his desk writing to Catherine. Rinaldi is rush-

Lobby cards promoting *A Farewell to Arms*, 1932. Both scenes are posed for the publicity but correspond approximately with the scene when Frederic leaves for the front and later when Rinaldi has censored Frederic's mail. The card above dates from the 1938 re-release of the picture, the card below from 1932—thus the different styles of art lettering.

ing him, for he is anxious that they get to the brothel before it is crowded. Frederic is not interested in going anyway. Not knowing he is married, Rinaldi cannot understand his friend's devotion to Catherine. All Rinaldi sees is that his friend no longer has wild good times as in the old days. Besides, the movie hints as the novel does not, Rinaldi is slightly jealous ( jealousy being a simple motivation that the audience can readily sense). So Rinaldi decides he must interfere with this too serious love affair. As ranking officer of his unit, it is Rinaldi's responsibility to censor the mail. Rinaldi sorts out all Frederic and Catherine's mail to each other and has it returned.

Months have passed before the fade-in to the next scene. Frederic is talking to the priest. He is terribly worried about Catherine. In all this time he has not had a single letter from her. And today all the letters he had mailed to her in Milan, thirty-two of them, came back stamped "Return to Sender. Person Unknown." Frederic has no idea that she has gone to Switzerland, and he fears something terrible has happened to her. He has not been able to get any information about her at all. Leave-of-absence has been forbidden since battle maneuvers have begun to the north. Nevertheless, Frederic has decided that he must go to Milan to find her. That is desertion, the priest tells him; he will be caught. He *must* not do this! "Yes, I must. That's what I wanted to tell you, Padre. What does this war mean to me any more? What does anything mean but finding her?"

Hemingway thought that the movie's premise for Frederic Henry's desertion was preposterous. The movie hero deserts, he said, because his girlfriend wouldn't write him any letters. When he goes to look for her, the entire army tags along so he won't get lonely.[17] Hemingway apparently found the battle sequence that follows quite incoherent: night shots of troop movements so confusedly intercut with shots of Frederic making his escape that the audience could hardly tell that he was trying to go the other way. Hemingway was sore that the circumstances of Frederic's desertion as they are developed in the novel were not in the movie at all.

If one is not so concerned that the battle sequence in the movie changes the book, it seems like very exciting film, with bombardment and strafing, artillery, machine guns, and planes. There is much glare, noise, and the music of Valkyries riding. It is an impressive montage—really virtuosic directing. For such a sequence as this the movie won an Academy Award for Best Cinematography and for Best Sound.

Through the montage, images of the cross and the crucifixion appear over and over: a church steeple is toppled in the flare of an explosion; crosses on graves are overturned by bomb blasts; a soldier's corpse hangs over barbed wire with arms outstretched. This was Borzage's antiwar statement that war represents a recrucifixion of Christ. Of course in its expressionism and symbolism the battle sequence was very different from the book.

Frederic is almost arrested by the battle police. He swims the river to escape their fire and, as in the novel, hides on a train to Milan. In the movie it is now Ferguson who continues the trouble for the lovers that Rinaldi began. It is late at night when Frederic sneaks into her room in the nurses' quarters. She understands that he has deserted and is desperate to find Catherine. She hates Frederic now: "I hope they catch you. I hope they shoot you! Pay you back for what you've done to her! Making her have a baby!" This is the first Frederic has heard of the baby. If it occurred to him to tell Ferguson that he and Catherine are married, presumably she would calm down. And one would think that simply for Catherine's sake, Ferguson would tell Frederic that she is in Switzerland, for she knows that Catherine loves him and that the whole plan was for him to join her there as soon as he could. But Ferguson is nearly hysterical now. Frederic begs for help: "Where? Where? Oh, for pity's sake, tell me, Fergy." She still refuses. All the noise in Ferguson's room has awakened the other nurses, and Frederic has to flee.

Frederic thinks of another plan. He places a notice in the personals column of the Milan newspaper telling Catherine to meet him in Stresa. By the kind of extraordinary coincidence commonplace and allowable in melodrama, Rinaldi, though he is still at the front, finds a copy of this paper and happens to read the advertisement. He believes that Frederic must have been shell-shocked in the battle, lost his memory, and wandered away. He will go to his friend's rescue, to find him before the military police arrest and execute him.

When he finds Frederic, Rinaldi realizes how serious a mistake it was for him to try to keep true lovers apart. Obviously Frederic is frantically in love with Catherine, and when Frederic tells him that Catherine is pregnant, Rinaldi, behaving like a decent fellow again for all the trouble he has caused, knows that they must be reunited. Without admitting to Frederic that he has intercepted their letters, Rinaldi tells him that Catherine is across the lake, in Brissago. (It never occurs to Frederic to wonder how Rinaldi could know where she is.) Frederic borrows a rowboat and heads for Switzerland.

Meanwhile, in Switzerland, Catherine is coming back to the hotel from a walk. Though she knows there is never anything for her at the mail desk, she checks anyway. Yes, the mail clerk says, today *twenty* letters have come for her. She is ecstatic that at last she has heard from Frederic; then seeing that the packet contains only all her own letters to Frederic—REJECTED BY CENSOR—she swoons.

When next the audience sees her, she has been rushed to the hospital, her fall apparently having induced the complicated, premature labor from which she will die. Now the film intercuts between shots of Catherine in the hospital, weakly calling for Frederic, and shots of Frederic desperately rowing across the lake. (This is the race against time, found in innumerable movies.) Frederic arrives at the hospital just as Catherine is being wheeled into the operating room. After the delivery, she survives only long enough to play the death scene.

Hemingway seems to have been seriously worried that anyone would ever want to read his novel after seeing such a picture as this. In later years it remained something of a wonder to him that people continued to read the book despite what Hollywood had done to it.[18] Hemingway really ought not have troubled himself in that regard, futilely disputing a matter of taste. Very possibly more people read *A Farewell to Arms* in 1933—in the Scribner's edition, the $1.25 Modern Library edition, or the 75¢ Grosset and Dunlap "photoplay" edition, with end papers a collage of movie stills—than had read it in any of the several years since its first publication.[19] Maybe some of his new readers felt that the movie was more enjoyable than the book; for some people, almost any movie is better than almost any book. On balance, presumably the movie enhanced Hemingway's popular reputation vastly. Many in this mass audience had never heard of a Hemingway title before, and here was *A Farewell to Arms* being nominated for an Academy Award as Best Picture. It did not win; *Cavalcade* (Fox, 1933), adapted from Noel Coward's play, was Best Picture that year. But the nomination was a kind of honor for the author nevertheless.

*A Farewell to Arms* kept making money for the rest of the decade, in re-release twice. World War II dated it some and diminished its value as a movie property. In 1949 Warner Brothers made an inexpensive trade for the rights, but only produced *Force of Arms* (1951), which was only slightly like *A Farewell to Arms*, not really an adaptation. (The passing similarity between *Force of Arms*, and *A Farewell to Arms* is mentioned in the Preface to this book.)

Then in November, 1955, Hemingway received a cablegram from David O. Selznick: "Happy advise you have brought *A Farewell to Arms* for my return to production and hope to do job that will please you."[20] It can hardly be imagined that Hemingway was happy to hear the news. On the positive side, this would mean no one would be seeing the Borzage version for a very long time, for Selznick would recall all television prints showing as the "late movie" and have them destroyed. On the negative side, this time Hemingway was not even getting paid for what new indignities the book might have to suffer.

Selznick was very genuinely glad to have the movie rights. But his courteous message to Hemingway notwithstanding, Selznick really had little confidence that Hemingway would be pleased with the new version. In a memo to his director John Huston he wrote, "I certainly want Hemingway to like the picture, if this is at all possible, which I doubt, because—as those who worked on *The Sun Also Rises* and *The Old Man and the Sea* learned—if a character goes from Cafe A to Cafe B, instead of Cafe B to Cafe A, or if a boat heads north instead of south, Hemingway is upset."[21] Selznick could not see himself being "slavish" to the book that way.

Lobby cards for the two versions of *A Farewell to Arms*, 1932 and 1958.

Ben Hecht's first script was a close adaptation, and Selznick thought it was "worthless." Each time he and Hecht revised the script, it drifted further from Hemingway's text. This was a trend that John Huston, who was trying to protect Hemingway's interest, found objectionable. Selznick had to remind Huston again and again that the novel was not "Holy Writ," and that there was not going to be any "Papa-worshipping groveling on this picture."[22] Eventually Huston had to be replaced by Charles Vidor, who had an attitude toward the script closer to Selznick's own.

Selznick claimed to believe that Hemingway was a splendid writer. It was just that Hemingway was not a movie producer. "I have the greatest respect in the world for Hemingway, but my ego—and also my record—doesn't permit me to think that Hemingway can prepare a better motion picture than I can. On the contrary, I know damn well he can't." He also thought *A Farewell to Arms* was a wonderful book, though flawed by "sloppy introductions of characters and careless handling of time elements, etc. (It is not clear what Selznick meant by "sloppy" and "careless".) The problem was that the book was not right for the movies in every way. Selznick would use the book insofar as it had "the qualifications . . . for motion picture purposes," then throw it away.[23]

Stated economically, the purpose of a motion picture is to turn profits as high as possible by pleasing an audience as large as possible. As for Borzage before him, Selznick's problem was to enhance the mass appeal of a sophisticated novel by giving it more of the qualities of a popular movie.

Selznick would give his picture a very different look, however, Styles in the movies had changed. No one made a "woman's picture" anymore, or at least did not admit it was such.

Much more so than Borzage, Selznick was a producer of spectacles. Borzage had not had the budget to make his *A Farewell to Arms* an "epic." He shot the picture entirely on the studio lot (except for one sequence filmed in the Southern Pacific train yard). Selznick would spend $5 million to shoot on European locations. Press releases would speak pridefully of lavish battle sequences that required twenty-eight freight cars filled with props and equipment to be railroaded into the Italian Alps. Counting villagers and troops from Italian army units, the movie had a cast of 11,000—or so it was said. Audiences could not get wide-screen, color extravaganzas like this on a television screen. The fifties was a good decade at the box office for big pictures.

The spectacle was certainly not a new style of movie; it had appealed to previous generations of movie-goers. Selznick was in the tradition of DeMille and Griffith. Indeed, dramatic spectacle was ancient. Aristotle discussed the use of spectacle in classical Greek drama. He had a low opinion of it as an element of drama: "The Spectacle has, indeed, an emotional attraction of its own, but, of all the parts, it is the least artistic, and connected least with the art of poetry. For the power of Tragedy, we may be sure, is felt even apart from representation and actors. Besides, the production of spectacular effects depends more on the art of the stage machinist than on the poet."[24] Selznick was like the stage machinist, adding the emotional appeal of spectacle which was apart from the power of tragedy in the novel itself.

For spectacular effects, *Gone With the Wind* (MGM, 1939) had been an easier novel to work with, because spectacle had been written into the book. *A Farewell to Arms* was not written in so large an epic scale. Selznick believed Hemingway's story had *potential* to film as spectacularly as *Gone With the Wind.* The movie's publicity said that *A Farewell to Arms* was "as big or bigger than [Selznick's] Southern epic." But Selznick, Vidor, and Hecht had to find their own ways, not Hemingway's, to fill the screen with extravaganza.

Selznick's adaptation of chapter 8 of the novel—the scene in which Frederic says good-by to Catherine before going up to the front and accepts the St. Anthony's medal—is a good illustration of the epic style. In Hemingway's version, the scene takes place on the hospital's front steps. In Borzage's version, it takes place, with some tears, in the entrance hall. In Selznick's version, it is played in a vast village square jammed with townspeople assembled to see the troops off for the glorious offensive. A military brass band is marching past. Whole regiments of troops are mustering into formation. A huge convoy of military vehicles lumbers through. The ambulances move at slow pace. Frederic (played by Rock

Jennifer Jones as Catherine Barkley saying farewell to Frederic as he leaves for the front. Publicity still, courtesy of Twentieth Century-Fox.

Hudson) keeps glancing into the crowds of parents and children and peasant girls to catch a glimpse of Catherine (Jennifer Jones), if she is there. Meanwhile, Catherine—so fresh and pretty, the white veil of her nurse's headdress setting her apart from the peasants in their drab greys and browns—desperately pushes against the crowd. She is miserably confused because all the ambulances look alike. Finally, she glimpses Frederic, and, now weeping with happiness, she calls out his name over the din of the crowd. Frederic rushes to meet her. They embrace and kiss; then Frederic hurries back to his ambulance. Over the march music and the shouting of the crowd Catherine calls to him, "I'll be waiting . . . I'll be waiting."

In the pages that follow in the novel, Hemingway describes the convoy moving into the mountains. As Frederic sees it:

> The road climbed steeply going up and back and back and forth through chestnut woods to level finally along a ridge. . . . I looked to the north at the two ranges of mountains, green and dark to the snow-

> line and then white and lovely in the sun. Ahead there was a rounded turn-off in the road to the right and looking down I could see the road dropping through the trees. There were troops on this road and motor trucks and mules with mountain guns as we went down, keeping to the side.

The description goes on like this to end chapter 8 and begin chapter 9. It was not exactly the picture of Alpine troops moving into the mountains that Selznick had in mind. Selznick required an even more picturesque sequence, with more military pageantry, more action, and more human interest. Thus the movie audience sees buglers on Alpine peaks trumpeting calls to the miniature armies assembling in the valleys far below. Crowds gather on the roadside to cheer on their brave soldiers. Nuns distribute parcels of food. Pretty girls hand out gay mountain wildflowers, which the soldiers jauntily stick in the barrels of their rifles. The infantry resolutely marches up the snowy roads. Their uniforms have a quaint foreign look to them, especially the Tyrolean caps. Some men smoke big curved pipes or zestily sing Alpine songs. (Selznick sent a memo to his composer about this. He wanted the effect of thousands of voices coming up from the valley. It was not to sound like an opera chorus, but like real soldiers singing.)[25] No one is yodeling, but these soldiers look like sometimes they do. Some men trudge with heavy artillery pieces strapped on their backs. A pack mule is hoisted by block and tackle over the side of a precipice. A soup kitchen is set up in a cave, and a hastily painted banner identifies it as the Villa Rossa brothel, much to the amusement of the troops. An altar is set up by the roadside, and men fall out of line to kneel and accept the blessing of the priest, who raises his crucifix against the vista of mountain peaks. The Hemingway text mentioned Austrian observation balloons. They would have been good. Selznick must not have been able to arrange for any Austrian observation balloons.

Eventually Selznick returned to the book for the sequence of action that climaxes with Frederic's being wounded. Before that, Selznick added another scene for the sake of spectacle in which the hero seems more glamorously daring than he ever does in the novel. He climbs to the ridge where the artillery is placed so that he can survey enemy gun positions on the opposing slopes, more in the attitude of a commanding general than a lieutenant in the ambulance corps. Shells begin to scream overhead. Frederic's place now is with his men. In a daredevil stunt he climbs onto the cable car and is reeled down the mountainside. Suddenly, as the enemy gunners take aim, the entire war is focused on him. Shells explode perilously near. But this war is only a Hollywood war, a dangerous winter sport on the slope of a splendidly beautiful winter resort.

This was not Selznick's final statement about the war. That would come in a much more elaborate sequence later in the movie—the retreat from Caporetto, which bears approximately the same relationship to his *A Farewell to Arms* as the burning of Atlanta bears to *Gone With the Wind.* Selznick gave the sequence his most lavish worry. In a memo to his director Selznick asked that the casting office make available a great assortment of infants and small children (even twins, because Selznick knew statistics that proved twins were more often seen in Italy than in any other country). Also he wanted old men and women, and cripples and blind people. He worried whether the scene had enough dogs and cats, or too many umbrellas.[26]

His spectacle version of chapters 27–30 begins with the bombardment of the town of Orsino. It is night, and it is sheeting rain (thus the many umbrellas). Shells scream into the village, blowing up buildings. Houses burn out of control. People are evacuating the town in a state of mass hysteria. There is a pandemonium of animal noises.

Back at the hospital Frederic and his men have loaded their ambulance with equipment. There are too many patients to be moved. Either they will be taken as prisoners or killed if the hospital is bombed—an idea of German atrocity not in the book. (Here Selznick was using over again a fearful scene from *Gone With the Wind.*) In a more important departure from the book, Frederic and Rinaldi urge their young friend the priest, who is named Father Galli in the screenplay, to leave with them. He refuses. He has "higher orders" from his God to stay with the abandoned men. When the ambulances leave and the bombs fall nearer, the wounded men start to panic. Father Galli's courage calms them. They follow the lead of his voice in singing a hymn as the hospital explodes. The novel does not say what happens to the priest. Selznick used him as an Italian hero to cover with glory (like the American chaplains of the torpedoed *Dorchester* in World War II).

When day comes and the rain stops, Frederic's ambulance is part of an endless column of suffering humanity crowded onto the road to Udine. The refugees trudge along near exhaustion. Some pull carts and wagons. Most are carrying all that they have left in the world on their backs.

Some lucky few have piled onto military vehicles for a ride. Bonello, one of Frederic's men, is sitting on the tailgate of their ambulance. He sees a young woman with an infant in her arms. She is about to collapse with fatigue. Bonello leads her to the ambulance so that she can ride in his place. A husky peasant is sitting there now. Bonello orders him off; the peasant shoves him with his foot. Bonello pulls him down, and they roll over and over together down an embankment.The young woman climbs wearily onto the ambulance. No one in the crowd more than glances at the men fighting. Bonello is on top of him now, and, insane with rage, he slowly and deliberately strangles him to death. Bonello gets to his feet and staggers towards the ambulance, but then faints with exhaustion. (In the book, Bonello eventually walks off hoping to be taken prisoner by the Germans rather than risk being killed by Italians.) The film cuts to a close shot of the young woman with the infant. She has fallen asleep. Her baby slowly slips from her arms into the roadway. No one notices. The woman sleeps on as the ambulance continues up the road.

The next scene is night. Frederic's ambulance loses a tire, so he and his men have to start walking. Aymo, one of the drivers, is a comic character in the movie. A stock type, he is the soldier who somehow always has it very soft. All this time Aymo has been asleep in the ambulance. Now, just as it seems he is in for some bad luck, a truck loaded with the Villa Rossa girls drives by. One of them, Esmeralda, recognizes Aymo as one of her favorites. She waves and calls to him. Aymo runs to the truck, and the girls pull him aboard. (In the novel Aymo is shot and killed by the rearguard of his own troops because they are frightened and shoot at anyone.)

After this minute of comic relief, the pathetic spectacle of despairing and dying refugees continues.The exodus goes on through driving rain. Carts and wagons are stuck in the mire now. A little boy drops his toy truck in the mud and toddles to retrieve it. His mother, insensitive to everything but their need to survive, grabs his hand and drags him on. A woman collapses in the roadway. Another woman is frantically calling for her husband. A very old lady has fallen, and her husband struggles to lift her. He is very feeble, but no one helps him. A young mother lies dead in the mud at the edge of the road, her baby still nursing her breast.

There was a theme to this Selznick version of the retreat. The Caporetto sequence showed that war is hell, as Sherman said, who burned Atlanta, as in *Gone With the Wind.*

The Caporetto section ends with chapter 30 in the novel. The retreat has been throttled at the crossing of a river bridge. The military police have set up a drumhead court martial and are arresting both high-ranking officers who are not with their troops and anyone suspected of being a German in Italian uniform. Frederic is seized because he speaks Italian with a foreign accent, which could mean that he is an infiltrator. A lieutenant colonel is also arrested. The questions to him are perfunctory.

> "It is you and such as you that have let the barbarians onto the sacred soil of the fatherland."
>
> "I beg your pardon," said the lieutenant-colonel.
>
> "It is because of treachery such as yours that we have lost the fruits of victory."
>
> "Have you ever been in a retreat?" the lieutenant-colonel asked.
>
> "Italy should never retreat."
>
> We stood there in the rain and listened to this. We were facing the officers and the prisoner stood in front and a little to one side of us.
>
> "If you are going to shoot me," the lieutenant-colonel said, "please shoot me at once without further questioning. The questioning is stupid." He made the sign of the cross. The officers spoke together. One wrote something on a pad of paper.
>
> "Abandoned his troops, ordered to be shot," he said.
>
> Two carabinieri took the lieutenant-colonel to the river bank. He

Scenes from the retreat from Caporetto in the Selznick production of *A Farewell to Arms*. With this sequence Selznick hoped to rival the epic scale of *Gone With the Wind*. Publicity stills, courtesy of Twentieth Century-Fox.

> walked in the rain, an old man with his hat off, a carabinieri on either side. I did not watch them shoot him but I heard the shots. They were questioning some one else. This officer too was separated from his troops. He was not allowed to make an explanation. He cried when they read the sentence from the pad of paper, and they were questioning another when they shot him. They made a point of being intent on questioning the next man while the man who had been questioned before was being shot. In this way there was obviously nothing they could do about it. . . . We stood in the rain and were taken out one at a time to be questioned and shot. So far they had shot every one they had questioned. The questioners had that beautiful detachment and devotion to stern justice of men dealing in death without being in any danger of it.

When the guards' attention is distracted for a moment, Frederic runs for it: "I ducked down, pushed between two men, and ran for the river, my head down. I tripped at the edge and went in with a splash."

Of this passage Alfred Kazin has said: "Caporetto, the great episode of the Italian officers being taken out of the line of retreat and shot by military police, stands out in *A Farewell to Arms* because it is a Goya painting of the horrors of war. The expected response is built into the material. The emotions involved are purely tragic, never disturbing, confusing, uncertain."[27]

In the Hecht-Selznick screenplay of this scene, there is no holding to a line of Hemingway's theme, and the control of tragedy becomes raving pathos. The characters are different for the Hollywood version. Rinaldi is with Frederic in the movie retreat, and they are both arrested—Frederic because he speaks with an accent, Rinaldi because he is a major separated from his unit. (In the novel Rinaldi is a lieutenant.) There is also this difference: the first officer to be questioned by the court really *is* a German agitator or spy. He claims, in a faint German accent, that his division is the Nineteenth, but the court catches him in that lie, for the Nineteenth Division was pulled out of action ten days before. The spy is sentenced to death, then pleads to exchange his confession for the mercy of the court. "No! Wait! I will talk—Wait! I will talk!" "Take him away," the court orders.

Then Rinaldi is questioned. He is maddened by fatigue and by the horrors he has witnessed. Near hysteria, he confesses that he is a coward. Though a doctor, he deserted the hospital at Gorizia and the men dying there. Now he wants to be shot. It is even with relief that he hears his condemnation pronounced. Frederic is aghast. He pleads with the court officers: "Major Rinaldi's sick! He's sick, I tell you!" The officers do not pay any attention. Rinaldi is led to a chair and seated. A blindfold is placed across his eyes, but he bravely pulls it away. He places his hand on a crucifix that a priest holds. As Frederic watches with horror, Rinaldi smiles at him and calls, "Goody-bye, puppy, I am joining Father Galli!" The rifles fire at command. Rinaldi slumps violently in the chair.

Donald Barthelme has written a short story of gallows humor titled "Some of Us Had Been Threatening Our Friend Colby." "Because of the way he had been behaving," Colby's friends have decided that they must hang him as an example to other friends who might go "too far." Since it is his execution, Colby ought to have a say in the manner of it. When Colby asks if he might not have a firing squad instead of a hanging, his friends say that, no, he cannot: "A firing squad would just be an ego trip for Colby, the blindfold and last-cigarette bit, and . . . Colby was in enough hot water already without trying to 'upstage' everyone with unnecessary theatrics." The execution of Rinaldi is "theatrics," even to the blindfold bit. It is sensationalism, too, in that the movie seems excited for the chance to show an execution that Hemingway left off scene.

If Hemingway's novel represents a significant statement in modern literature about war, it is because of the Caporetto section. In *The Red Badge of Courage* Stephen Crane dramatized the possibility that heroism may be a condition of irony. Hemingway demonstrated that heroism may be a condition of absurdity. In the Introduction to his own 1942 anthology *Men at War,* Hemingway said that he was a man who hated war profoundly. To show this, he included the last three chapters of the Caporetto retreat to express something essential about what he thought of war. Not all literary historians have recognized *A Farewell to Arms* as an antiwar novel. Although Eugene Löhrke included the Caporetto chapters in the 1930 anthology *Armageddon: The World War in Litera-*

*ture,* he described the novel as "thin, pointless and weak," an "acid and shallow comedy."[28] Leslie Fiedler expressed a much more standard opinion in his Introduction to an edition of Jaroslav Hasek's *Good Soldier Schweik,* where he identified *A Farewell to Arms* as a "classic prototype once and for all" of the anti-war novel.[29]

David O. Selznick did not think that *A Farewell to Arms* was a conspicuously important book about the experience of war. Selznick knew that there was great commercial value, as well as enormous production expense, to all the sensationalism and pathos of the war sequences. For motion picture purposes, however, the book was essentially a love story, and the war was only an impressive background for the love story. One of the disputes between Selznick and Huston was caused by the director's too great an interest in military concerns at the expense of the love story.[30] In another memo Selznick wrote that the picture had to be "Love, Love, Love," and there was not enough yet.[31] To correct the fault, he and Hecht would have to improve Hemingway's material by creating new scenes for the lovers.

The screenplay has Frederic and Catherine spend an afternoon swimming and boating at the lake, a scene whose only point was to show Catherine playing for Frederic (and the audience) in her old-fashioned bathing suit. Late in the production a series of short scenes was added to the Switzerland sequence—all of them out-of-doors, so as to take advantage of the magnificent mountain scenery. Frederic and Catherine go for a sleigh ride, build a snowman, practice yodeling on a mountain trail. On New Year's Eve they join in the circle of a children's party in a quaint Alpine village square. When spring comes, they pick wildflowers in a mountain pass. Nothing happens with respect to plot or character development in these scenes; they are only romantic decorations.

Selznick and Hecht might have added any number of such scenes without changing the character of the relationship between Frederic and Catherine as it stands in the novel. But in fact they *wanted* to change it. Selznick did not like Hemingway's conception of the love story. It was some kind of fantasy based on "some cockeyed concept."[32] It was not realistic enough to suit Selznick, which was to say that Frederic and Catherine do not behave as lovers do in the movies. So Selznick and Hecht proceeded to alter Hemingway's scenes to conform with a Hollywood sense of realism.

For example, the screenplay allows Frederic and Catherine to meet under the same circumstances as in the novel; there is none of the silliness of a first encounter in an air-raid shelter, as in the Borzage version. Still, Hemingway's dialogue in this scene must not have sounded right for the movies. Frederic is not trying very hard to make a good first impression. He is almost rude.

> "How do you do?" Miss Barkley said. "You're not an Italian, are you?"
> "Oh, no." . . .
> "What an odd thing—to be in the Italian army."
> "It's not really the army. It's only the ambulance."
> "It's very odd though. Why did you do it?"
> "I don't know," I said, "There isn't always an explanation for everything."
> "Oh, isn't there? I was brought up to think there was."
> "That's awfully nice."
> "*Do* we have to go on and talk this way?"
> "No," I said.
> "That's a relief, isn't it?"

Hemingway guessed that Selznick dared not let a movie hero be "gauche" to a girl.[33] The dialogue of the screenplay has him more polite and affable.

> CATHERINE: Isn't it rather odd—for an American to be in the Italian army?
> FREDERIC: It's not really the army, it's only the ambulance.
> CATHERINE: It's very odd, though. Why did you do it?
> FREDERIC Oh, I missed out on a job as a war correspondent. I didn't particularly want to kill anybody—so I tried the Red Cross—to have a look.
> CATHERINE: To have a look—!
> FREDERIC: Yes. I may want to do some writing. They assigned me to the auto-ambulance. (With a smile) End of story.

Of course Catherine and almost every woman in the audience is going to be easily attracted to such a man. He is gentle (not wanting to kill anybody), but courageous, too (wanting to be a war correspondent). In the novel Frederic is in Italy studying architecture. In the movie, somewhat more glamorously and mysteriously, he writes.

In the novel when Frederic and Catherine first talk about being in love they are only playing a game, as they both are perfectly well aware.

> She looked at me, "And do you love me?"
> "Yes."
> "You did say you love me, didn't you?"
> "Yes," I lied. "I love you." I had not said it before.

Selznick and Hecht thought Frederic ought to be passionately earnest in this scene. "I'm not playing any games," he says in the screenplay; "I'm in love with you." The audience may be perfectly sure he has loved her since first sight.

As soon as that has been said, the movie can make them lovers. Their second evening together they walk in the hospital garden. Rain starts, and they take shelter in a conservatory. Catherine is frightened by the rain because, as in the novel, she sometimes in dreams sees herself dead in the rain. Also she is feeling sad about her fiancé who was killed early in the war. Frederic comforts her. She responds to his very ardent kiss, and they make love on the greenhouse floor (the camera discreetly turning away to observe the rain on the windows). To this moment, including their first meeting the evening before and their garden stroll this evening, they have been in each other's company for perhaps ten minutes.

Frank Borzage and his writers had arranged to marry Frederic and Catherine at almost the earliest possible opportunity after the seduction scene—not the morning after, but as soon as they are reunited at the Milan hospital. The "wedding scene" comes later by several months in the Selznick-Hecht screenplay. Frederic is almost completely recovered from his leg wounds when he takes Catherine to the race track for the afternoon, a scene that corresponds approximately to chapter 19 of the novel. Catherine tells Frederic that she is pregnant. They discuss the fact that they cannot be married officially, since army regulations would require that Catherine be sent back to England. They can only exchange their vows in a private way. From the loudspeakers at the grandstand comes an announcement of a new victory at the front. The crowd cheers, and another brass band begins to play:

CATHERINE: (her eyes shining): Isn't that fine wedding music? (holding his hand.) I, Catherine, take thee, Frederic, for my wedded husband.

FREDERIC: (looks at her tenderly and adoringly): To have and to hold . . . till death do us part.
(They look at each other devotedly. Frederic lifts her hand, kisses her wedding ring finger. Catherine kisses his hand and repeats:)

CATHERINE: Till death do us part.

There is still an hour of movie left on the reels when they marry. Sooner than they expect they are parted, when Frederic's leave is cancelled and he is sent to the front again. Even as the lovers repeat the line "Till death do us part," the audience should be able to expect the sad end to their love story.

Selznick seems never to have considered having the screenplay spare Catherine's life. The death scene was to be the movie's greatest dramatic opportunity for Rock Hudson and especially for Jennifer Jones, who was Selznick's wife. The final minutes of Selznick's version became even longer, more sentimental than Borzage's. As Frederic and Catherine say their farewells to each other there is even more sobbing than in the earlier movie. When Catherine dies, Frederic breaks down completely. The doctor and nurses leave him alone as he kisses her corpse (which, by Hecht's morbid script direction, is already strangely cold and gray):

FREDERIC: (sobbing) Darling, my wonderful darling. You'll never leave me. You're with me till I die—my darling—till I die. (He bends over and kisses her. Then he raises his head slightly, struck with grief-stricken terror.)

FREDERIC: Cold. Cold. (He moves back, looks at her, sobs.) You're so cold, Cat . . . like a statue. (He straightens up, slowly, and moves away. The camera holds on Catherine's face.)

Then the camera follows Frederic on his walk back to the hotel in the rain. It thunders, and Catherine's voice, in Frederic's memory, is heard on the soundtrack: "I'm not a bit afraid, darling; I just hate it." Frederic walks nearer the camera, and Catherine speaks again, in reprise of another scene: "Oh, won't it be fun? There will be three of us." The scene fades to a shot of Catherine beside Frederic's hospital bed the first night they pretended they were married: "We're going to have a strange life. But it's the only life I want." Now Frederic walks near enough so the audience can see the rain and tears on his face.

Selznick worried that the death scene might be too extreme: "A scene of blubbering schmaltz may, I fear, lead us into the most severe kind of criticism from Hemingway, from critics, from lovers of the book, and from those millions of people who expect *A Farewell to Arms* to have the unique qualities of Hemingway."[34] It may be that Hemingway never saw the ending. A. E. Hotchner says that when he and Hemingway saw the movie together, they walked out after thirty-five minutes.[35] Many critics thought the ending was in poor taste. One said it was "endless sentimentality"; another called it "a maudlin wake."[36] Selznick was badly disappointed by the reviews. They had something to do with why he never made another picture.[37]

The critics did not wreck the commercial success of the picture. Because it had been so expensive to finish, costing much more than the $5 million which had been budgeted, the net profits were far below Selznick's wish. Regardless of that, it was one of the ten top grossing movies of the year. Evidently the "millions of people," not counting "lovers of the book," who only *expected* the movie to match the book did not know the difference.

Selznick was proud of his reputation as an adapter of "celebrated books," like *Rebecca*, by Daphne du Maurier, and *Anna Karenina* (Selznick did not especially discriminate between the merit of the novels he filmed). In each instance the movie success had required a blatant deception: "I succeeded in convincing audiences that I *had* been a slave to the book, so that there was no resentment."[38] The publicity was the public's assurance that the movie was "faithful—a credit to Selznick." In remarks quoted for the slick souvenir program of *A Farewell to Arms*, Selznick took the respectful position that the only way to make a successful movie from a novel was to leave the author's writing as written:

> I have never been able to understand why some adapters and producers insist upon throwing away something of proved appeal to substitute things of their own creation. It is a form of ego which unfortunately and unfairly has drawn upon all of Hollywood the wrath of

> the reading world for many years. I don't hold with the theory that the difference in medium necessitates a difference in storytelling, or even a difference in the basic construction of individual scenes. Clearly, the only proper way of approaching the transcription of a great work into motion picture form is to try to retain the original.

In 1935 Selznick had adapted *David Copperfield*. As if he had learned a contemptible manner of success from the Dickens satire, like the hand-wringing Uriah Heep, Selznick could act the role of the "humble individual."

For her 1939 book *America At the Movies*, for the chapter on adaptation, "The Vampire Art," Margaret Farrand Thorpe quoted Selznick on the subject of the illusion that adapters have to create when they work from a well-known book.

> The biggest job in adapting a well-beloved work is that of getting it down to the length of a feature film. And I have discovered that the public will forgive you for any number of omissions—particularly of subordinate material which is not directly connected with the main plot—but it won't forgive you for deliberate changes. For that reason I have found it best to make the bridging scenes which span the omissions as suggestive as possible. That is, by picking up dialogue and even phrases from other parts of the book and using such to construct the bridging scenes, the audience is given the illusion of seeing and hearing that with which they are already familiar.[39]

Adaptation sounds like very close work, as Selznick describes it; like an expert tailor reweaving a hole by picking up threads to stitch an invisible mend in a three-hundred-dollar Harris Tweed coat.

If Selznick had said this with respect to his production of *A Farewell to Arms*, one would have to dismiss the statement as blandishment merely. Selznick *did* make deliberate changes, and crude ones.

And it is simply not as difficult to create the illusion of a respectful adaptation as Selznick pretends, certainly not with a book like *A Farewell to Arms*. The public could be easily deceived about *A Farewell to Arms*, for they did not know the book very well. The novel was published more than twenty-five years before the movie came out—far too long ago for it to have the familiarity of a best-seller, not long enough ago to have the familiarity of a classic. It was not a schoolbook, nor a fond book of childhood. It was read closely in some college classes, but those who knew the book well did not comprise a large enough number of people to matter to Selznick. Had Selznick been adapting *The Old Man and the Sea,* then he might have needed to trouble himself about the public's knowing the book. With an adaptation of *A Farewell to Arms,* however, it was surely true that more of Selznick's audience remembered the original *movie,* as old as it was, than remembered the book. That comparison was in almost every way to the advantage of the old movie, which was better directed and much, much better acted. (Hemingway himself did not like the old movie, but Gregory Hemingway remembers his father saying more than once that Borzage's version was better than Selznick's.)

No, *A Farewell to Arms* was not the "well-beloved work" which Selznick spoke of as being so hard for adapters to film. *After* the Hollywood version *A Farewell to Arms* could become a well-known novel, even without being read. There were not many people in a position to appreciate the movie adaptation for being like the novel, even had that been so. But there were very many people who, seeing the movie, might imagine the novel was like it. And if they would imagine that the novel had rather the same quality of glamorous love in war as the movie, then Hemingway was a writer to like and admire. So it was that Hollywood, even with its bad movies, continued to number for Hemingway new admirers who were likely to appreciate his fiction in no other way.

CHAPTER IV

# Action Adventure: *To Have and Have Not*

Publicists for *A Farewell to Arms* announced that Paramount's 1932 picture heralded a "New Era! A Rebirth of Romance," as was the headline for one newspaper story. The article quoted Helen Hayes (presumably the statement was written for her) as she expressed her admiration of Hemingway for his having written so wonderfully simple a love story. "How different it is," she concluded happily, "from the hard-boiled films—the gangster, racketeer, night club and newspaper stories that have been so successful in the recent past!" Eventually Hemingway provided Hollywood with many other properties which, in the simple ways that his works were used for the movies, became wonderfully simple love stories. But there were Hemingway properties for the hard-boiled gangster movies as well. This other style of Hemingway movie began when Hollywood discovered his 1937 novel *To Have and Have Not*. Here was material that instead of being romantic and pathetic was cynical and tough.

The book *To Have and Have Not* was never as famous as *A Farewell to Arms*. Nevertheless, using a different title each time, Hollywood filmed *To Have and Have Not* in three different versions and borrowed material from it for movies beyond these three. Hollywood got more running-time from this novel than from *A Farewell to Arms*, and so much footage screened for so many audiences had a great deal to do with establishing Hemingway's reputation as a tough-guy writer.

Not to literary critics nor to movie producers did *To Have and Have Not* seem as important a work of literature as *A Farewell to Arms*. With the adaptations of *A Farewell to Arms* Hollywood had pretended to have some respect for a great novel; advertisements had tried to persuade the public that the book had been treated in a way Hemingway and his admirers would approve of. By contrast, there was hardly even the pretense of literary dignity attending the Hollywood versions of *To Have and Have Not*.

The novel's first chapter was easy to adapt almost along a straight line with what Hemingway wrote. Harry Morgan, the protagonist of *To Have and Have Not*, is trying to make a reasonably honest living running a charter boat operation out of Key West across to Havana, mostly for tourists and sport fishermen. Like many other people during the depression, he is not doing very well. In Havana, three Cuban revolutionaries offer him three thousand dollars to get them off the island and into the States. Morgan refuses because that kind of politics and that kind of smuggling is too dangerous. As the Cubans walk out of the waterfront cafe where they have been talking, they are machine-gunned in the street, the bullets spraying through the window, shattering bottles along the bar where Morgan stands.

Morgan clears out and goes down to his boat. He is taking an American named Johnson out fishing again. Johnson is not a very likable fellow, and not a good fisherman either. Johnson will not listen to what Morgan tries to tell him about fighting a marlin and ends up losing Morgan's expensive rod and reel. At first Johnson refuses to pay for the tackle, then finally agrees to settle his entire account, the next day, after the bank opens. He skips the bank visit, though, and takes a flight back to the States without paying anything.

William Faulkner (he was in Hollywood working for Warner Brothers) and Jules Furthman developed the screenplay with very close directions from producer-director Howard Hawks. They did some rearranging so that the fishing sequence with Johnson comes sooner. Afterwards Morgan has a drink at the barroom of a hotel and is offered a job carrying illegal passengers. Morgan refuses. Then, in a variation on Hemingway's story line, Morgan discovers that Johnson intends to skip without settling his debt. Morgan calls him on it, and Johnson agrees to sign over $800 worth of travelers' checks. Just at that moment the men who tried to hire Morgan's boat are machinegunned in the street. The stray bullets tear up the barroom and kill Johnson before his signature validates the checks.

The killing of Johnson was perhaps a cheaper melodramatic contrivance than Hemingway would have been inclined to use. However, it is not a very significant difference between the novel and the movie, especially since Johnson has no further purpose in the novel. His thematic significance—as one of the "haves" without regard for the condition of the "have nots"—is the same in both versions.

Any sameness did not last long. Nothing after the opening minutes seemed much like Hemingway's material at all. James Agee said in his review of *To Have and Have Not,* "It has so little to do with Ernest Hemingway's novel that I see no point in discussing its faithfulness!"[1] There were certain things about the movie that the critics did like, especially Humphrey Bogart's style as Harry Morgan and everything about the new starlet, Lauren Bacall. Still, they did not think it was much of an adaptation of Hemingway.[2]

Hawks was sensitive and defensive about the criticism that the movie had betrayed the book, almost as if he had not expected reviewers to care about that. In a *Cahiers du Cinema* interview years afterwards, Hawks found an opportunity to clear himself of blame. Asked why he made a movie so different from the book, Hawks claimed that he and Hemingway had planned the changes together:

> Once when Hemingway and I were hunting together, I told him I could take his worst story and make a movie out of it. Hemingway asked me what was his worst story. "*To Have and Have Not,*" I said. Hemingway explained that he had written the story in one sitting when he needed money, and that I couldn't make a movie out of it. I said I'd try, and while we hunted, we discussed it. . . . After four or five days of discussion I left. Faulkner and Jules Furthman then wrote a script incorporating the ideas which Hemingway and I had evolved on our hunting trip.[3]

Hawks repeated the story, with minor variations, in several interviews.[4] It is a story to relish telling, as it has Hawks bearding the lion. Still, the story leaves one skeptical about Hemingway's acquiescence to Hawks's suggestion that *To Have and Have Not* was his worst book. Hemingway had always felt that the widespread critical abuse of this novel was undeserved. It is also odd that Hemingway should have deprecated the book as being hack work, for actually Hemingway had spent several long months of 1936 working on it, and as he wrote he had great confidence that it represented a major achievement.[5] It seems from Hawks's account that Hemingway was a little surprised that it would occur to anyone to film *To Have and Have Not*. In fact Hemingway had *already* sold the film rights to Howard Hughes—in 1941, for $10,000. Obviously Hughes thought a movie could be made of *To Have and Have Not*.

When they talked about what could be done with the story, Hemingway and Hawks had some fun with dirty jokes about how Morgan excited his wife with the stump of his amputated arm. (In the book Morgan loses his arm as a consequence of a vicious gunshot wound.) Morgan would not be an amputee in the movie, but, according to Hawks, Hemingway agreed the movie should have a girl for Morgan. "We decided that the best way to tell the story was not to show the hero growing old, but show how he had met the girl, and, in short, show everything that happened before the beginning of the novel."[6] One is inclined to doubt that they really had an agreement like this.

The novel shows Morgan being destroyed but not "growing old"; the events of the novel's three sections span less than a year. The novel does not say how Morgan and his wife, Marie, met, but it could not possibly have been the way it happens in the movie. For one thing, the book has it that Morgan's wife is two years older than he is (forty-five as against forty-three); calculated by the difference in age between Lauren Bacall and Bogart, the movie has Marie twenty-five years younger than Morgan. And, as has been noted, the movie begins at the same place as does the novel, not before. Marie first enters the story when Morgan catches her with Johnson's wallet, which she stole to keep from being stranded on the island. Morgan does not want Marie to steal any of the money that Johnson owes him. In the wallet are travelers' checks that mean Johnson was lying when he said he would not have any money until the bank opened the next day. In a way it is lucky for

Lobby cards for *To Have and Have Not*.

Morgan that Marie is, this one time, a thief, since otherwise he would not have known Johnson is a cheat. Of course that makes no difference after Johnson is shot and cannot sign the checks. But Morgan and Marie are collaborators from then on; they are a pair.

Morgan himself does not think that the relation will last a long time. It is difficult for him to imagine that his life has a permanent place for a woman. As soon as he has enough money, he buys Marie a plane ticket away from the place. She cashes it in; she would rather stay and have Morgan. By the end of the movie it is decided that at least they will leave the island together and start their next adventure together. *To Have and Have Not* is far from being a sentimental movie romance, and they do not in so many words talk about being in love.

Anyone who has seen *To Have and Have Not* would have difficulty imagining the movie without Marie's part in it. Her scenes with Morgan (James Agee called them a "series of leisurely mating duels") are the best material in the script, as they exchange lines of smoldering innuendo and smoke cigarettes.[7]

And yet for all her time on camera, the character of Marie has very little to do with the main plot of the screenplay. Her part could have been written in after the main story line had been laid out.

How did the screenplay originate, if not in discussion between Hawks and Hemingway about Morgan and Marie? Prior to the movie's release Hawks said nothing to the press concerning talks with Hemingway about making this picture (even though any use of Hemingway's name was excellent promotion). Hawks's initial position was that he was going to have to disregard the book if he were to make a good movie. Hawks said that he agreed with the critics who judged that the book was not worth very much. Also, he said, it showed little promise as movie material since it was too much a proletarian novel of the thirties. Steinbeck's *Grapes of Wrath* had been filmed in 1940, but now there was a war going on, and no one was interested in seeing a movie about the class struggle between the "haves" and the "have nots," let alone about a minor revolution in Cuba. Hawks had simply wanted the property as a vehicle for Humphrey Bogart, Warner Brothers' most popular actor. That is why Hawks, using Warner Brothers' money, had been willing to buy the rights for *To Have and Have Not* from Howard Hughes for $80,000, which was eight times what Hughes had paid. "That's what I bought," Hawks admitted, "the character and, of course, the title."[8] If the proletarian interest of the novel were discarded, then the title made no obvious sense. (Or perhaps like the title *A Farewell to Arms*, it could be interpreted as a romantic theme—to have and have not each other.) That barely mattered since any Hemingway title was valuable property the year after the tremendous success of the movie *For Whom the Bell Tolls*.

The first thing to be decided about the adaptation was a change of place. Because it was a war year, Hawks explained, complicated and sensitive issues of diplomacy were involved in the choice of location. Political relations with Caribbean governments were delicate, and the U.S. State Department did not want to offend Latin American sensibilities, especially since the new "Good Neighbor Policy" was in effect. The Office of the Coordinator of Inter-American Affairs had reviewed Hawks's plan for the production, "advised against the use of the Cuban locale of the story and warned that such a background, with implication of insurrection, would most likely deprive the picture of an Office of Censorship export license, which meant the studio would lose the profits of foreign distribution." Hawks was told the only place in the Caribbean vicinity he could locate the story was the island of Martinique, since that was French territory and out of the jurisdiction of the Office of Inter-American Affairs. That suggestion "immediately struck a responsive chord. Why not switch the locale [from Cuba] to contemporary Martinique, retain the main character . . . and make the background conflict that between the Vichy French and the de Gaullists?"[9] That, Hawks said, was how he, Furthman, and Faulkner conceived the idea for their new version of Hemingway's story. That was why, in the opening sequence, the men who want to hire Morgan's boat were Free French rather than Cuban.

Political considerations explain why the background was changed but not why the story line was so very much altered. A character in John Steinbeck's novel *The Wayward Bus* describes a way that Hollywood sometimes works: "You get a new wrinkle and you're fixed. You don't want to go radical. Just a wrinkle, like they call it in Hollywood, a switcheroo. That's with the story. You take a picture that's made dough and you work a switcheroo—not too much, just enough, and you've got something then." Warner Brothers' most successful picture of 1943 was *Casablanca,* which won Academy Awards for Best Picture (over *For Whom the Bell Tolls*), Best Director (Michael Curtiz) and Best Screenplay. Bogart was nominated as Best Actor. (Paul Lukas won that award, for his role in *Watch on the Rhine.*) Whether or not the terms "wrinkle" or "switcheroo" were ever current in Hollywood, they approximate what happened between *Casablanca* and *To Have and Have Not,* which of course is another hard-boiled drama of Resistance movement intrigue. Certainly the studio was completely happy that *To Have and Have Not* was so very much like *Casablanca.* When the studio's publicity chief saw a preview he sent a notice out to the staff: "Polish up the picks, shovels and pans for the gold mine on the way in Howard Hawks's production of Ernest Hemingway's *To Have and Have Not,* which we sneaked last night and which is not only a second *Casablanca* but two and a half times what *Casablanca* was."[10]

*To Have and Have Not* seems at least as much an adaptation of *Casablanca* as of the Hemingway novel. To appreciate this, of course, one has to know *Casablanca.* In that movie an American named Rick Blaine owns a nightclub in Casablanca, a Moroccan city teeming with refugees trying to obtain exit permits to Allied countries. The political situation in the city is volatile. Rick has allegiance neither to the Vichy government, which controls the city, nor to the Free French underground. So everybody comes to Rick's place, because there is an atmosphere of tense neutrality there.[11] Rick has not always been disinterested in political matters, but since a love affair in Paris that ended badly at the time of the Occupation, he has protected himself in a shell of cynicism that allows loyalty only to his own best interests.

Then an important Resistance leader, Victor Laszlo, comes to Casablanca with his wife Ilsa. Laszlo has escaped from a concentration camp and hopes to return via Casablanca to Lisbon, where he will resume his fight against Fascism. The Vichy French and the Gestapo know he is in Casablanca and are determined that he will never leave the city. The Gaullist underground approaches Rick to ask him to use his influence to arrange Laszlo's flight. However, even when Rick comes into possession of two safe conduct passes that Laszlo and Ilsa could use, he refuses to help them. He does not like Laszlo, for a very personal reason. Though Laszlo does not know it, Ilsa was the girl who deserted Rick in Paris. What Rick does not know is that Ilsa was already married to Laszlo at the time. She had supposed he had been killed when the Gestapo captured him. While with Rick in Paris, she learned that Laszlo had survived, and her sense of loyalty and duty forced her to return to him, although she no longer loved him. Ilsa eventually tells Rick this entire story. Now that she is finally back with Rick, she thinks she will abandon her dedication to the Cause and remain with him.

In the meanwhile, Rick has gradually been turning against the Vichy government. He is learning that no man has the right to think only of himself or to remain neutral in a war against Fascism. He decides to help Laszlo in every way he can. At first Ilsa refuses to escape with Laszlo. Then, at the end of the movie, Rick convinces her she must go with him, that Laszlo must never know of their affair, lest in losing her Laszlo lose his will and strength to continue the Resistance struggle.

From the opening shots there are points of resemblance between *Casablanca* and *To Have and Have Not*. Just as *Casablanca* opens with a map of Europe and North Africa spread across the screen, *To Have and Have Not* opens with a map of the Caribbean showing the island of Martinique and its city of Fort de France. Like Casablanca, Fort de France is Vichy territory subjected to internecine warfare between the German sympathizers and the Resistance. In Fort de France there is a hotel which is the central setting for the screenplay. The nightclub in this hotel is not quite as "swell" a place as "Rick's" in *Casablanca*, but it is like a remodeling of an old scene. The musical mood at the club is about the same (Hoagy Carmichael is the piano-player/singer in *To Have and Have Not*, as was Dooley Wilson in *Casablanca*). More important, the political mood at both places is about the same.

Of course Harry Morgan does not own this place; he is at the club because he has a room at this hotel. That is hardly a more significant difference than that Morgan wears khakis whereas Rick Blaine wore a tuxedo. They are the same men in essential ways. Like Rick, Morgan is an American, tough and cynical—about women no less than anything else. There are hints in the script that there once was a love affair that ended badly. (For example, as Marie sniffs the stopper of her bottle of perfume, she pries, "Remind you of somebody . . .?" "A little," Morgan admits.) Morgan minds his own business and looks after only himself and his alcoholic mate, Eddy (played by Walter Brennan). He does not want to get mixed up in local politics.

Then Morgan is approached by a group of Gaullists who want him to pilot his boat on a mission that could significantly aid the cause of the Free French in the Carribean. A Resistance leader must be smuggled, not out of Fort de France (as Laszlo had to be smuggled out of Casablanca), but into Fort de France, from the island of Anguilla. At first Morgan refuses. Then when he is out the money Johnson had owed him, he changes his mind. He agrees to make the secret night rendezvous with Paul De Bursac—and with De Bursac, his beautiful wife, Helene. During the crossing from Anguilla they are challenged by the Coast Guard of the National Security force, who are the Fascists on the island. Morgan blasts out the patrol boat's searchlight and escapes. In the gunfire De Bursac is wounded in the shoulder. Morgan sees that De Bursac and Helene are safely hidden in the wine cellar of the hotel in Fort de France. There is no doctor who can be trusted, so it has to be Morgan who probes for the bullet and treats De Bursac's wound.

De Bursac needs Morgan's help in an even more desperate way. De Bursac had arranged a $5,000 bribe of an official at the prison of Devil's Island, where still another key Gaullist leader is being held. De Bursac needs someone to pilot a boat to Devil's Island, off the coast of Venezuela, and back.

Morgan wants nothing more to do with De Bursac and his war. Gradually, however, Morgan is learning what Fascism is all about as he sees the ruthlessness and brutality of the Gestapo-like Security Police.

Captain Renard (played by Dan Seymour, who had a brief appearance in *Casablanca*) and his henchmen are searching for De Bursac by now. Renard is investigating the incident of the battle with the patrol boat the night before. He believes Morgan carried passengers. If Morgan will not inform him of De Bursac's whereabouts, perhaps Eddy will. Renard has taken Eddy in for questioning, but he will let him dry out for a while first. If he is desperate enough for a drink he will talk.

Now Morgan has been pushed too far. He is not going to let them use Eddy. In the climactic scene of the movie, as if reaching for a match in a table drawer Morgan reaches for a pistol instead, and firing through the table kills one of the guards. He threatens to pistolwhip Renard to death unless he telephones headquarters to order Eddy's release. Then Morgan forces Renard to sign safe conduct passes (as in *Casablanca*) that will clear their boat from the port of Martinique. The movie ends as Morgan and De Bursac, with Marie and Helene, and Eddy, about to begin the adventure to Devil's Island.

The ending is the weakest part of the script. It seems to cut off without finishing the story. Also, the sense of the danger of the mission to Devil's Island is confused with the feeling that this is a lark of an ocean holiday for Morgan and Marie, with Eddy along to carry their bags.

Hawks kept changing his mind about the script. (Faulkner, who was usually a calm writer even in Hollywood, felt tense trying to keep up with new plans.)[12] At one point Hawks developed a long and completely different ending for the script. It was never filmed, but it is interesting to read in its script form. This discarded ending would have brought the movie almost as close to the novel as it had been at the beginning, but at the same time it would have made the movie's resemblance to *Cassablanca* even more obvious.

Plots of Hawks's movies can be exceedingly complicated. The original ending is difficult to follow unless one understands that in the script Helene (played by Dolores Moran) was a much more important character than she is in the version that finally came to the screen. She was to have been a character very much like Ilsa—that is, married to the Resistance leader, De Bursac, but in love with another man, Morgan, for whom she is almost ready to abandon the Cause. By the time the script was revised, filmed, and edited, most of the lines of this relationship were erased. They are in release version faintly, however, and they have to be traced before a summary of the original ending makes sense.

We must go back to the scene of the night crossing from Anguilla when Morgan first met De Bursac and Helene. Morgan has not much liked De Bursac from that beginning. He had been vaunted as a Resistance fighter, but in the fight with the patrol boat it seemed to Morgan that he was almost ready to surrender. Morgan is wrong in his impression that De Bursac has a coward's streak, but he will not learn that until later.

Morgan is aggravated by the presence of Helene. He cannot see a good reason why she has to be along. Still, she is obviously a very sensual woman, and Morgan is attracted to her, partly because De Bursac seems too weak a man to hold on to her.

On her side, Helene is contemptuous of Morgan, because he is not an idealist at all, because he acts like a mercenary. When her husband was wounded she thought Morgan acted like a brute. "Leave him where he is," Morgan had said; "I don't want him bleeding all over my cushions." (Such is the tone of Morgan's tough talk.) After Morgan shows the compassion to care for De Bursac's wound, however, her feelings seem to change completely: "You can't make me angry with you any more," Helene says; "I don't know why. You could do anything to me. I wouldn't care." Morgan's response: "Of all the screwy dames." Helene is on her way to becoming intensely in love with Morgan.

Marie overhears Helene's line. When she is alone with Morgan the next time, Marie taunts him, imitating Helene: "You could do anything to me. I wouldn't care." Morgan has no strings attached to him, though. He tells Marie to walk around him one time. She doesn't understand what he means, but she does as he says. Then she gets the point—there are no strings. But she is beginning to burn about the woman Morgan keeps calling "Cheesecake," while he calls her only "Slim."

Marie is not going to lose Morgan, but she might have to share him. Morgan and Helene have a private conversation when Helene comes to his room—provocatively—to take a bath (there being no tub in the cellar where she and her husband are hiding). Morgan tells her that he and Slim are pulling out tonight. Does Helene want to come? Helene doesn't understand for a moment. Does he think that she would abandon her husband? No one would blame her, Morgan is thinking, if De Bursac is the coward he seems. But Helene does not want Morgan's sympathy. She loves her husband, even if he is weak. She never will leave, no matter what. Morgan grins at the way she is so sure. "Never?" he asks, then kisses her hard. She seems to respond. "Never be too sure," he suggests. At that moment Marie interrupts them to warn that Renard is on his way up to the room. Then is the shooting that climaxes the movie as it was finally released.

As familiar as *To Have and Have Not* is to movie buffs (no doubt it is the most famous Hemingway feature), no one could guess that by the original plan of the discarded script, the movie was to continue in a way that would have Lauren Bacall soon *betray* Bogart—her fury like that of a woman scorned. By this version of the script, before the adventure to Devil's Island De Bursac must recover the $5,000 that he has hidden back at Anguilla; only he knows where. Morgan and Eddy will take him across by boat. Marie knows the plan. (She even knows it is Helene's rouge on Morgan's handkerchief.) It is not for the Cause that Morgan is doing it—he wants the $5,000. He is not going to steal the money from De Bursac. He doesn't have to, he says. The money is Helene's, too, and Helene is going with him, and bringing the money.

At the same jetty of land where they met De Bursac the first time, Morgan and Eddy wait at anchor until he returns with the money. Several figures emerge from the darkness and leap to the stern of the boat. De Bursac is one; Renard, with a heavy automatic, is another; a bodyguard, with a Thompson gun, is the third. Eddy tries to warn Morgan and is slammed in the chest by three bursts from the machinegun. Eddy dies.

To think again of the Hemingway source, in chapter 18 of the novel Morgan is in with a gang of vicious Cuban revolutionaries who have robbed a Key West bank. When they board Morgan's boat, one of them machineguns his mate Albert, exactly the way Eddy is killed in the movie. Morgan knows now he is going to be killed, as soon as he has piloted their escape to within sight of Havana. As he dumps Albert's body overboard, he manages to kick overboard the machinegun. There are still many of them against Morgan alone, but Morgan has his own machinegun below deck with the engines.

It is nearly the same situation now in the movie. Morgan dumps Eddy's body, and he dumps the gun. Renard then shoots his own henchman, and that body goes under. It is not a political matter with Renard anymore. He simply wants the $5,000 and has no intention of sharing it with anyone. Of course he will murder Morgan and De Bursac when they are within sight of land. The odds for Morgan in the movie are much better than his odds in the book. Renard is armed, but Morgan has the machinegun below deck. And Morgan also has De Bursac. Then the engines stop. Morgan goes below to see to the problem; De Bursac distracts Renard's attention for a moment. An instant later, Renard reacts, firing one bullet at Morgan. Morgan's gun flares three or four times, blasting Renard back against the coaming. The automatic falls out of his hand, and he slumps dead on the deck.

In the novel, the last shot at the stomach kills Morgan. But by the convention of movies that can miraculously spare heroes' lives, Morgan is only wounded. Before he dumped Eddy's body, he took as a keepsake the bottle opener that Eddy always hung round his neck. Now that bottle opener has saved Morgan's life, deflected the bullet. It shows a deep gouge.

The discarded script had one more scene. It is the next morning with the fade-in to Morgan's room at the hotel. Helene enters very concerned. Has he been badly hurt? No, it is only a slight gash. Helene remarks that Paul seems so different since he has come back. He has been praising Morgan to her. He has said that Morgan is going to Devil's Island. That had not been Helene's understanding. She had thought she was leaving with Morgan herself. What changed his mind? Helene wants to know. "I don't know," Morgan says frankly; "Guess I like him better than I do you." He does not spell it out to her more than that, but it is very clear what has happened. Morgan respects De Bursac now. It took guts for De Bursac to shut off the engines. Renard might have shot him right then. And by this time, De Bursac has had a chance to explain to Morgan why he had been willing to surrender to the patrol boat the first night returning from Anguilla. It was not that he was afraid of dying. He alone knew where the bribery money was hidden, and if he died with that secret, the plan to save the greater leader was finished. The Security Police would probably order his execution, but perhaps in the meanwhile he would find the chance to pass the secret to a comrade. Morgan can see how wrong he had been. It seems that he knows you do not shame a strong man, or betray a man who has fought with you, by taking his wife.

So Helene will stay with the hero of the Resistance Cause, as Ilsa stayed with Laszlo. They will say their good-bys now and finish it with a kiss between friends.

Marie enters as they kiss. The kiss does not look very much like a simple good-by to her. But Helene senses that Morgan prefers the blonde to her. She gracefully surrenders the field, wishes Marie luck with Morgan, and gives Marie a strand of pearls. Marie is bewildered by the gift, so Helene quotes Shakespeare for her as she exits: "The robbed who smiles steals something from the thief."

Marie has a confession to make to Morgan. She notices the bullet-marked "church key" around Morgan's neck. Without being told she knows that Eddy is gone. How did Renard know that Morgan, De Bursac, and Eddy had gone back to Anguilla? Marie admits it. *She* tipped off Renard. But Morgan had already guessed it. It does not matter between them. He doesn't blame her, he says. "I would have done the same thing myself." He closes his eyes, very tired, and holds onto her hand. Marie starts crying with happiness, she kisses his hand, and watches his face relax into sleep.

This original ending for *To Have and Have Not* was hardly believable, and Hawks used good judgment in cutting the story shorter without getting into anything about Marie's jealousy that leads to her betrayal of Morgan. Lauren Bacall would have been completely out of character behaving in so erratic a way. Who could have believed that Morgan would dismiss Marie's responsibility for Eddy's death so lightly? It seems an impossible statement when Morgan, trying to see it from Marie's point of view, says, "I would have done the same thing myself."

Hawks said that Hemingway liked the picture, that he never complained about the changes. The thing that made him sore was that he got gypped, receiving only $10,000 from the sale of the book while the movie people went on to make very big profits.

The studio had the right to use the property over again, in whatever way. Jerry Wald produced an adaptation of Maxwell Anderson's play *Key Largo* for Warner Brothers in 1948. Wald took some of Hemingway's material—the gun fight on the boat—for the finish of that movie. *Key Largo* was another Bogart picture. Bogart survived in this version, too, managing to pilot the shot-up boat back to port, where waits the girl, again played by Lauren Bacall.

Bogart would play the Rick Blaine or Harry Morgan type of character yet again, in *Sirocco* (Columbia, 1951). The political background for that movie was the Syrian nationalist revolution againt French imperialism. Harry Smith, the Bogart character, owns a gambling club in Damascus, a city the French are holding under martial law. Smith is a profiteer and has no politics. Gradually, however, he becomes involved in aiding the negotiations of a French colonel who is trying to arrange a truce. Smith becomes involved, too, with the colonel's mistress, who needs an exit to Cairo. And so on, in the manner of *Casablanca* and *To Have and Have Not*.

In fact, Bogart was asked if he would be interested in playing Harry Morgan in a second version of *To Have and Have Not* that would use the material left unexplored by the Hawks adaptation. Bogart was receptive to the idea, which came to him from one of the studio's writers, Ranald MacDougall.

But the studio said no to MacDougall's proposal. They already had their money's worth from *To Have and Have Not*. Anyway, it was too soon for a remake, especially with the same face as Morgan. They could put a different title on the remake and still use Hemingway's name. On the other hand, Hemingway's name did not have the draw at the box office it had enjoyed after the success of *For Whom the Bell Tolls*. Hemingway had not published a new novel since 1941.

There was an additional consideration. Now was beginning the era of "communist-anticommunist psychosis" (Allen Ginsberg's expression in "Wichita Vortex Sutra"). Congress was looking at Hollywood movies and Hollywood personalities for un-American themes and radical sympathies. Studios were guarding themselves against the accusation that their movies were in any way critical of the existing social order. *To Have and Have Not* was exactly the kind of material Hollywood wanted to avoid. The very title sounded like an indictment of the capitalist system. And a central thematic idea of it—that a man alone has no chance—was at least vaguely un-American.

Despite these various reactionary problems, Ranald MacDougall was able to find some interest in the project. John Garfield wanted the role of Morgan, and producer Jerry Wald wanted the rest of a book he had partly exploited in making *Key Largo*. So the studio gave MacDougall six weeks to try to write the script he called *The Breaking Point*. Director Michael Curtiz (*Casablanca*) liked it when he read it. Finally, Jack Warner, without much confidence, agreed to a $600,000 production budget and an eight-week shooting schedule beginning in April, 1950. Such was the start of what would become one of the more interesting and intelligent Hemingway features, though in some obvious ways it did not follow the book.

MacDougall's script changed the settings of the novel from Key West and Havana to Newport, California, and a small, unnamed town on the Mexican coast. Newport was a town a little like Key West, and, since it was convenient to Hollywood, it was economical to shoot the locations there. Mexican exteriors were shot in Newport as well.

There are no Mexican or Latin revolutionaries in the movie—nothing political at all. The social scene is the relatively stable and just middle-class society of 1950. There is crime, but it is nothing, the movie seems to suggest, that the law of a well-ordered society cannot control.

In the opening sequence of *The Breaking Point*, a Mr. Hannagan (Johnson of the novel) has chartered Morgan's boat to take him fishing along the Mexican coast. Actually, Hannagan is less interested in the fishing than in having a private cruise with his girlfriend, Leona Charles (played by Patricia Neal). When the blonde shows too much interest in Morgan, Hannagan deserts her in a Mexican town and flies back to the States without settling the fee with Morgan.

There is no character Leona Charles in the novel, though she faintly resembles Dorothy Hollis, mistress of the owner of the yacht *Irydia IV* in chapter 24. Leona—whom the tough talk of the movie's advertising called "the danger dame"—is used in the screenplay to develop a domestic dilemma that has no relation to the novel. In the movie Morgan has a sweet and pretty wife named Lucy (played by Phyllis Thaxter) who is very unlike Marie in the novel. A more domesticated character than is the typical hero of a tough-guy picture, Morgan is a devoted husband and father of two girls he thinks the world of. (In the novel Morgan does not think

Lobby card for *The Breaking Point*, 1950, the fine second movie version of *To Have and Have Not*.

much of his daughters, an attitude that could not be allowed to stand in the movie lest the audience's sympathy for Morgan be alienated.)

The Morgan family has its typical problems. After twelve years some of the excitement has gone out of the marriage. Naturally, Lucy is jealous when she finds out her husband was stranded in Mexico with Leona. She thinks that Leona's glamour is a serious threat to her marriage. Lucy and Morgan have a quarrel later in the story, and Morgan walks out on her, thinking he might as well go ahead and have an affair with Leona. Then he changes his mind; his loyalty to Lucy is stronger than the temptation.

The Morgans' other problem is money. When Hannagan skips out on Morgan in Mexico, Morgan decides to take the risk of making a smuggling deal with Mr. Sing, who, as in the novel (chapters 2–5), arranges illegal entry to the States for Chinese refugees. In the novel Morgan gets the money from Mr. Sing, then strangles him to death—breaks his neck. He is not going to risk any trouble from the likes of Mr. Sing. Then Morgan orders his cargo of twelve Chinamen off his boat and leaves them stranded in Cuba. His conscience does not bother him about that, since the alternative was to shoot all twelve of them. He is not going to take anything into the country that can talk.

It does not happen exactly this way in the movie. The screenplay makes Morgan a more sympathetic hero. He puts the Chinese back on shore but never considers the possibility of killing them. Mr. Sing does get killed, but Morgan was only defending himself in a life or death struggle. After the Chinese are boarded, Mr. Sing, with an oily smile, tells Morgan that there have been "unexpected expenses," so he will not be paying Morgan as much as he promised. Morgan says the deal is off. Mr. Sing shrugs, reaches into his coat pocket, as if for the rest of the money, and draws a gleaming pistol. Morgan grabs his gun and pulls him into the boat. Five wild shots are fired as Morgan and Sing wrestle on the deck. Morgan tries to bend the gun away from Sing's grip. The gun goes off. Sing is dead.

Leona, watching the fight, is very impressed and excited by Morgan's power. Morgan himself also feels something very like a sexual exhilaration as he kills Mr. Sing. The screenplay writer, MacDougall, could not write this into his script explicitly, but that was his understanding of Morgan as he tried to develop the character. Morgan's pleasure in violence represented a sexual gratification.

MacDougall had another thesis about Morgan's character that he wanted to dramatize. Morgan had been a Marine during the war, had been trained to kill, had been toughened to it, and finally had learned to take pleasure in it. This is the first time since the war that Morgan has had anything to do with killing, and it frightens him that he experiences the same kind of thrill as when he was killing Japs in the Philippines. He tells Leona about the time he saw torpedoes sink a Jap transport. It turned over and sank. The guys inside started yelling. You could hear it a half mile off. They started banging on the hull inside. You could still hear them after the ship went down. "You think after a thing like that killing [Mr. Sing] bothers me?" He is sure that he would kill him again.

Hemingway knew about the brutalizing effect of war on the individual. Pablo was thus brutalized when he led the capture of the Fascist town in *For Whom the Bell Tolls*. In *To Have and Have Not*, Roberto, the Cuban who murders Morgan's mate, is brutalized this way. One of the other Cubans says of Roberto, "You know he doesn't mean to do wrong. It's just what that phase of the revolution has done to him." And the veterans who hang around Freddy's Bar in Key West and crack open each other's skulls in vicious brawls are, in the words of the novel, "the completely brutalized ones." The Vets are important to Hemingway. What is to become of them? What is society's responsibility to them, having battered their minds?

This was a theme of the novel that MacDougall saw as crucially relevant to the time 1950. Morgan of *The Breaking Point* is a veteran whose capacity for violence society had glorified a few years before. Since the war, society has not made a place for him. He has not been completely successful in trying to adapt to a world of civilian decency and domesticity. There is an impressive metaphoric statement of the idea in the shooting script. When Morgan brings his boat back from Mexico he passes the gigantic "mothball fleet" of decommissioned war ships moored in San Diego harbor. Morgan's mate, Wesley, is talking to Leona: "The 'mothball fleet.' Stuff nobody had any use for after the war. When we needed those things they were great. Now everybody says what a waste and leaves them there to rot. Like Harry—he's in mothballs too."

Even when he is home with Lucy and his girls, lying awake nights, Morgan remembers the war. Lucy tries to get him to forget it and live as he has to live now: "The war's over! Long ago! You got a wife and two kids to think about—keeping us together—getting us enough to eat, and clothes for our backs—that is the biggest war there is, and you better realize it!" He does realize it, painfully much. That is the tension of it: the frustration and the rage and the knowing he can kill: "It's a war all right, and I'm scared. I'm scared of the grocery man—that he won't give me a pint of milk when I need it, and I'll kill him for it." He is that close to the breaking point, as the title means.

When Jack Warner saw the preview of *The Breaking Point* in a studio screening room, he directed that all these lines be edited out of the movie. The film could show the mothball fleet, but there was not going to be any symbolism about it. Morgan was not going to talk about murdering the grocery man, or even remember the war and all the dead Japs. There would be nothing in his picture that could possibly be construed as a criticism of America's treatment of its veterans or a suggestion that veterans were psychologically warped, emotionally unstable, or potentially dangerous.

In the movie as Jack Warner finally approved it, what seems to be bothering Morgan is only the difficult decision of whether to keep trying to make it with the boat business or give it up to become a partner with his father-in-law on a lettuce farm. Lucy pleads with him to do that. Morgan will not listen. Even if he liked the idea of a quiet farm life, they need money to start over again.

"All I got left to peddle is guts. And I'm not so sure I got any. I have to find out." He is thinking about an offer when he says that. Gangsters want him to pilot the get-away boat after a robbery. They are not plotting an ordinary bank robbery, as in the novel; something much more elaborate and daring had to be masterminded for the Hollywood version. They plan to hit the cash room of the race track during the two minutes the horses are running and the guards' attention is distracted. Oscar Levant read the details of the plan in the shooting script and told Jerry Wald, "Don't bother making the picture. Let's do the robbery."

Of course Lucy does not want her husband to get mixed up with anything that has to do with guns and crime. Though she does not know the details, she does know there is going to be trouble and threatens to leave Harry if he goes ahead with it. To Morgan it seems that he has no choice.

The script shows that Morgan is excited by the dangers of the crime. In the expurgated release print, he is not thinking to be part of the crime or the violence. Whereas Morgan in the novel plans to get out into the Gulf Stream, kill the Cubans, and keep the money, Morgan of the movie, who is a cleaner hero, plans to capture the gang and collect the reward.

All of it happens differently from what he planned. The gunmen kill Wesley, his mate, as they board the boat, and Morgan figures they intend to kill him, too, as soon as he has served his purpose. He has two pistols hidden below deck with the engines, and he waits for a moment of surprise. When the shooting is over, everyone is dead except Morgan, and he is almost dead. He lies bleeding on the deck, shot in the arm and stomach. In voice-over he is heard thinking: "One thing to spoil it. One thing to go wrong. Murdering rat. Who woulda thought I hadn't gotten him. A man alone—a man alone ain't got no chance."

The lines are as close to parallel with the novel as could be said in decent speech. In the novel Morgan believes at first that he does have a chance: "I'm a son of a bitch," he said, his lips against the planking. "I'm a gone son of a bitch now. I got to cut the engines or we'll all burn up, he thought. I got a chance still. I got a kind of a chance. Jesus Christ. One thing to spoil it. One thing to go wrong. God damn it. Oh, God *damn* that Cuban bastard. Who'd have thought I hadn't got him?" A while later, for he is a long time dying, he does not believe he has any chance at all: "No matter how a man alone ain't got no bloody fucking chance."

In both the novel and movie, Morgan is still alive when the Coast Guard finds his boat adrift and tows it to shore. According to the novel, an ambulance rushes him to the hospital where he dies in surgery. Marie takes the girls back home, not able to tell them yet that their father is dead:

> "How's Daddy?" one of the girls asked.
> Marie did not answer.
> "How's Daddy, Mother?"
> "Don't talk to me," Marie said. "Just don't talk to me."
> "But—"
> "Shut up, Honey," said Marie. "Just shut up and pray for him."

The ending works differently in the movie. MacDougall wanted to suggest a psychosexual importance to the arm wound: Morgan of the novel was wounded in book 2, the rum-running episode, and lost his arm. To MacDougall the amputation seemed to have Freudian implications, as a symbolic castration. In the movie, therefore, when the doctor explains to Morgan that he will have to lose his arm to save his life, Morgan thinks his manliness and his intimate life with Lucy are ruined. He refuses to give permission for the operation.

Lucy is allowed to talk to him for a few minutes when they bring him ashore. With violins underscoring their dialogue, Lucy brings back his will to live and promises she will think him just as much a man with only one arm. After the ambulance rushes him to the hospital, Lucy comforts the girls: "He'll be all right! You'll see. I know Harry. He'll be all right. Wait and see." She holds the children tightly. "But you'll have to pray for him. You have to pray very hard now."

MacDougall's script followed this with a scene at the hospital based on the scene in the book where the surgeon tells Lucy that Morgan has died on the operating table. The scene was not filmed. MacDougall hoped the audience would understand that Morgan does die. Director Michael Curtiz, on the other hand, hoped that the cut would soften the effect of the ending, to make the movie less positive about Morgan's death. It would have been a very tough-minded audience that could believe Morgan would die with his daughters praying so hard. Morgan is not really alone anymore. He might, therefore, have a chance after all.

Whatever the audience assumes may happen to Morgan, the movie ends sadly with a last minute of film improvised during the shooting. Police begin to disperse the crowd gathered at the dock. No one pays any attention to the little black boy, Wesley's son, who does not yet know that his father has been murdered. He stands at the end of the pier looking around and out to sea, wondering what has happened.[13]

Hemingway sent notes to Jerry Wald and John Garfield saying that *The Breaking Point* suited him. Critics, too, were satisfied. In the *New York Times* Bosley Crowther did not mind overstating that the screenplay was "right down the original groove."[14] Ironically, despite the reviewers' respect for the movie, even though it was named to several lists of the best movies of the year, the studio never had much confidence in it, or else continued to think it too radical in social theme. It was withdrawn from circulation rather soon, and what profits it made came from European circulation.

MacDougall believed that there might be still another movie using only the "Have" characters of *To Have and Have Not*. Warners was not interested in the idea and sold the film rights to 7-Arts Productions as part of an inexpensive package deal of unimportant properties. Then in 1958, when three other Hemingway movies were in production or release, it seemed the right time to capitalize on a market for Hemingway material.

Those three other movies—*The Old Man and the Sea*, *The Sun Also Rises*, and *A Farewell to Arms*—were all major productions, big, expensive color movies. 7-Arts had to find a way to draw attention away from them and make this cheap remake of *To Have and Have Not* seem conspicuous. Controversy was one way to do it, if the movie could have a controversial title, for example. The first script version, drafted by Ben Hecht, screenwriter for the Selznick *Farewell to Arms*, had the peculiar title *Rub My Back*. Producer Clarence Greene changed that title to *One Trip Across*, which had been Hemingway's title for book 1 of the novel when it had first been published separately in *Cosmopolitan* in 1934.[15] Studio press agents put out a rumor that because Hemingway intended to block the use of that title (no sensible reason given), Greene would change it. It would be called *Ernest Hemingway's Gun Runners*. The updated version of Hemingway's old plot was to be about revolution in Cuba, and would involve gun-smuggling rather than rum-running. This was standard movie fare. In *Sirocco* (Columbia, 1951), Bogart had been selling guns to the Syrians to fight the French. In *We Were Strangers* (Columbia, 1949), John Garfield had been involved in a revolution in Cuba and an attempt to assassinate Cuban dictator Machado. Audie Murphy, the new Harry Morgan, was doing the same things the other Morgan players had done. But the war in Damascus had been 1925 and the Machado plot 1933. In 1957 there was a revolution going on in Cuba right then. A few newspaper stories appeared claiming that Hemingway was protesting the new movie title *Ernest Hemingway's Gun Runners* on the grounds that it implied his support of Castro's movement to overthrow the Batista regime and that he himself was involved with operations in contraband weapons. The studio probably fabricated this threat of legal action, too, in order to draw attention to the title, which finally dropped Hemingway's name.

This was not the most ludicrous part of the pretended feuding. Greene had insisted that a model with no movie experience be given a part; according to a news release, her name was Gita Hall Hemingway. Then that story was dropped and the rumor spread that Hemingway threatened legal action to prevent the use of his name.

Hemingway's alleged hostility to the production was all very unfair, Greene was quoted in *Variety* as saying, because Hemingway had not even read the script. He would find this adaptation was "more faithful to Hemingway's characterizations and the personal interrelations than was the original film."[16]

Director Don Siegel wished his producer had not invited any comparisons. Siegel had not wanted to make the picture because the earlier adaptations were certain to seem better.

> "I realized how utterly ludicrous it was for me to remake *To Have and Have Not* and *The Breaking Point*, both of which had superior stories, both of which had superior money, both of which had superior time. I thought it was absolutely stupid to remake *To Have and Have Not*

> and *The Breaking Point*. . . . I was very much against it, but I needed the money. . . . I'm sure the picture isn't any good."[17]

The opinion was shared by Daniel Mainwaring, whom Siegel hired to write the screenplay after Ben Hecht and then Paul Monash had drafted unacceptable versions.

Without much enthusiasm for the movie or, for that matter, the novel, Siegel and Mainwaring went back to the Hemingway version to appropriate the Key West and Havana locales and the background of revolution. They also took several of Hemingway's minor characters who had not been used in previous adaptations. They also studied MacDougall's script for *The Breaking Point* and borrowed what they could use from it.

They changed the hero's name. Sam Martin (Audie Murphy) runs a marginally profitable charter boat service out of Key West. He has a sexy wife (Patricia Owens) named Lucy (her name taken from *The Breaking Point*). They have not been married very long, and there are no children. Martin has named his boat the *Lucy M*.

Trouble begins when Sam takes a Mr. Peterson fishing. He loses a valuable rod and reel. Just as he is about to write a check to settle his debts, the police arrest him for passing worthless checks. The loss is critical. Sam pawns his last reel, tries to gamble back his loss at the craps table, and loses.

The fellow who is doing all the winning that night is a smooth operator named Hanagan (again a name borrowed from *The Breaking Point*, though spelled differently in the script). Hanagan likes the way Martin handles himself and sees him as a man who might need money badly enough to get into something illegal.

Sam, in fact, is a very clean-living fellow; the only dishonest thing he has ever done is play in an illegal crap game once in a while. But Hanagan is willing to pay a lot of money to someone who will smuggle him into Havana without the authorities knowing about it, and Sam takes the job.

There is a girl along, Hanagan's mistress, Eva (this was the role for Gita Hall Hemingway). The night they are in Havana Eva makes a heavy play for Sam in what seems to begin a triangular subplot like that of *The Breaking Point*. She does not get very far.

While this is going on, Hanagan is off on his own negotiating the sale of machine guns to Cuban revolutionaries. On the way back to the boat to meet Sam and Eva, Hanagan kills a Cuban soldier who stops him to check his identification. Knowing to expect sudden trouble, Sam already has his boat's engines turning when Hanagan runs down to the pier with a crowd of Cubans in pursuit.

Sam himself does not know about the murder until Coast Guard authorities in Florida question him about his activities the night before. A boat like Sam's had been described by Cuban officials. Luckily, there is no proof, and Sam is able to talk himself clear.

Sam knows his association with Hanagan is leading him into serious trouble. He cannot stop it now, though, because his boat has been confiscated for payment of debts. Hanagan buys the boat himself and offers to give it back to Sam plus an additional five thousand dollars if Sam will use the boat to carry an unspecified cargo to Cuba.

Hanagan, two of his henchmen, and Carlos, one of the revolutionaries to whom the guns are being sold, are to make the crossing with Sam. At sea, Carlos accidentally discovers that the crates are filled with scrap iron. So that Carlos cannot warn his people of the double-cross, Hanagan's men kill him. Soon after this, Hanagan discovers that Sam's mate, Harvey, has stowed away. Now Harvey will have to be killed, too, because a rummy cannot be trusted to keep quiet. This is the limit for Sam; he will not let his friend be killed. Harvey jumps overboard and starts to swim for a nearby island. Sam races the boat in the other direction, then spins the wheel to throw Hanagan and his men off balance. He grabs his automatic rifle, and, with the boat racing uncontrolled, full throttle towards a smashup on the jagged rocks ahead, shoots it out with Hanagan and his men. Hanagan is killed, after he fires one point-blank shot at Sam.

Both Siegel and Mainwarning had wanted the bullet to kill Sam Martin, but Clarence Greene, the producer, had final say on the matter. He was a producer of the old school that preferred invincible heroes, and he remembered, besides, that Morgan had survived in earlier versions. Therefore, Sam is only wounded in the shoulder.

He manages to bring the boat under control and picks up Harvey from the water. Harvey sees all the blood;

HARVEY: Ah—look what they done to you. Are you hurt bad, Sam?
SAM: I'm all right. You just get a hold of that wheel. Head us back to Key West.

* * * * *

HARVEY: You sure you're all right?
SAM: You just get me home to Lucy.

That is the last line of the script. The film cuts to shots of Lucy at the edge of the beach looking out to sea, hearing the seagulls, knowing her man is coming home.

Though lacking dignity, *The Gun Runners* almost seems like serious drama compared to the next movie about Harry Morgan, boat jockey, as one Hollywood writer liked to call him. In its next Hollywood version *To Have and Have Not* would have thirteen musical numbers and Elvis Presley as star.

*Girls! Girls! Girls!* was produced for Paramount in 1962 by Hal Wallis, producer of *Casablanca* as well. It is not clear who was remembering which picture, and probably the musical people never looked at the Hemingway book. Still, some similarities among several movies are manifest. Ross Carpenter (Elvis Presley) runs a sport fishing boat in unspecified waters. In the opening sequence he is marlin fishing with a bad sportsman named, for a switch, Mr. Morgan. His wife (the Leona character of *The Breaking Point*, Eva of *The Gun Runners*) is excited by Ross. She knows that he needs money badly, because he doesn't own the boat and the man who does own it has to be selling. Ross, who is a clean-living fellow though he does sing rock-and-roll, wants no part of her kind of trade. Then a tough character named Johnson buys the *West Wind* to make her part of his tuna boat fleet. Johnson is not a crook, but he is taking mean advantage of Ross, and he is trying to steal Ross's new girl—not the Morgan broad, the cutie with the blonde pony-tail. The climax comes when Ross commandeers his old boat, has a fistfight with Johnson, and recovers the sweetheart. She is rich, it turns out, and will buy Ross his boat when they marry.

In March, 1977, another real Hemingway movie came out, *Islands in the Stream,* which also has to be compared with *To Have and Have Not.* The reviewer for *Time* remembered the old Hawks picture as having endured very well all the years, because Hawks "tossed out most of the original novel and wrenched the rest into a racy adventure yarn." After seeing *Islands in the Stream* the reviewer was tempted to say, "Come back, Howard Hawks."[18]

The reviewer might not have realized the irony of his comparison. The makers of *Islands in the Stream* also discarded material from their novel (though not nearly as much as did Hawks). And especially in one long sequence of the movie, they replaced part of *Islands in the Stream* with material from the novel *To Have and Have Not.*

The books have similar structures, which is why it was possible to transfer material from one to the other. Both books are put together as sets of three chapter sequences, related to each other but not tightly. While they were revising an early version of the screenplay for *Islands in the Stream,* it seemed to writer Denne Petitclerc, director Franklin Schaffner, and producer Peter Bart, that the third part of the novel was not going to work well on film. Suddenly to put Hudson in quasinaval command of his yacht, the yacht now a sub-chaser, seemed, confusedly, to be starting a new story line for a different movie. It would have taken many minutes of film to provide an explanation of how Hudson came to have this assignment. Chapter 1 of book 3 in the novel begins in the middle of things with the tracking of the sub already having begun. The same effect in the movie theater might have seemed like the old days when a projectionist occasionally would skip one of the reels.

This is the situation in the third part of the movie. Hudson (played by George C. Scott) has learned that his oldest son, Tommy, a war pilot in the RCAF, has been shot down in flames. Despairing utterly, Hudson decides to leave his island where it is too painful continually to remember. He will stay on the mainland to paint and forget, and sometimes his younger boys will be with him.

In midstream of the crossing Hudson finds his friend Captain Ralph's boat disabled and listing. Captain Ralph has been making

IF IT'S BEEN TOO LONG SINCE YOU'VE SEEN A REALLY GOOD MOVIE... SEE "ISLANDS IN THE STREAM".

Paramount Pictures Presents

George C. Scott

A Franklin J. Schaffner Film

"Islands in the Stream"

A Bart/Palevsky Production

Based Upon The Novel By Ernest Hemingway Screenplay By Denne Bart Petitclerc

Produced By Peter Bart and Max Palevsky Directed By Franklin J. Schaffner

Music Jerry Goldsmith Services By Connaught Productions Panavision® In Color A Paramount Picture

PG

Read the Bantam Paperback

Newspaper ad for *Islands in the Stream*. In this image, as some columnists noted, George C. Scott bears a resemblance to Hemingway.

crossings to rescue Jewish refugees who have managed to escape from Europe to these islands. The night before a German submarine had surfaced, boarded Ralph's boat to raid his supplies, then shot him up. Now Hudson is involved in a war he had thought to escape and forget.

One version of Petitclerc's script developed the moral problem of Hudson's duty, whether or not he is now bound to get the refugees to American land, despite the risk that there might be a gun fight with American patrol boats. Also, his boat could be impounded, and he could be jailed for carrying aliens with no papers. By one possible finish to the movie, Hudson would fight it out with the Dade County sheriff and his deputies.

A simple circumstance of landscape blocked that turn of plot and obviated that moral question. At the Kauai, Hawaii, location for the filming of *Islands*, there was no stretch of land that looked anything like Key West or Miami. Now the script would have Hudson taking the refugees to Cuba, as Morgan returned Mr. Sing's Chinese. There was danger there, too, from Cuban patrols searching for spies and saboteurs. Captain Ralph warns Hudson: "They shoot fast. If they get you, they get a medal. They are very fond of getting medals."

The passengers are boarded. Hudson's mate, Eddy, has a Browning automatic rifle.

HUDSON: Don't shoot that thing, unless I tell you. I don't want anybody getting hurt.
EDDY: Okay, Chief. Jesus, it's like the old days when we used to run booze from here.

Like the old days, one could say, of *To Have and Have Not*.

The line is almost like a cue for the firing of a flare from a Cuban patrol boat. A Spanish voice over a bull-horn commands their surrender. Hudson throws open the throttles as Eddy starts firing the Browning. Cuban guns answer. Tracer bullets drum against the bulkhead, tear up Hudson's cockpit, shatter glass. Hudson's splintered boat surges away. Hours later, in the shallow channel through jungle foliage where he had thought to hide or elude, Hudson is killed.

Mary Hemingway discussed Hudson's fate with her husband while he was writing the ending for the book. She asked him not to kill Hudson—or at least to give him a chance to survive. When Hemingway read the ending to her, she felt that he had written it to please her after all and had given Hudson "a kind of a chance" (Morgan's words in *To Have and Have Not*). The boat might get to one of the islands where they can fly in a good surgeon. When eventually Mrs. Hemingway herself edited the manuscript for publication, she still understood that Hudson could live. He is not yet dead, after all, at the last lines of the book.

She explained her interpretation of her husband's intention to the movie people and suggested that perhaps Hudson ought not die in the gunfight. By an early version of the script, indeed the last scene of the movie would have been in a hospital room where

Hudson is recovering from his wounds. That version was discarded. Finally Hollywood killed the tough Hemingway hero.

Hudson dies the death that Morgan might have died in all the movies that went before, bleeding to death on the deck of what is really the same boat. Of course, Hudson and Morgan do not die identical deaths. Morgan is shot in the stomach by a side arm at short range. Hudson is shot in the back by .50 caliber bullets from a Cuban gunboat. Morgan has the longer time suffering. Hudson does not die alone, since Joseph and Willy of his crew are with him (Eddy has already been killed). If that is an extension of an old Hemingway theme, even a man *not* alone has "no bloody fucking chance."

There is nothing that Joseph can do to keep Hudson from dying. Joseph is weeping or nearly weeping (the book does not say so, but one sees this on the screen) when, to try to stop it, he says lines such as these (here quoted from the movie script, adapted slightly from the book): "Tom, I'm going to fix you up good. You lay quiet now. . . . Tom, I love you, you son of a bitch. Try to understand if you can. . . . Tom, don't you die."

Hemingway, in a sense, knew about adaptations and remakes. Catherine Barkley, like Morgan and Hudson, also died of a visceral wound, bleeding to death. "It seems she had one hemorrhage after another. They couldn't stop it." Joseph's pleading with Hudson is a scene very similar to Frederic Henry's telling Catherine over and again that she will not die and cannot die and that she is going to be all right.

Catherine is perfectly without illusion about this and says very directly that she really is going to die. Morgan understands this also, as does Hudson. Hudson does not think that he is going to be saved. "He looked up and there was the sky that he had always loved and he looked across the great lagoon that he was sure, now, he would never paint and he eased his position a little to lessen the pain." When it is certain, Hemingway characters do not have illusions about their not dying. That is a belief for old movies.

CHAPTER V

# Hemingway Entertainment in the Hollywood Style

Gertrude Stein said, "If you have an audience it's not art."[1] That sounds like an eccentric condition for a definition of art, but she did not mean that art could not have an audience. Rather she meant (perhaps) that the artist's commitment had to be to what his art required instead of what his audience wanted. If in this sense you had an audience, it was entertainment, not art.

To offer an overly simple distinction such as professors write up in chalk-talk on blackboards, Hemingway was an artist and the movie producers were entertainers. Not everyone would be inclined to accept this distinction, especially not the movie people. How could one make money in movies if they were beyond what most people understood and enjoyed? And what importance did art have anyway if people did not understand it or like it? Such was producer Frank Borzage's point of view: "It is one of the duties of a director to make his picture financially successful; which is another way of saying he must please his audience. An 'arty' picture is usually misnamed. Real art can be understood by you and I and everyone else."[2]

Borzage had been able to make *A Farewell to Arms* into such "real art" as anyone could understand. He kept what entertainment qualities he found in the book, then tried to make the novel more popular by adding other qualities that the audience liked. That was giving a book the "Hollywood treatment," as the term used to be.

A menswear shop in Paris, Tobias, has a sign the width of the storefront, in block letters, in English—"The Authentic Hollywood Style." So with the movies there was a certain Hollywood look, which sometimes was a little more showy than Hemingway's writing.

With Hemingway around to check on the script, it was difficult to change the story of *The Old Man and the Sea*. But it was possible to intensify the scenic qualities of the book. As a movie, *The Old Man and the Sea* could be more beautiful than the book.

Hemingway writes of Santiago rowing out to sea:

> [The old man] began to row out of the harbor into the dark. There were other boats from the other beaches going out to sea and the old man heard the dip and push of their oars even though he could not see them now that the moon was below the hills.
>
> Sometimes someone would speak in a boat. But most of the boats were silent except for the dip of the oars.

Cinematographer James Wong Howe made it a lovelier passage. The audience sees the horizon turning a deep Warnercolor rose in the dawn light. The fishermen seem shadowy figures as they file down to the shore and slip their boats into the water. Softly they chant a native song as they paddle out to sea. A lantern glows and bobs on the bow of each boat. This was a nice effect, reviewers agreed, and surely pleasing to the audience. Insofar as the movie presumed to be authentic Hemingway, however, the scene was almost gratuitously beautiful (to say nothing of the fact, which would have rankled Hemingway, that it was a Hawaiian beach instead of Cuban). The cinematography of some other scenes as well came close to being overly picturesque.

Other Hemingway books lent themselves to commercial improvement in the same way. As has been observed, it was easy for Selznick to heighten the scenic effects of *A Farewell to Arms*. It was to his profit to be able to describe the movie in the advertising copy as having been "majestically filmed in the actual Hemingway locales of the Italian Alps, Milan, Lake Como, Switzerland, and Rome." These were not all "actual Hemingway locales"—Lake Como and Rome are not places in the novel. The audience did not know or care about that, but was probably grateful that the Hollywood-sponsored tour of the book included visits there.

*The Sun Also Rises* was another of the scenic Hemingway movies, which was one of the things Hemingway did not like about the Hollywood version. He said the movie was a "splashy Cook's tour of Europe's lost generation bistros, bullfights, and more bistros."[3] There was a fair amount of tourism in the novel to begin with, which prompted Scott Fitzgerald to quip in his notebook, "*This Side of Paradise*: A Romance and a Reading List. *The Sun Also Rises*: A Romance and a Guide Book."[4] The book has Paris, Pamplona, Madrid, the Spanish countryside: "Europe's most famous name places," the movie publicity called them. This was "Hemingway's colorful world." To exploit the glamour of foreign scenery, the movie spends much more time than does the book on such sights as the fiesta, the running of the bulls, the parades, the rau-rau dancing, the fireworks. The movie provided a vicarious travel experience for an audience that might never travel otherwise. Jake Barnes in the novel says ironically, "All countries look just like the moving pictures."

"The Short Happy Life of Francis Macomber" (filmed as *The Macomber Affair*) and *The Snows of Kilimanjaro* offered the audience the exotic splendors of African scenery. The screen version of *The Snows of Kilimanjaro* was really a world travel adventure. There are scenes in Paris, described in the publicity as "the city of a million delights"; in Madrid, "with the excitement of the bull ring and the tempo of the Spanish dancers"; along the Riviera, "wonderland of revelry and romance"; and Africa, with its "hippopotami-teeming waters" and the magnificent Mt. Kilimanjaro. Much of the wonderful scenery was fake. The towering image of Kilimanjaro was only a painting on the wall behind a Hollywood sound stage. As for the African scenery of *The Macomber Affair*, Nairobi was really the village of Tecate, Mexico. The scrub plain outside Tecate was transformed into an African veldt by the contrivance of twenty-three plaster trees, eighteen plaster ant hills, and six plaster sand dunes. After the location shooting was finished, the property crew purportedly had the graciousness to leave the ant hills behind with the expectation that the villagers could use them as tortilla ovens.

Both the 1945 movie of *To Have and Have Not* and the 1957 remake had pretend Caribbean locations. Advertising for *The Gun Runners* promised that the movie would transport the audience "from the secret coves of Florida to the intrigue-ridden heart of Havana!"

*Hemingway's Adventures of a Young Man,* adapted by A. E. Hotchner from a selection of Nick Adams stories, was perhaps the Hemingway movie most like a travelogue. Most of the scenic effects were uncalled for since the Nick Adams stories are among Hemingway's least descriptive writing. (In "Big Two-Hearted River" scenery is described in detail for its symbolic value, but this was not one of the stories Hotchner used.) The movie opens with a panorama of the Michigan lake country, as described in the shooting script: "The morning mist is gently drifting up from the lake as the camera catches, in the morning sky, a thick V-flight of ducks coming low and calling to each other. The flight of ducks looms larger and larger until it fills the screen—then, circling once, the ducks drop lightly down to rest on the lake's surface."

A series of shots follows of Nick and his father fishing, hunting, and camping together in the woods, almost in the style of an advertising film promoting the wonders of Michigan as a vacation land. In the last shot of this sequence, a camera mounted in a helicopter swoops suddenly down into the heart of the wilderness with a vertiginous, Cinerama-like effect.

A long sequence in the movie narrates Nick Adams's adventures in Italy. Nick has been wounded in the war, and while he convalesces, his nurse gives him long wheelchair tours through the city of Verona. The audience sees statues, fountains, and elegant buildings: the Loggia del Consiglia ("Camera should make us aware of the awesome beauty of the Renaissance buildings of the Piazza," the shooting script notes), the Scaligieri Tombs, the Theatre Romano, the Piazza Della Erbe, the Piazza San Zeno, and so on. Producer Jerry Wald knew that the audience would appreciate the tourist attractions of Verona, though for all these scenes have to do with Hemingway the movie might as well have been shot at a studio lot. None of the Nick Adams stories, nor any other Hemingway work, is set in Verona.

The studio maintained that it was out of respect for Hemingway's specific directions that this part of the movie was filmed in and around Verona. Hemingway—according to a press release—had told Hotchner to have the movie people stay away from Milan because Milan had become "a horrible city." It would be better, he said, to go to Verona, where Nick had been a soldier and where he went hunting wild duck. Hemingway might have conferred with Hotchner about locations, but it may be seriously doubted that Hemingway would have liked the meaningless scenic effects of the movie. In her review of *Hemingway's Adventures of a Young Man*, Pauline Kael complained with good cause that the "DeLuxe-colored calendar art" of the movie was one of the things about it that made the critic "want to cry out that this is the film equivalent of everything Hemingway was trying to eliminate from his writing."[5]

"Go to movies and see the world" used to be a Hollywood publicity slogan. It was an especially good selling angle with Hemingway since the public identified him as a world traveler and adventurer. To give a big-screen, technicolor-bright treatment to the travel aspect of his fiction was an obvious way to exploit its escapist appeal.

Another standard way for screenwriters to popularize Hemingway's material was to heighten the action of his plots. Just as the movies gave the impression that Hemingway's fiction was filled with the glamorous adventure of world travel, so too they gave the impression that it was "action packed" with excitement, which is of course a primary requisite of escapist entertainment.

Sometimes it might have seemed to the movie people that Hemingway had missed very obvious opportunities for something exciting to happen. In the story "My Old Man," the boy's father is killed in a collision of horses in a steeple chase. It is an accident, though as the boy learns from overhearing a conversation after the race, his father had a bad reputation as a jockey. He was a "crook" and "had it coming to him." The 1950 movie version *Under My Skin* (originally titled "The Big Fall") predictably elaborated the father's involvement with the underworld of racetrack gamblers. Dan Butler (played by John Garfield) makes a deal to throw the race with a gangster named Louis Bork. But Bork knows that Butler has a good mount, could win the race, and is capable of double-crossing the mob, which in fact is exactly what Butler intends. So Bork hires another one of the jockeys to make sure there is no double-cross. If it seems like Butler might win, the other jockey will cause a collision and stop him that way. Thus in the movie there is not only the excitement of the race, but also the excitement of the duel between riders, something like the chariot race in *Ben-Hur* (MGM, 1926, 1959) without Roman spectacle. Jumping the last obstacle, their horses crash. The other rider is thrown and killed. Then moments after Butler crosses the finish line to win, the riderless horse collides with his. Butler is thrown and killed, too.

Hemingway predicted that Hollywood would have to change the opening of *For Whom the Bell Tolls* because there was not action enough. He told one of his friends, "They'll have to do it Hollywood style, you'll see, the scriptwriters will blow the train right off, instead of opening quietly in the forest as I wrote it."[6] The movie did open with the train being blasted sky-high.

Not even Hemingway's last chapter was exciting enough for the movie version. These are some of the changes made at the fight for the bridge:

1. The movie includes scenes of Pilar, Augustin, Primitivo, and Fernando battling the Fascists at the sawmill. At one point, Fernando takes careful aim at an enemy soldier. Fernando's rifle clicks empty, and at that moment he is shot in the belly. There is a close shot of him doubled over in agony. The enemy soldier peers cautiously around the circular saw. Pilar shoots him, grins vengefully, and recocks her gun. Eventually the guerrillas retreat from the mill. On signal, they throw grenades through the window, blowing the building to smithereens. None of this action is in the book.

2. The movie also has scenes of Pablo, Rafael, and men from the band of Elias fighting the Fascists at the guard-post. By one of the fast series of movie clichés, Pablo sneaks up behind a sentry, seizes him by the throat, and throttles him to death.

3. After Jordan has sniped the sentry at his end of the bridge, he runs onto the road carrying the packs of dynamite, as in the book. What happens next is different. Jordan does not see that the other sentry is raising his rifle and taking careful aim. The gentle An-

selmo, sentimentalized in the movie, has delayed killing his man. Now, at the last instant, he fires, and the sentry collapses. Hemingway gave Anselmo no such moment of weakness.

4. Early in the novel the gypsy Rafael had boasted that someday he would destroy a Fascist tank. He is only boasting, as is his way:

> ". . . He is a gypsy [said Anselmo]. So if he catches rabbits he says it is foxes. If he catches a fox he would say it was an elephant."
>
> "And if I catch an elephant?" the gypsy asked and showed his white teeth again and winked at Robert Jordan.
>
> "You'd say it was a tank," Anselmo told him. "I'll get a tank," the gypsy told him.
>
> "I will get a tank. And you can say it is what you please."
>
> "Gypsies talk much and kill little," Anselmo told him.

Rafael does not get his tank; he gets only a truck. After Jordan has blown the bridge, the gypsy, a fine marksman, knocks a truck out of action by shooting a tire, then smashing the radiator. In the Hollywood version Rafael *does* get his tank. He hides behind a boulder as the tank passes. He clambers to the turret and drops a grenade into the slit, jumping off behind rocks as the tank lumbers on down the road and explodes. That is the way tank warfare has to be fought in the movies. Then running towards the camera shouting his triumph—"I got me a tank!"—Rafael is riddled with machine gun fire. His death was another Hollywood exaggeration. In the novel Rafael is one of the guerrilla band left surviving at the end.

5. In a war movie, there must be revenge on the tank for killing Rafael. It happens this way. In the book, there is nothing on the bridge when Jordan and Anselmo blow it. Not so in the movie. As Jordan and Anselmo stand ready to pull their wires to the grenades and dynamite on the girders, the tanks are already starting to cross, machineguns firing. Anselmo has another moment of weakness and seems paralyzed. Jordan dashes from cover into the field of tank fire, seizes Anselmo's wire, runs back to his cover and pulls. The dynamite blows. The entire center section of bridge drops out, and the tank that killed Rafael topples into the gorge.

There were various other standard action situations that Hollywood could work into Hemingway's story lines. One was the heroic rescue to show the hero to all the advantage that was his due as movie star. In the sequence of *Hemingway's Adventures of a Young Man* that covers Nick Adams's exploits in the war, Nick recklessly, daringly drives his ambulance across no-man's-land to rescue his commander from a bombarded building where he is trapped under fallen beams. The major is still breathing. Nick carries him to the ambulance and races back toward his own lines. An enemy shell wrecks the ambulance, and Nick has to carry the major the rest of the way on his back. There is no such situation in any of the Nick Adams stories.[7]

In *The Snows of Kilimanjaro*, a writer named Harry is dying from gangrene, which started with an infection caused when he neglected to treat a scratch he got when stalking through thorn bushes to photograph a herd of waterbuck. The Hollywood version causes the infection in a sequence of danger. There is the thorn scratch first. Then a short time afterwards, Harry and his wife are out in native boats on a lake chasing a herd of hippopotami. One of the brutes jolts the second boat, knocking a native boy into the water. He screams in terror as the hippopotamus attacks. Harry dives in to rescue him. The film cuts to a shot of Harry carrying the boy, streaming blood, to safety on the lakeshore. Harry's wife says to him later: "And you insisted on carrying the boy in your arms all the way back to camp. And I'm sure it was from all his blood and dirt that you got the infection."

*Under My Skin* has a rescue very near the beginning of the movie. Dan Butler has been racing in Merano, Italy, and is in trouble with the gangsters there. It is time for Dan and Joe to clear out of the country. Some of the gang's strong-arm men show up at the hotel while they are packing. Joe gets away over the rooftops of the neighboring buildings, while Dan tries to talk himself out of trouble. There is a fight, and the police arrive just in time to save Butler from being beaten almost to death.

Sometimes the movie hero has to escape on his own, with no one to rescue him. There are escape sequences in several of the Hemingway gangster movies. In the story "The Killers," Hemingway's character Ole Andreson—"Swede"—has tried to drop out of sight into the town of Summit, Illinois, where he hopes the Chicago mob will not be able to find him. The story implies that the professional killers are after him because he double-crossed somebody. Writers for both the 1946 and 1964 movie versions followed the story's suggestion and constructed elaborate plots that turn on a double-cross. In the later movie, Johnny North, as "Swede" has been renamed, drives the get-away car in a Brinks robbery. He plans to keep the money himself and run away with his girl. But he has made the mistake of telling her the name of the motel where he intends they will spend the first night of their elopement from crime. Johnny does not know that Sheila is doubling a double-cross with the gangleader, Browning, whose woman she has been all along. When Johnny and Sheila arrive at the Pineywoods Motel with their suitcases of money, Browning is in the room waiting. Browning shoots Johnny point-blank but, incredibly, only wounds him. Gripping his bleeding side, Johnny staggers into the night and crashes through the woods with Browning in pursuit. He stumbles over a log and rolls down an embankment. Lying very still in his pain, he hears Browning and Sheila talking. They have the money; they will not take the time to look for him now. Browning will hire a couple of professional killers to track him down if he is not dead already. The scene was not very imaginative, of course. The run, the trip, the fall, the lying still made for a very routine pattern of movie escape. Of such conventional action of tested and proven effectiveness were easy movies made.

To rerun a scene from *A Farewell to Arms*, Frederic Henry's escape from the court martial at the bridge is exaggerated for Selznick's version into an old-movie cliché. In the novel he runs for the river, trips at the edge, and splashes in. The Hollywood hero is not so clumsy in his escape. The court is convened in a tent. Frederic Henry shoves two guards from their feet, smashes the lanterns to plunge the tent into darkness (in many, many movie fights the hero douses the lights), and dashes out. With the carabinieri firing, he races across the perilous open ties of a railway trestle and dives into the river with almost championship form.

Once he is with Catherine again, Frederic knows that they are still not safe until they have fled Italy for Switzerland. In the night, in the storm, they row across the lake to Swiss waters. It is a dangerous crossing, with minutes of tension when there might be a challenge from a guard in a patrol boat: "I pulled close up to the shore and lay quiet. The chugging came closer; then we saw the motor boat in the rain a little astern of us. There were four *guardia di finanza* in the stern. . . . They all looked sleepy so early in the morning. . . . The motor boat chugged on and out of sight in the rain." The suspense is heightened in the Selznick movie as the boat's searchlight cuts and probes through the shoreline reeds where Frederic and Catherine lie low and breathless.

Denne Petitclerc's script for *Islands in the Stream* plays many scenes of the novel for higher excitement than the original story. The night of the queen's birthday celebration, Hudson is drunk and acting wild, recklessly firing phosphorous flares with the Verey pistol. He is in a bad mood, almost sick with anxiety about his sons' arrival the next day. (In the novel, it is Hudson's crony, Frank Hart, who is behaving badly and firing the flares. Some of the friends of the book are not characters in the movie.) One of the flares arcs onto the porch of the commissioner's house and burns there, while his servants rush around to beat it out. (Frank Hart aims for the commissioner's porch, but the flare does not carry that far.) Hudson loads again, and the pistol fires accidentally. The flare caroms off the inside stern rail and lands blazing at Hudson's feet.

The most desperate moment of the "Bimini" section of *Islands in the Stream* is when Hudson's boy, skin-diving, is attacked by a hammerhead shark. Hudson watches the fin glide and wobble towards Tommy. He knows he has only three shells in the Mannlicher Schoenauer. The first two shots miss: "Thomas Hudson was trying to be loose but steady, trying to hold his breath and not to think of anything but the shot; to squeeze and keep just a touch ahead and at the base of the fin which was wobbling more now than it had at the start when he heard the submachine gun start firing from the stern and saw water start to spout all around the fin." Eddy is firing the automatic weapon. He slams the shark seconds before it strikes. The movie is different from this only in small ways. Of course the camera cannot show what the book can say is in Hudson's mind—that there are three bullets left. Instead the camera shows him reach to the cartridge box to reload and discover, in instant terror, that the box is empty. The fear in watching the scene on film is somewhat different, too, in that Hudson's weapon is empty before the burst of the machine gun is heard.

Probably it was good judgment not to exaggerate the excitement of the sequence beyond this, because it could seem like a weak imitation of the horror of *Jaws*. Of course the shark was difficult enough to film realistically anyway, with the fake fin pulled on tow-line and a swimmer in rubber suit. Presumably, Hemingway, having so low a tolerance for screen illusion, would have hated the rubber shark like he hated the rubber marlin in *The Old Man and the Sea*.

The "At Sea" section of *Islands in the Stream* took the most drastic revisions. In the novel Hudson and his crew are relentlessly searching for the crew of a destroyed submarine. Hoping they can make contact with one of their wolf pack, the Germans have commandeered a turtle boat and are hiding in the shallow, narrow channels of the keys. It is not a reckless chase. Hudson's pursuit is slow, thoughtful tracking. "Continue searching carefully westward," the code message had come from Guantanamo.

For the faster pace of movie adventure, the situation is turned around, with Hudson the pursued rather than pursuer. The enemy has high-powered patrol boats. In chapter 14 of part 3, Hudson dares to steer into a channel, even though the tide is falling fast, because the Germans went in perhaps only an hour and a half before. Then Hudson's boat is grounded in mud and sand until the tide comes back in. The situation is adapted into a smash-up for the movie. Hudson's only way of escape into a blind channel is to scrape his keel across a reef. The speeding patrol boat follows and is splintered on the rocks. Half the enemy is destroyed.

In the novel, Hudson, as the commander and pilot of his boat, is fighting by the decisions he makes. Mostly it is his crew who fire the weapons and heave the bombs. Hudson is at the wheel when they are ambushed from the mangroves. The Germans are aiming at him first, of course, and the first bullets hit him: "Just then they opened on him. He did not see the blinking flash and he was hit before he heard the stutter of the gun and Gil was on his feet beside him. Antonio was firing tracers where he had seen the gun flash." To give the glory to the hero of the movie, in the screenplay more of the desperate action is given to Hudson himself. He sets the trap for the Germans, wading in the channel, emptying cans of gasoline on the water, leaving himself open to fire from the Cuban prow gun. At the last moment, Hudson fires a Verey flare on the gasoline (a variation on Hudson's drunken horseplay in the harbor the night of the queen's birthday). The river explodes into fire. The Cuban boat is blocked, but their machine gun fires through the flames and hits Morgan as he climbs to the bridge.

More rounds of ammunition are fired in the novel than in the movie, and more explosives are blasted. Grenades and fire extinguishers are packed with dynamite and junk metal. But the movie is more exciting. The movie sequences seem like footage from a James Bond thriller like *Thunderball* (UA, 1965). Or they are chapters from a movie serial of the Thirties—chapter 14, "Reef of Doom," chapter 15, "Wall of Fire."

The love story of *Islands in the Stream* was adapted with conspicuous restraint. In the last twenty pages of part 2 of the book "Cuba," Tommy's mother, Hudson's first wife, comes to the island. She is an actress, now on tour entertaining troops. She is going to marry someone else. She is still very beautiful; it is said that she is the most beautiful woman in the world. When Hudson sees her again there is a rush of love for her and an impatience to make love to her, as when Frederic Henry sees Catherine at the hospital in Milan and knows that he is in love with her. Everything is wonderful between them for a while again. After they make love, she asks about Tommy because she has not heard from him in weeks. Hudson has not known how to tell her that he has been killed in the war until she guesses what is true.

In the section of the movie titled "The Woman," the situation is reversed. It is Audrey (the name is for a different character in the novel) who already knows that Tommy is dead. (One reason for the change in the screenplay might have been in order to film Scott's acting across the seconds when he realizes why she has come. Facing away from the camera, he reflexively reaches for the chill at the base of his neck.) The movie does dramatize the old and long love between Hudson and Audrey and their intimacy that continues. But with the apprehension and the grief between them, there is not the arousal and glamour that love is supposed to have in the movies. The audience may watch and understand them as they are in love, but does not especially fantasize about them. The adapters used with dignity the relationship that Hemingway gave to the characters, but few people in the audience would appreciate that.

Some of the Hemingway novels were strong love stories to begin with: *The Sun Also Rises, A Farewell to Arms, For Whom the Bell Tolls*, and, though it has not yet been filmed, *Across the River and into the Trees*. Adapters of the other Hemingway properties were inclined to strengthen a love interest if it were weak, or even create a love story from the slightest possibility that Hemingway offered.

This was true of *The Old Man and the Sea*, unlikely though it may seem. Leland Hayward thought that he could improve on Hemingway's material in this way. There is the line in the book about the old man's wife, who has died: "Once there had been a tinted photograph of his wife on the wall, but he had taken it down because it made him too lonely to see it and it was on the shelf in the corner under his clean shirt." Hayward intended to keep that line. Then, in a later dream sequence, the movie could show the old man remembering the days long past when he had courted his wife. Even as a very short sequence, Hayward believed this would be an effective touch. Hemingway immediately killed the idea.

Other Hemingway stories admitted a love interest more readily. For both screenplay versions of "The Killers" the writers found it easy to introduce a girl into the Swede's complicated past. In the earlier movie Swede had two girls. There had been a nice girl, Lily (pure as a lily), who had loved him in the days he was trying to be a heavy-weight contender. Then he met Kitty (with the morals of an alley cat) who led him to crime and to grief. Kitty double-crosses Swede and abandons him for the gangleader she started with. Lily, by the irony of the plot, ends up married to the police lieutenant who once had been Swede's friend but had to do his duty when Swede started to go bad.

The plot of "My Old Man" had to be expanded anyway to make it last the length of a feature film. The story has a father and a son, but no mother. Hemingway does not account for her absence; perhaps she is dead. Whatever the circumstance, it was very easy for producer and screenplay writer Casey Robinson to use a common formula for a love story and have the boy become great friends with a woman just old enough to be his mother, thereby eventually bringing the woman and his father together. In *Under My Skin* the jockey, Dan Butler, and his boy Joe go to Paris where Dan hopes to find mounts at the Paris tracks. There they meet a beautiful woman named Paule, who is a singer at her own Left Bank nightclub. Years before, Paule had been infatuated with Dan Butler; he had been the most colorful jockey in Paris. He had ignored her then, though, and she had taken up with one of Dan's friends, Claude. Then Dan and Claude had gotten in serious trouble with gamblers. Dan fled to America, but Claude did not clear out soon enough and was murdered. Paule has despised Dan Butler ever since, mistakenly believing that Dan must have been indirectly responsible for Claude's death. Paule cannot help liking this boy, Joe, however, and they become very attached to each other. Gradually Paule realizes that a man as devoted to his son as Dan is must not be all bad. On Dan's side, he is bitter about women; the movie hints that his wife deserted him and Joe. At first, therefore, Dan thinks he is pleased with the friendship between Joe and Paule only for Joe's sake. Soon, however, Dan and Paule begin to fall in love. The three of them go to the country together to train the horse that Dan has bought. One morning at breakfast Joe asks innocently, "Say, Pop, why don't we get married to Polly?" The question is in the open now. Dan and Paule admit they love each other. If Dan wins the big race, they will marry and all go to America.

The story does not have the intense French passion that the publicity promised: "Ernest Hemingway's Best! A Story of Flesh and its Longings!"; or "John Garfield loves a French woman [Micheline Prell] the way a woman wants to be loved!" The passion in the movie amounts only to a single kiss. Still, for the purposes of entertainment, the script was much an improvement over Hemingway's story, which had no love angle at all.

Movie publicity, like the covers of "confession" magazines, tends to promise a more titillating experience than the audience actu-

The original one-sheet poster for *To Have and Have Not*, here badly creased with age. The BOGART lettering is in red, screened to salmon pink at the edges. The shading around the faces is sky-blue. The faces are in black and white, but Lauren Bacall's lips are the Bogart red. From the author's collection.

ally views. A poster for *To Have and Have Not* showed Bogart and Bacall in a giant close-up, a moment away from an intense kiss: "BOGART . . . with his kind of woman, in Ernest Hemingway's most daring man-woman story!" The movie is not daring at all. The book was sexually intimate in some Joycean passages, but not at all with the movie glamour connoted by "daring."

Advertisements described *Hemingway's Adventures of a Young Man* as an adolescent's first adventures with sex—"The Hungers of a Young Man's Springtime." Nick Adams was "In a hungry hurry to know the touch of a woman—the pride of manhood." The Nick Adams stories are not about excited teenage love and sex, except for "Ten Indians," which was not used for the script, and "The Summer People," which was not published until ten years after the movie was made. "The End of Something" is about Nick and a girlfriend, but their love, such as it may have been, is over before the story begins, and Nick is breaking up with her. For the screenplay, A. E. Hotchner appropriated Frederic Henry's love story in *A Farewell to Arms*, and innocently rewrote it with no sex at all.[8]

In the movie *The Macomber Affair*, a rich, spoiled woman (played by Joan Bennett) has a weak, cowardly husband (Robert Preston) who is displeasing to her in comparison with a new lover (Gregory Peck), who is more beautiful and virile. "The Short Happy Life of Francis Macomber" as Hemingway wrote it has adultery as one turn of plot, but it is not about what one would call a love affair. The white-hunter Wilson's attitude towards Margot Macomber is ambivalent. At any given moment he tends to think badly of her to about the same degree that he does not think badly of her husband. Then his attitude towards her will reverse, then shift again. His sexual instinct toward her seems almost dispassionate. He certainly does not love Margot Macomber, and she does not love him. In the movie version, Wilson and Margot *do* fall in love, as the audience could have predicted. Late in the movie Wilson admits that. The situation is the very same as in the story. Wilson and Macomber have wounded a buffalo, and they have to take the risk of going into the heavy brush after him to finish him off. Then the screenwriters inserted the following dialogue, which is not in the story, and not suggested by the meaning of the story. Macomber asks to wait a minute. He is afraid again, as he was when they had to stalk the wounded lion in yesterday's hunt. He has something he wants to ask Wilson. (In a way this does not seem the very best moment to bring up the subject of a woman, but the writers know that Macomber will have no chance to say anything at all after this.)

MACOMBER: Just tell me one thing.
WILSON: Anything.
MACOMBER: You've fallen in love with her, haven't you.
WILSON: Yes, I have.
MACOMBER: All I want is an even break.

They shake hands, for they are, after all, sportsmen. They have an understanding that they are equals now, since Macomber has discovered his courage, and from now on there will be a fair and even competition for Margot.

*The Macomber Affair* was a very accurate adaptation, all considered. It used almost all of Hemingway's dialogue (even repeated references to Mr. Wilson's ruddy complexion, which did not seem to describe Gregory Peck's appearance very well). Almost none of Hemingway's material was significantly changed, except that Gregory Peck and Joan Bennett had to be completely in love with each other. Hemingway's version of their relationship would have disappointed their millions of fans.

The event of the shooting is the same in the story and movie. Margot shoots at the wounded buffalo charging her husband and kills her husband instead. It is as good as murdering him, which perhaps is what she wanted to do. The story is almost perfectly ambiguous on that point, as is the movie.

The movie returns to Nairobi. There is a great deal of unpleasantness to go through. Wilson has to write a report and he himself is not completely sure whether or not Margot was trying to shoot at Francis Macomber. He does try to assure her that she will be able to get through the inquest. The last shots of the movie are of Margot walking by herself to the ordeal of the court. It was an effective ending and quite appropriate to the story. The audience never finds out—MURDER OR ACCIDENT?, which was one of the movie's advertising slogans. The publicity people perhaps exaggerated the matter. (To be sure, this might be called a fault of literary critics as well.) The publicity specialists suggested to theater managers that they promote interest in the picture by having a local lawyer lead a panel discussion about Margot's guilt.

To the movie's credit, the love interest was not allowed to ruin the ending. There are no throbbing promises about enduring love between Margot and Wilson, and about how they will marry when the inquest is over.

The movie ending does continue past the end of the story, which halts abruptly in the minutes after the shooting. Wilson is giving Mrs. Macomber a very hard time.

> "Why didn't you poison him? That's what they do in England."
> "Stop it. Stop it. Stop it," the woman cried.
> Wilson looked at her with his flat blue eyes.
> "I'm through now," he said. "I was a little angry. I'd begun to like your husband."
> "Oh, please stop it," she said. "Please, please stop it."
> "That's better," Wilson said. "Please is so much better. Now I'll stop."

That is the last line of the story. The screenplay did keep these lines, in almost the same wording, in almost as ironic a tone perhaps, but moved them to a scene between Wilson and Margot minutes before the inquest begins.

Gregory Hemingway remembers being with his father when he saw *The Macomber Affair*. The movie people sent a print over to Cuba, and the boy felt a little embarrassed that his father fell asleep during the movie when they had gone to that trouble. One cannot feel sure that Hemingway would have approved how the movie was ended, but clearly his own ending would not have worked on the screen. The suddenness of the ending is effective when seen on a page, but probably much too extreme when seen with actors playing it out. And it would have been a more confusing ending than movie audiences were used to.

This was sometimes a problem with Hemingway properties insofar as Hollywood was concerned. Their endings did not always have the heavy, sure weight of resolution, the swelling, orchestral finality that audiences expected most movies to have. It took a long while even for sophisticated critics to become used to reading the low and subtle endings to some of Hemingway's stories—"zero endings," as they have been called.[9]

Endings that are not clear and loud can seem to some people distressingly "modern." A television viewer wrote a letter to the editor of *TV Guide* complaining about modern movies: "I can tell you in short order why we would rather see old movies than new ones. Old movies have a plot, a story, something worth telling, and mainly they have an *ending*. So much of the drivel shown now rambles on and on. You wonder what it is trying to say and finally it just quits. No ending—just quits. Don't writers have sense to think up endings any more?"[10]

Hemingway created an old lady who complained to him about something very like this in a conversation in *Death in the Afternoon*. She is not very satisfied with the ending of a story Hemingway has just told her. "And is that all of the story? Is there not to be what we called in my youth a wow at the end?" "Ah, Madame," Hemingway answers, "it is years since I added the wow to the end of the story. Are you sure you are unhappy if the wow is omitted?" The old lady replies, "Frankly, sir, I prefer the wow." She could be speaking for the mass audience. For the sake of the old lady and the rest of the audience that shared her view, Hollywood filmed endings that were not only final but also emotionally intense.

One understands, then, why the effect of the ending of *For Whom the Bell Tolls* was not exactly what producer Sam Wood wanted for the 1943 Paramount adaptation. In the last chapter Robert Jordan's leg has been broken, so he cannot make the retreat with the other guerilla fighters after exploding the bridge. He stays behind on the pine slope of the mountain where he will be killed, though he may be able to delay the pursuit of the Fascist cavalry. The novel ends with Jordan sighting down the barrel of his submachine gun at the lieutenant who cautiously leads the cavalry patrol up the hillside. This was filmed almost exactly as Hemingway described it—with the camera aiming down the barrel to see Jordan's view. But the movie had to resolve the suspense into an emotional climax. The film cuts to a close shot of Jordan aiming directly into the camera. The weapon fires violently. The screen image dissolves in gunsmoke to a close shot of an iron bell whose

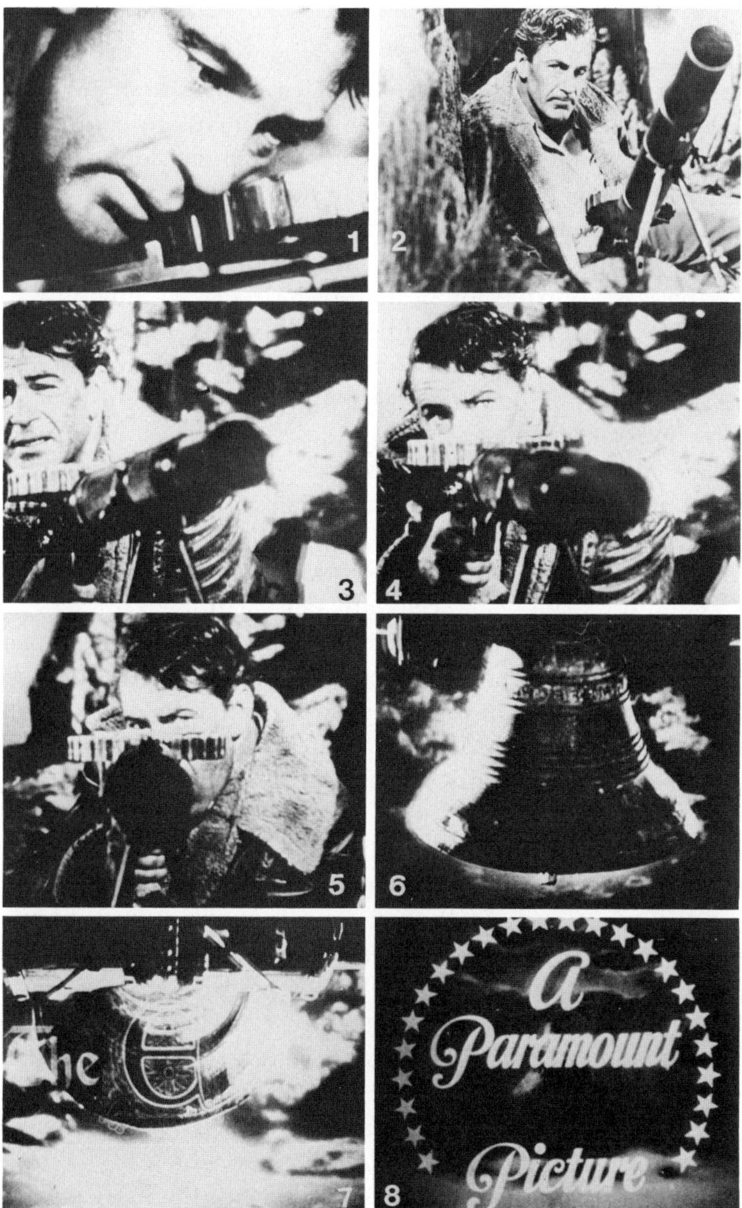


Gary Cooper as Robert Jordan, waiting in pain, sighting the cavalry coming in file up the slope, then swinging the Lewis gun into aim. At the instant after frame 5, the weapon fires and the screen is filled with smoke, which clears with the tolling bell. Frame 2, here shown for the sake of continuity, is not taken from the film print but is a publicity still—of extravagant sexual suggestiveness, one might remark.

From the motion picture *For Whom the Bell Tolls*. Courtesy of Universal Pictures.

resonant toll covers the noise of the gun. It is one of the great finishes in American film. Certainly it was "a wow at the end."

Louis Bromfield's ending for his earlier screenplay of *For Whom the Bell Tolls*, which was discarded, is anticlimatic by comparison. Jordan fires the machine gun at the cavalry on the slope. His fire is answered by a shell that digs up a shower of dirt. He sets his jaw, shifts the gun, then fires again. Another shell falls, now nearer to him. Jordan fires another burst from the machine gun, and suddenly there is an explosion of flame where the machine gun had stood. The movie screen is filled with smoke. The scene has changed as the smoke clears. Figures on horseback appear many miles away. Maria, Pilar, Pablo, and Augustin ride to the crest of a hill overlooking a village. It is Gredos, Pablo says. Maria, as if dazed, seems not to hear. Does she hear? Pilar asks. It is Gredos. They are safe. Maria seems to hear Jordan's voice encouraging her. He is with her. "As long as there is one of us there is both of us. Wherever you go, I go. We will go to America another time." Pilar asks again, does she hear? They are safe. As if awakening, Maria hears her. They ride down the valley as the picture fades. Not only does this last shot undercut the intensity of the tragedy at the moment of Jordan's firing, it is unnecessary. Without being shown, the audience would trust that Maria is safe and that there has been a purpose served by Jordan's sacrifice of himself to protect the retreat of the others.

In real life almost everyone dies without much great significance or compensation associated with his death, if not in vain. Movie audiences wish death in the matinee, when it must occur, to be different. In every particular way that it is extraordinary, Jordan's is a death for a great movie scene. Not only does he die for Maria, but he is also fighting against fascism. By the heroic circumstance that is given to him, he has a weapon, an ambush site, and his enemy coming up the hill in slow single file. He is not in unbearable pain, because the nerve is crushed. Also, he has the beautiful scenery of a wonderful morning in which to die. In the essay *Nature*, Ralph Waldo Emerson describes the marvelous circumstance by which nature, whose purpose is to confirm the virtue of noble acts, sometimes provides a splendorous setting for heroism.

> When a noble act is done,—perchance in a scene of great natural beauty; when Leonidas and his three hundred martyrs consume one day in dying, and the sun and the moon come each and look at them once in the steep defile of Thermopylae; when Arnold Winkelreid, in the high Alps, under the shadow of the avalanche, gathers in his side a sheaf of Austrian spears to break the line for his comrades; are not these heroes entitled to add the beauty of the scene to the beauty of the deed?

For all this, the separation of Jordan and Maria is no less sad. Rather, the sorrow is magnified to the scale of the heroic meaning and the heroic view.

In this sense one may see how much better and easier for the sake of a movie ending are the last pages of *For Whom the Bell Tolls* than the last pages of *A Farewell to Arms*. There is no splendid meaning to Catherine's death, and she dies in a stark hospital room.

Some of Hemingway's characters die good deaths and others do not. In *Islands in the Stream*, Hudson's oldest boy, Tommy, enlists as a pilot in the war. His plane is shot down by a flak ship over the English Channel. Hudson does not feel sure that he understands why his son had to be killed. "It's way past the things we know about," he says in the screenplay. When he tried to bail out, his parachute caught fire. There is a quality of terrible glory to his death.

In the novel, even before the war and Tommy's death the two younger brothers, David and Andrew, are also killed. Hudson receives the telegram about a motoring accident in Biarritz. The boys were with their mother, who was killed also. An early version of the screenplay tested the possibility of killing the boys in the movie, too. This was the same discarded script in which Hudson survives his wounds. The telegram comes to him at his hospital room: "YOUR SONS DAVID AND ANDREW . . . ." Director Franklin Schaffner decided that it would be completely inappropriate to end the movie this way. He could not kill everyone off; it would not be fair, he explained. It would batter the audience's feelings. "How long has it been since you've seen a really good movie?"—such was the theme of the publicity campaign for *Islands in the Stream*. "Since you saw a movie that said something about life and love that you will take with you in your heart and mind long after the evening's over." No one was going to take good feelings away from a movie in which David and Andrew are killed without reason.

The death of sons is very grim tragedy, especially when it is unfair. So is the death of a father. The adaptation of the story "My Old Man" into the movie *Under My Skin* shows very clearly how Hollywood could alter the force and direction of Hemingway's emotional vectors so as to avoid an ending that was too harsh. At the end of the story, after Joe overhears a conversation about his father's being a crook who had it coming to him, one of his father's friends tries to comfort the boy: "Don't you listen to what those bums said, Joe. Your old man was one swell guy." It does not seem to help Joe much to hear that. In the final line of the story he says, "Seems like when they get started they don't leave a guy nothing." It is not fair, and this feeling of complete negation is not in the movie at all. After he is thrown from his horse, Dan Butler is taken to the track emergency room where Joe is with him when he dies—a sadder scene than in the story. Joe will always be able to remember, however, that his father *won* the race, which is not as it happened in the story. Also, Joe will always know that his father died riding an honest race. Thus when his father's friend comforts him, it has important meaning.

GEORGE: Joe, your dad was a great jockey. He rode the greatest race I ever saw. He died winning honest. They can't take that away from him ever.

JOE: (Seeing the statue that memorializes great jockeys who have been killed): Will they put his name on the roll of honor.

GEORGE: They couldn't keep it off. He was a great jockey and a great guy.

Finally, whereas at the end of the story Joe is alone, at the end of the movie he has someone to be close to—the French girl, Paule, whom his father was going to marry. As they leave the track together, Paule tells Joe that they should honor his father's last wish and use the prize money to start a new life in America. She puts her arm around Joe's shoulder protectively at the final dissolve. It is a positive and forward-looking resolution.

For the happiest possible ending, screenwriter Casey Robinson might have let Dan Butler survive his fall from the horse—still destroy the horse, perhaps, but not the rider. Two years later, when Robinson wrote the screenplay for the movie version of *The Snows of Kilimanjaro*, he *did* save the hero whom Hemingway let die. In the story, a hyena, symbolizing death, is prowling around Harry's camp. It seems the beast has crept invisibly past the campfire, rested its head on the foot of the cot, then crouched on Harry's chest. "He could not speak to tell her [his wife] to make it go away and it crouched now, heavier, so he could not breathe. And then . . . suddenly it was all right and the weight was gone from his chest." Then it seems to be morning. A rescue plane lands and flies Harry out over the summit of Kilimanjaro. The flight is only the illusion of dream in the moment that Harry dies. In the Hollywood version, his wife's screams frighten the hyena away in the night. In the morning, the plane really does land for the rescue.

Robinson offered a defense to those who might accuse him of compromising the integrity of the story by giving it a safe and happy ending that would not distress the audience. In the first place, Robinson explained, he and producer Darryl F. Zanuck had decided that the dream flight would not film well, that Hemingway's effect would not come across on the screen. One could argue about that. Of course, they were not shooting in Tanganyika and did not have Mount Kilimanjaro to fly a plane over. The effect would have required an elaborate process shot.

Robinson further explained that he and Zanuck believed that the story had "the most tender, most hopeful, and the happiest conclusion that Hemingway could devise," as if Hemingway wanted to grant his hero at least that much for having suffered a profoundly honest appraisal of his ruined career as a writer. The decision to let the hero survive in the movie version was, by specious reasoning, in keeping with Hemingway's intention, "which was to say that any of us have earned a fitting reward if we have the honesty to add up our mistakes and a deeply felt wish to correct them. The suggestion that this reward take the form of a second chance seems a more satisfying interpretation of Mr. Hemingway's thought than would be a cinematic ride in any airplane."[11] To Hemingway it seemed simply that the movie's meaning was opposite to the story's. He said the movie was one-third Zanuck's, one-third Robinson's, and one-third his.[12] Wherever else he found his share, it was not at the end.

Most of the audience would have had no idea that Robinson and Zanuck had changed the endng of the story so drastically. Could a survey have been made of the audience's preference for one ending over the other, however, most of the audience probably would have selected the Hollywood ending, and not only because the hero lives happily afterwards. They also would have liked the movie's implicit moral. There is a moral meaning to the story as Hemingway wrote it, having to do with an artist's uncompromising commitment to his art. That would not have meant much to the general public. Better as a thought for the movies was Robinson's moral about our deserving a second chance in life if we admit our mistakes. It was virtually a Christian idea.

Though no one went to the movies for the sake of moral instruction, the public readily approved movies which suggested, not preached, a moral point—if it was a simple and familiar point, like about second chances, or winning honest in *Under My Skin*. Likewise *The Gun Runners* had a clear little lesson near the end. Sam Martin's mate Harvey is overjoyed that Sam is not a gun runner after all. "I knew you couldn't go through with it. You know, Sam? Because like I always said, a man can't go bad if it ain't in him to go bad. And it just ain't in you—even if you tried."

*The Old Man and the Sea* was excellent for the movies in this regard. Hemingway had written a wisdom-like idea for Spencer Tracy to express: "Man is not made for defeat. A man can be destroyed but not defeated." The studio intended this to sound like a religious, even a biblical truth. One newspaper display ad showed Tracy gazing reverently toward the sky, his face bathed in light. The copy read:

In the beginning God created Heaven and earth. And the earth was without form and void; and darkness was upon the face of the deep—and the spirit of God moved upon the face of the waters.

THIS WAS THE BEGINNING

AND GOD CREATED MAN

Here is Mr. Ernest Hemingway's magnificent portrayal of man,

OF MAN'S HOPE

OF MAN'S FAITH

The story of man's courage, of Man's eternal Determination.

IN THIS ATOMIC AGE—MAN CAN BE DESTROYED—BUT NEVER DEFEATED!

THIS IS WHERE OUR STORY BEGINS

Never in the history of the screen a picture so rich in spiritual and emotional values!

This was like Elmer Gantry preaching in the Bomb Age, as if after the nuclear blasts there would still be a meaningful distinction between having been defeated or merely destroyed.

Hollywood had to adjust the moral theme of *The Sun Also Rises* so that the audience would understand it and approve of it. The characters belong to "the lost generation." They are "lost" in the sense of being doomed and are sometimes sorry and sometimes almost gleeful about it, as the gentlemen songsters of the Whiffenpoof song are damned from here to eternity. They also are lost in the sense of being without direction. The old values and ideals that were guidance to previous generations do not seem relevant any more, having been pretty well ruined by the war. Yet the characters, notably Jake Barnes but also Brett Ashley, are not perfectly content to live without ideals. They are looking for something to replace what was ruined. They want, for example, a system of morality to replace the Christian morality that does not work for them.

Jake Barnes is a philosophical drunk. One night during the Pamplona festival he comes back to his room very late and very drunk. Unable to sleep, he starts thinking very ethically about the way that they all have been treating Robert Cohn, whom they all dislike. Mike Campbell has been behaving especially badly toward Cohn: "I liked to see him hurt Cohn. I wished he would not do it, though, because afterward it made me disgusted at myself. That was morality; things that make you disgusted afterward. No, that must be immorality." That is the system of morality that Hemingway believed in for the purpose of this book. Right conduct is what makes you feel good afterwards; wrong conduct is what makes you disgusted.

Peter Viertel could not use this passage when he wrote the screenplay for Zanuck's 1956 movie version of *The Sun Also Rises*. The idea that anything that makes you feel good is moral (which is the way that the idea would have been misinterpreted) would have displeased the movie congregation.

Right after Jake has defined morality (rather, immorality) to himself, he mocks the idea, comprehensive cynic that he is. "What a lot of bilge I could think up at night. What rot, I could hear Brett say it. What rot!"

That is exactly Brett's word for it when, later in the book, Jake begins to wax religious with her, though he is not really being serious about it. It is the last day of the Pamplona festival, and the fights might be very difficult for Romero. For one thing, the wind is stiff, which makes the cape work dangerous. Also, Romero is badly hurt, from the beating Cohn gave him. Brett and Jake are talking about such matters when Brett sees the St. Fermin chapel and thinks that she will go inside "to pray a little for him or something." There are many people praying inside, and they kneel down, too. In a very little while Brett is ready to leave. "Come on," she whispered throatily. "Let's get out of here. Makes me damned nervous." The praying is not successful. (Jake had gone in to pray when he first arrived in Pamplona, but that was not successful either.) Brett is not sure why she gets "so nervy in church." She explains it as having to do with being "damned bad for a religious atmosphere." Also, she has "the wrong type face." She says that she has never gotten anything that she prayed for. Has Jake?

> "Oh, yes."
> "Oh, rot," said Brett. "Maybe it works for some people though. You don't look very religious, Jake."
> "I'm pretty religious."
> "Oh, rot," said Brett. "Don't start proselyting today. Today's going to be bad enough as it is."

Perhaps it should have been said of the movie, "Don't start proselyting. It's going to be bad enough as it is." The scene of Brett going into the cathedral to pray is completely different in tone in the movie. She is very devout about it, as is Jake. (You can tell from the way he crosses himself.) They are alone in the cathedral, except for an unseen, quite glorious choir, which, strangely, is singing a service for an empty building. The music enhances the religious value of the picture. Leaving the place, Brett does not make any remarks about how church makes her damned nervous, or any of that.

Hemingway was not trying to preach in his novel, but by the circumstances of the book's ending he does have Brett come to discover that there might be something of nearly religious value without there being God. The situation leading to the final minutes of the movie is approximately the same as it is in the final pages of the novel. Brett's torrid affair with the bullfighter Romero is over. She sent him away, not because the sex of it was less than she imagined it would be, but because she began feeling guilty about ruining him. Now, afterwards, in one way Brett feels miserable because Romero is gone. In another way she feels better, because she has done the moral thing. This is what she tries to explain to Jake when he responds to her urgent telegram to come find her in Madrid. This is where the meaning of the movie's dialogue separates from the book's.

| BOOK | MOVIE |
|---|---|
| [Jake and Brett are drinking martinis at the bar of her hotel. Brett is speaking:] | [Jake and Brett are riding in a taxi through the streets of Madrid.] |
| "You know it makes one feel rather good deciding not to be a bitch." | BRETT: You know, it does make one feel good to behave decently. |
| "Yes." | JAKE: (smiling) Strange, isn't it. |
| "It's sort of what we have instead of God." | BRETT: It's sort of what we have instead of God. |
| "Some people have God," I said. "Quite a lot." | JAKE: Some people have God. Quite a lot. |
| "He never worked very well with me." | BRETT: He never worked very well with me. |

| | |
|---|---|
| "Should we have another martini?" | JAKE: Maybe you didn't really try.<br>BRETT: Maybe not.<br>(She moves closer to him. They sit quietly for an instant.) |

All the changes are related to the same moral difference. A bar is not the proper place for a discussion about God. It makes it seem as if they are not seriously wanting to know about God, and indeed they are not in the novel. Jake drops the subject: "Should we have another martini?" It would have been shocking to many people to see Jake so indifferent to God as to be drinking another martini. In the movie version, by contrast, Jake almost sounds like he is ready to witness for God. By the tone of his line "Strange, isn't it," and by his smile as he says it, the screenplay has Jake register a trace of moral superiority, as if he is pleased to have known something all along that Brett is just now beginning to fathom. It is not an attitude towards Brett that Hemingway's Jake ever would take. With his line "Maybe you didn't really try," Jake is chiding Brett for not having God. She admits that maybe it is her fault, and her new awareness of God brings her closer to Jake. As she sits quietly it seems that she must be thinking how she must try God harder after this.

Now the movie audience can understand, if it pleases, that God is the answer to all their problems, as if the purpose of Hemingway's novel were the expression of that Christian trust. It is a very comforting belief, and Brett leans her head against Jake's shoulder to say her last line in the movie:

BRETT: There must be an answer for us—somewhere.
JAKE: (in a low, solemn voice) I am sure there is.

There is none of this hopeful godliness in the novel. Nothing is going to change the fact of Jake's genital wound, and nothing is going to make Brett into the kind of woman who can be satisfied with Jake's love without the physical expression of it. At the end they share no feeling except a cynical awareness of the futility of it all. "Oh, Jake," Brett said [in the novel], "we could have had such a damned fine time together." "Yes," I said. "Isn't it pretty to think so."

The shooting script directed that the sun should come out from behind heavy clouds during the last shots of the movie. That would have been clear symbolic dramatization that God is hearing all this. That trite effect was not filmed, but the audience would still understand that there is a shining future for Jake and Brett. A resonant narrator's voice is heard on the soundtrack reading in modernized English a short form of the epigraph for the novel: "One generation passes away and another generation comes; but the earth abides forever. The sun also rises." Music swells.

Twentieth Century-Fox suggested to theater managers that they ask local clergymen to preach sermons on the famous Ecclesiastes text from which Hemingway took his title. If the sermon were given the Sunday of opening week, it would be a strong promotion for the movie. It did not particularly matter how text was interpreted from the pulpit. The idea was that anything the ministers said would seem like an endorsement of the morality of *The Sun Also Rises*. Moral sanction was important, especially because of some of the other things that could be said about this particular book.

For this was another side to the way Hollywood popularized Hemingway's material. Hollywood had to position Hemingway's writing and his reputation close to the general public's sense of right and goodness. Adapters could enhance a moral meaning of a book, or make one up. And they could take any immoral meaning away. Stated more generally, as adapters improved the entertainment value of any given novel or story by giving it those qualities that the audience liked to see and hear in a movie, so too could they improve a book's movie value by removing anything that the audience might not wish to hear or see. This was the fundamental principle of Hollywood censorship.

CHAPTER VI

# Hemingway Censored

"Again 20th Century-Fox breaks tradition as it brings you Hemingway's boldest love story that no one dared film until now," claimed the advertisements for *The Sun Also Rises*, although there had never been a Hemingway book that Hollywood had not dared to film. "The Hemingway love story that shocked the world! The theme so daring, so delicate, it could not be put on film until now!" In tone such copy resembled the blurb of a cheap paperback edition of *The Sun Also Rises*, whose lurid cover tried to entice readers with the promise of sleazy vice within: "Only Hemingway, master of unspoken secrets, could successfully tackle this daring theme, . . . could weave this shattering novel of dissipation and passion in pleasure-mad Europe."

Of course *The Sun Also Rises* was a book with a reputation, which had something to do with why it was a "pre-sold" movie title, a very valuable property. There must have been a huge number of people who over the years knew hardly anything about the novel except that it had a daring theme.

Hemingway's mother, a completely genteel, religious woman, read the book and thought it was a dubious distinction for her son that he should have written what she called "one of the filthiest books of the year."[1] Even today, more than fifty years later, many people read the book for the first time and react against it for the same reasons that she did. Now it is usually college students who read the book, and this is not especially true of their reaction to the book. When high school students are assigned the book, however, their parents are sometimes distressed, as the teacher finds out.

Mrs. Hemingway might have been better satisfied with the morality of the movie (though it seems she was not the sort of woman who went to the movies, and she died before the movie of *The Sun Also Rises* came out). Movies were made for people who had rather conservative sensibilities about decency in entertainment. Sometimes movie publicity was intended to arouse people's prurient curiosity. But audiences could fairly well depend that there would not be very much that was morally shocking, even daring, in Hollywood features.

Starting in 1930, right at the beginning of the era of sound film, Hollywood began to write for itself a moral code by which to protect itself from public outrage against the corrupting influence of the movies. The Motion Picture Code of Production gave specific and absolute proscriptions against the inclusion of certain kinds of material in movies and gave strong warning that certain other subjects be treated with restraint and good taste.[2] An administrative office was created to see that the industry followed the guidelines of the code. Decade by decade into the 1960s a more liberal interpretation was given to most articles of the code; during that period the code was rewritten a number of times. But in 1956, when *The Sun Also Rises* went into production, the Motion Picture Code was still a very stern document.

The novel version of *The Sun Also Rises* violated the code in many ways. Still, it would be difficult to argue that the violations were more extravagant than the violations caused by various other Hemingway novels and stories. There were not especially subtle moral problems for screenplay writer Peter Viertel to work out as he adjusted the book to fit the requirements of a movie.

Obviously what was most sensational about the sex of *The Sun Also Rises* was Jake's sexual incapacitation, his genital wound. The novel's first reference to the problem comes in a conversation between Jake and a prostitute he has picked up because he is bored and vaguely wants company at dinner. They are in a taxi on the way to a restaurant that he likes:

> She cuddled against me and I put my arm around her. She looked up to be kissed. She touched me with one hand and I put her hand away.
> "Never mind."
> "What's the matter? You sick?"
> "Yes."

During their meal the girl, Georgette, directly asks Jake what is the matter with him, and he says he was hurt in the war. The movie leaves out the taxi ride, and of course, Georgette's sexual touch. It does retain Jake's remark that he was hurt in the war.

Later that night, in his room alone unable to sleep, Jake remembers the occasion in the hospital in Milan when he learned about the consequences of his wound:

> That was where the liaison colonel came to visit me. That was funny. That was about the first funny thing. I was all bandaged up. But they had told him about it. Then he made that wonderful speech: "You, a foreigner, an Englishman" (any foreigner was an Englishman) "have given more than your life." What a speech! I would like to have it illuminated to hang in the office. He never laughed. He was putting himself in my place, I guess. "Che mala fortuna! Che mala fortuna."

This scene, in flashback, is played straight, even solemnly, in the movie, as if a comic treatment of such a matter would offend the audience as being in poor taste. Lady Brett, who was then Jake's nurse according to the movie version of the story (a borrowing of an idea from *A Farewell to Arms*), rolls him in his wheelchair onto the hospital terrace. Jake looks hearty enough, though he has bandages, as on his right hand, which apparently have nothing to do with his problem. Jake waits there alone until he is joined by the chief surgeon, who wears a British uniform and smokes a pipe. Jake wants to know if he is going to be all right. Tactful as Britishers are, the doctor explains:

> DOCTOR: (He has taken his pipe out of his mouth.) Of course you'll be all right. There will be certain after effects from your wound, but that's to be expected. (Jake seems not to be listening to him.) The important thing is that the shell fragment which entered your back missed your spine. So you'll be able to walk and move about absolutely normally.

Having told Jake the good news first, the movie doctor continues. "However," he pauses for a long moment, "You're going to be impotent."

The novel does not use the word "impotent" in this passage. Perhaps it was felt that the movie had to be perfectly direct or the audience would miss the point. Be that as it may, in a 1957 picture "impotent" had a strong effect, as if the word had never been spoken in a movie before. One movie critic was so surprised by the use of the word that he said, "One has the sense of an historical occasion."[3]

If the movie had treated so private a matter in a comic way or in a crude, tasteless way, the code administrators probably would have withheld their seal of approval until the scene was acceptably corrected by editing. Nothing in the wording of the code specifically disallowed the subject of impotency, however, so it was not necessary for Viertel to alter the premise of Jake's characterization.

The code contained a very strong section on sex, the first article of which stated, "Adultery and illicit sex, sometimes necessary plot material, shall not be explicitly treated, nor shall they be justified or made to seem right and permissible." Sometimes the movie-makers had to think about their material in the most touchy ways in order to suggest disapproval of immoral sex.

Georgette, the *poule*, is a difficult character in this regard, of course. In the novel Jake does not pay Georgette for any sexual favor. On the other hand, he does not exactly disapprove of her. He has taken her to the Bal Musette for dancing. There he meets up with Brett, and he leaves with Brett. Georgette does not see him leave; she is having a gay time dancing with others. There is a point of correct conduct in Jake's mind about leaving her this way. By inviting her for the evening, even for dancing, he is committed to paying her, unless, of course, she goes off with someone else, having lost interest in Jake. What Jake does is to put a fifty franc note in an envelope, which he leaves with the proprietor. If Georgette asks for Jake, the proprietor will give her the envelope; otherwise he will save it for Jake.

This was not so easily arranged in the movie. Jake still thinks to leave fifty francs for Georgette with the proprietor. But that gesture suggests, perhaps, that Jake does not disapprove of Georgette's way of making money. It might even mean that if Jake had not met Brett he would have stayed with Georgette for more of her company. Viertel tried several versions of the scene. In one state of the script he wrote a passage of dialogue, in French, between Georgette and the proprietor. Georgette does notice Jake leave with

Brett, and the proprietor does give her the money. Still, she is perturbed that Jake left with a lady, and she wants to know why. The proprietor shrugs his shoulders: "C'est l'amour." Georgette is cynical: "L'amour? Huh!" ("Huh" is not a French expletive, actually.) And she tears up the note. It is stupid to do that, the proprietor remarks. "Oui, peut-être," Georgette agrees after a moment and starts to pick up the pieces of the bill as the camera cuts away. But this scene still did not leave it clear for the audience that Jake would not have stayed with Georgette in any case. Different dialogue was written for the movie as finally released. Georgette comes up to Jake as he is leaving so early.

| | |
|---|---|
| JAKE: | I'm a working man. |
| GEORGETTE: | I'm a working girl. |
| JAKE: | But we keep different hours. . . . Bon soir. |

His disapproval of prostitution is in the almost stern tone of his voice.

Speaking of Jake and Brett now, they are sexually very intimate only at one point in the book, and about that scene Hemingway is completely discreet. Brett has brought her friend Count Mippipopolous with her to visit Jake's rooms. Seeing that Jake is feeling very low, Brett sends the count on an errand. She comes back to Jake where he is lying on the bed: "'Sent him for champagne. He loves to go for champagne.' Then later. 'Do you feel better, darling? Is the head any better?'" Between Brett's line "He loves to go for champagne" and the transitional "Then later," Hemingway leaves them in privacy. There was really no need for them to have privacy in the movie. During the equivalent minutes in the screen version, Jake and Brett just have a drink.

Brett has other lovers in the novel: Robert Cohn, Mike Campbell, to whom she is engaged, and the bullfighter Romero. In the novel there are no sex scenes between Brett and any of these characters, because the novel is narrated by Jake in the first person, and Jake is not present for such scenes. He does not know that Brett and Robert Cohn were lovers until their short affair is over. The movie is still more discreet about Brett's sleeping around. The movie does not indicate, for example, that while in Pamplona she is sharing a hotel room with Mike Campbell. The plot would be incomprehensible if it were not clear that she runs off with Romero. But she is miserable after that affair. The movie therefore does not seem to condone her relationship with him; running off like that with someone does not make you happy. And besides, it is after the affair with Romero that Brett feels especially dissatisfied with her life and begins to seek a religious value.

What the movie does with the relationship between Brett and Robert, especially from Robert's position, is more complicated. Not only must a movie not seem to condone illicit sex, it was supposed to uphold "the sanctity of the institution of marriage and the home." Robert Cohn has been living with Frances Cline. At the beginning of the movie, as at the beginning of the novel, Cohn has decided that he is tired of his relationship with Frances. He leaves her when he becomes infatuated with Brett and begins following her doggedly. At the end of the movie, unlike the novel, Robert tells Jake that he thinks he ought to try to make a go of it with Frances after all. It seems that he might settle down: "I'm going to see Frances and try to straighten things out. (He pauses.) I just hope I'm not too late." Like Brett, Robert has discovered that running off with someone does not make you happy.

The code's sections on vulgarity, obscenity, and blasphemy and profanity meant that some changes had to be made in Hemingway's dialogue. These were not especially major changes and did not greatly alter the tone of the book. But "bitch," for example, was a vulgar word, and Brett could not be allowed to say "You know it makes one feel rather good deciding not to be a bitch," even though she is expressing a very decent feeling. In one scene of the novel, Mike Campbell, drunk and loud, is taunting the bullfighter: "Tell him the bulls have no balls." The line in the movie is "Tell him the bulls have no horns!" (Scribner's had been sensitive to the word *balls*, too, and the word *horns* was substituted in editions of *The Sun Also Rises* printed before the 1950s.) In the book Mike continues, "Tell him Brett wants to see him put on those green pants," which in the movie sounds less suggestive as "Tell him Brett wants to see him in those green pants again." In the book, as soon as Romero leaves, Brett does admit that he excites her: "My God! he's a lovely boy. . . . And how I would love to see him get into those clothes. He must use a shoe-horn!" This is changed to "He's charming—polite and gentle—something you wouldn't expect at all." There is no suggestion that Brett is aroused.

Most people think of movie censorship as pertaining to high-minded sexual conduct and decent speech. Actually, the code dealt with many matters other than these. For example, the code specifically cited bullfighting as a "wrong entertainment" that "lowers the whole living conditions and moral ideals of a race." Baseball and golf were identified as "healthful" sports that promoted "healthful reactions," whereas bullfighting (also cockfighting and bear baiting) promoted "unhealthy reactions." Bullfights in the movies, therefore, had to be chiefly costume pageants in Spanish reds and golds, with trumpet fanfares, and without much blood and slaughter. The actual penetration of the sword into the bull's carcass could not be shown, nor the slitting of its throat finally to kill it, nor the carving off of its ear as a presentation trophy. In the movie of *The Sun Also Rises* Brett does not get the bull's ear.

One way in which the book presents Robert Cohn's character was another sensitive point. Cohn sometimes seems obnoxious to the others because they think he acts Jewish. They think his aggressiveness, his sense of superiority, and the way sometimes he seems to indulge in his suffering have something to do with his being Jewish. Two different sections of the code—the article on religion and the article on national feelings—stopped any anti-Semitic slurs against Cohn. The movie in no way identifies him as Jewish (unless by the sound of his name). Every place the book used the word *Jewish* the movie substituted the word *intellectual*. So in the movie, for example, Cohn is said to offend people by his "intellectual superiority."

One wants to have a historical view of the censorship issue, whether one is discussing the censorship of movies or of books. Hemingway had to submit to certain restrictions when he published a book, and these restrictions presumably influenced the way he thought about material he might write. Most such restrictions do not exist today. And today there must be very little in Hemingway's writing that could not be filmed as it is printed—

depending, to be sure, on what "rating" the producers would be willing to accept. One could guess, indeed, that any new Hemingway movies yet to be made will be more sexually direct than their books.

The two Hollywood versions of *A Farewell to Arms* give an interesting historical perspective on censorship. The code had already been formulated when the Borzage version came out at the end of 1932. But producers were still learning where the boundaries of interpretation of the code had to lie, how far they could go. One might suppose that *A Farewell to Arms* would be a simpler book for the movies twenty-five years later, when the Selznick version came out, except that Selznick was not quite so adept as Borzage at seeing in advance where little problems of morals and good taste could make complications for his movie.

One of the publicity pieces used with the original Paramount *Farewell to Arms* seems symbolic of how matters stood with movie censorship in those days. In order to sell what the pressbook called "the Romance Theme of a Love-Filled Picture!" a theater manager could order a life-size cardboard "stand-up" to set in his lobby. Frederic and Rinaldi as cut-out figures stand surrounded by a half-dozen girls in feather boas and negligees. The cardboard girls were there to entice into the movie those passers-by who liked to think that movies were sometimes a little more wicked than they ought to be. But the stand-up also showed an inset photo of Catherine's face in an expression of shock at what she is seeing. Women might see the display as a suggestion that the movie takes Catherine's disapproving point of view.

This display piece was only a come-on; there is no such scene in the movie, with Frederic, Rinaldi, all the Villa Rossa girls, and Catherine aghast. The code had something to say about prostitutes and brothels. The movie went only a little further than the spirit of the code seemed to intend. The code proscribed dramatization of relations with prostitutes. "Brothels and houses of ill-fame," because "so closely and thoroughly associated with sexual life or with sexual sin," were "dangerous and bad dramatic locations." As described in an earlier chapter, the Borzage *Farewell to Arms* does have an early scene at the brothel. But the girl Frederic is teasing with is not expressly identified as a prostitute. By the oblique camera angle used in this scene, the audience sees only parts of her—her foot, ankle, and, for a moment, her calf in silk stocking. In 1932 that might have seemed a faintly exciting glimpse of her flesh.

The large censorship issue with a *A Farewell to Arms* was that Frederic and Catherine become lovers without being married. Their relationship through most of the novel is one of "impure love," to use a phrase of the code.[4]

Usually censorship problems were anticipated before a movie was filmed; they were worked out in the various stages of script. Cuts might be made in editing. Other cuts might have to be made at the suggestion of the administrators of the code. Even after that, while the movie was in national distribution, other cuts might be made by state and local boards of review. *A Farewell to Arms* seems to have had a complicated, confused censorship history, more so than most pictures.

Borzage and his writers had seen the obvious way to morally improve Hemingway's book, by marrying Frederic and Catherine

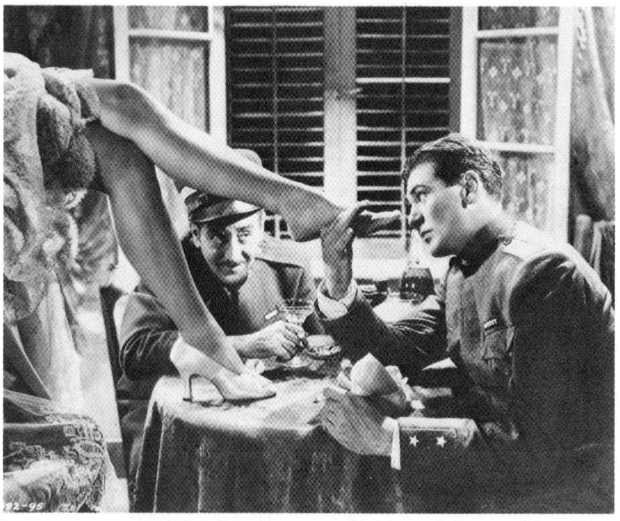

Gary Cooper as Frederic Henry flirts with a prostitute in the brothel scene of the Paramount *Farewell to Arms* (1932). This scene was edited out of some prints of the film. Publicity still courtesy of Paramount.

at a very early opportunity. That is the scene described earlier, the extraordinary wedding in which their friend the priest whispers the marriage ceremony while they hold hands and imagine that they hear organ music and smell orange blossoms. The priest is happy now, and he gives them his blessing. "Goodbye, and be happy, both of you."

In at least the original issue of the movie, the scene continues when the priest goes out. Catherine has to stand behind the door when suddenly Miss Van Campen, the head nurse, comes in looking for her. Frederic pretends she's not there. As soon as they are alone again, Frederic blows out the candle. Catherine is hesitant. She must not stay, she says; he has his operation in the morning. "It's our wedding night!" Frederic pleads. Catherine, still playing, reminds him that he has a dose of castor oil to be taking. Frederic says that he'll take anything from her, if she'll stay. Catherine gives in now and laughs: "Oh, darling, darling! I want what you want. There isn't any me any more—just what you want." The camera turns away from them now, across the balcony to the town. Lights from the gun batteries are searching the sky.

CATHERINE: (her voice heard off camera) Don't I make a lovely wife?
FREDERIC: (off) Such a lovely wife.
*Dissolve to*: medium shot, balcony, lights flashing over rooftops.
CATHERINE: (off) Feel our hearts beat.
FREDERIC: (off) No wonder my heart beats. I'm mad about you.
*Fade Out.*

This is quoting from the "Release Dialogue Script," dated December 7, 1932. A release dialogue script usually means an actual transcription of a release print, as might be made by a stenographer. At least one print of the movie containing this scene does still exist. But most prints one might find today, renting or buying the movie, do not have this "wedding night" scene.

Unfortunately, there seems to be no way of telling now when this deep cut was made. Perhaps it was not made until *A Farewell to Arms* went into rerelease later in the decade. Perhaps it was not made until the movie went into television release. Or it might be that Borzage decided to make the cut even before all the multiple prints were made for the first national distribution.

What *is* known is that Borzage did worry about the audience's moral reaction to this entire wedding and wedding night sequence. Was this a legitimate marriage? Would Catholics, he might have wondered, accept it as a valid sacrament? For Borzage had to worry not only about the code but also the powerful Catholic Legion of Decency, whose movie ratings were respected by many non-Catholics, too. If the legion disapproved or condemned a movie, its profits were certain to fall.

It suddenly occurred to Borzage, after all the shooting was finished, that, like a nervous bridegroom, he had forgotten the *ring*. The audience might not be sure it was a real wedding if there was no ring. Borzage recalled the cast to shoot the wedding sequence all over again, this time with a ring. (In later scenes of the movie, already filmed, Catherine would not have a ring on her hand, but that was a little wrong detail Borzage could not hope to correct.) Helen Hayes thought that the problem was perfectly silly and refused to play the scene over again.

Borzage had thought of something else to worry about. Catherine becomes pregnant in the continuation of plot. How was the audience to be sure that her baby was conceived after their wedding and not during the night in the park when she was seduced?

Borzage and his writers solved the problems of the ring and the date at the same time. The film fades away from the wedding night scene (Frederic and Catherine talking softly about their hearts beating) into a "calendar shot." The names of the months, in little dancing letters, fade in and out of a background—July, August, September, October. Four months leave Catherine a decent interval for knowing she is pregnant. Then a strange image, an "insert shot" superimposed: a man's hand, disembodied, slipping a wedding ring on a girl's finger. It was not Helen Hayes's finger, but the audience could not tell that. The image was a simple symbol that Frederic and Catherine really were married.

Comparing a later print of the movie with the original print one finds that other changes were made for decency's sake. The seduction scene was trimmed. The film had cut away as Catherine was crying "No! No, wait!" In the next shot of Catherine she is faintly hysterical about what has happened. Frederic is worried about it,

This publicity still could serve as Catherine's wedding portrait, for in her nurse's uniform she is married in white. One notices, however, that she wears no ring, an oversight that the director Frank Borzage later tried to correct.

too—"Why didn't you tell me?" That conversation was cut out because their sexual intimacy was too strongly implied. After the moment of struggle, the audience next sees Catherine when it is morning. And if the audience really wanted to believe so, it could seem that Catherine had been able to push Frederic away.

Such cuts were made with extreme delicacy. When Frederic recovers from his leg wounds he is sent back to the front. He and Catherine spend their last hours together in a room of the hotel across from the station. Frederic hears the train whistle and quotes the lines "But at my back I always hear / Time's winged chariot drawing near." "I know that poem," Hemingway's Catherine responds, smart girl that she is. "It's by Marvell. But it's about a girl who wouldn't live with a man." Borzage had his Catherine say the line exactly that way, but later the phrase "live with a man" seemed too strong. In late prints of the movie Catherine says only who wrote the poem, *not* what it's about.

The Borzage *Farewell to Arms* seems never to have had any word said about it as an immoral or even improper movie. The Catholic Legion of Decency gave it its "A" rating—"morally unobjectionable." Movie reviewers found nothing objectionable to remark. Only years later, in the next Hollywood version, did *A Farewell to Arms* become somewhat offensive material.

In some ways it is not especially clear that the Selznick *Farewell to Arms*, with a script by Ben Hecht, is more sexually daring than the Borzage version. Selznick's seduction scene, for example, which takes place in a greenhouse rather than outdoors in a park, is hardly any more explicit. In the entire duration of the movie Selznick included much more footage of Frederic and Catherine kissing and holding each other, but Selznick's camera still did not show them lying together in bed. Neither did Selznick show Catherine undressed, although in one scene at dawn in the hospital room her hair is down and she is not wearing the apron to her uniform. In another scene Miss Van Campen walks in on Frederic and Catherine, and except that Ferguson had warned her friend a minute before, Catherine would have been caught without her nurse's veil pinned in her hair.

An important difference is that in the later movie Frederic and

Catherine talk openly about their not being married. There is a light teasing about it between them. Catherine herself laughs at the idea of being "an honest woman." She says frankly that she is not embarrassed about not being married, though she means, of course, that her relationship with Frederic already feels sacred. During the scene at the racetrack they do act out their marriage ceremony to themselves. No priest gives them his blessing, however, and by the time they privately exchange vows, Catherine is already pregnant. In these ways the movie seemed almost to flout the audience's conservative moral standard.

Selznick found he had wide trouble. The movie critic for the *Herald Tribune*, headlining his review "Hemingway Is Vulgarized," felt that (sure as he was that Hemingway had not *written* a dirty book) *A Farewell to Arms* was "an incredibly offensive film." The adapters had gone "out of their way, again and again, to include the unnecessary smutty detail." The audience was lured into the theater "on the boast that it is a great 'American classic,' only to see 160 minutes of fondling and . . . to hear a lot of dirty talk."[5] The critic specifically cited as "dirty talk" the line "I never felt like a whore before." As in the novel, Catherine admits this in the hotel room before Frederic goes back to war. All other times in the story Catherine is very content with the morality of their love. She has only this one bad moment, because of all the red plush and the mirrors in the room, and soon she feels better again. Another line of dirty talk was the phrase "sleeping together" ("This was the price you paid for sleeping together") in the passage where Frederic is frightened by the danger of Catherine's labor.

Selznick had feared such a reaction to some of the language. Finally he decided that he could put over the idea that the picture had a very obvious moral theme: Frederic's monologue, in fear for Catherine's life, shows a very deft cutting around the controversial line.

| NOVEL (*Frederic thinking*) | MOVIE (*Frederic in monologue*) |
|---|---|
| Poor, poor Cat. And this was the price you paid for sleeping together. . . . Catherine had a good time of pregnancy. It wasn't bad. She was hardly ever sick. She | Poor Cat. Poor dear Cat. This was the price you paid for sleeping together. She didn't have a bad time when she was pregnant. She had a good time. She was |

| | |
|---|---|
| was not awfully uncomfortable until toward the last. So now they got her in the end. You never got away with anything. Get away hell! It would have been the same if we had been married fifty times. | hardly ever sick. She wasn't even very uncomfortable—until—toward the last. But you never get away with anything. Get away hell! They get you in the end. Maybe they're going to get her in the end, too. |

Hemingway lets it occur to Frederic that this might be the reason Catherine is suffering and perhaps dying—as if the wage of sin really is death, "the price you paid for sleeping together." Then he denies it absolutely: "It would have been the same if we had been married fifty times." That line is not spoken in the movie. Selznick thought that earlier in his career he would never have dared use the expression "sleeping together"; it was "very strong meat." The line would cause no trouble, though, he was sure, "because the picture is a strong moral preachment in any terms, including those of the Code and censorship."[6] The movie passed with the code office. It did not quite pass with the Legion of Decency, which judged there was "not sufficiently clear moral compensation for the undue emphasis on illicit love." The legion gave the picture its "B" rating, "morally objectionable in part for all."

There had been a very different kind of censorship issue—without reference to the code or the Legion—with the filming of the Caporetto sequence of *A Farewell to Arms*. Caporetto, in October, 1917, had been a disastrous Italian defeat. The Germans and Austrians took more than 250,000 prisoners while the Italians retreated. Hemingway had not represented the Italians in a glorious light, as has been noted. There is chaos during the retreat, with some officers abandoning their units, and some of the infantry soldiers talking as if they wished for defeat and throwing their weapons away. The conduct of the court martial is shameful.

Mussolini banned the novel when it was published. He threatened to ban the Borzage movie version as well. Filming had already begun when Mussolini sent word to Paramount, through the Italian embassy in Washington, that if the movie were an offense to Italy, he would ban the exhibition in his country not only of this movie but of *all* American movies.[7] It was an economic threat of considerable substance.

The ultimatum made a difference in how the battle sequence had to be shot and edited. In their first script Garrett and Glazer had described certain shots which now Borzage could not allow to be used: for example, a shot of Italian officers at headquarters charting the course of the army's *retreat* on battle maps; or, what would seem a flagrant insult, a symbolic insert shot of a herd of bleating sheep in stampede.

In deference to Mussolini, the place name "Caporetto" is not spoken in the dialogue. In fact Borzage decided that the safe thing to do was to refer to some other battle in which the Italians were victors. In film footage of battle, amid all the shells bursting, it is sometimes difficult to tell which side is winning anyway. Troops in retreat, if reasonably orderly, look about the same as troops in advance. In the months after Caporetto the Italian army heroically defended the Piave River. And from the Piave line the Italians and their allies fought the last great offensive in that theater of the war. After the main titles and before the opening shots a legend was projected on the screen for the audience to read: "Disaster as well as victory is written on the record of the World War, but high on the rolls of glory two names are inscribed—The Marne and The Piave." Late in the movie there is an insert shot of a newspaper headline reporting the victory: ITALIAN ARMIES SUCCESSFUL IN GREAT PIAVE OFFENSIVE. When the movie went into circulation, theater managers in major cities took out newspaper ads urging Italian-Americans to see "the valiant stand" of Italian troops at the Piave. *Il Duce* must have been pleased.

Selznick also had to worry about the Italian attitude towards Caporetto. There was no threat from the Italian government this time. Nevertheless, because he was shooting the picture in Italy and using Italian army units by the government's courtesy, Selznick did present the script for government approval and did comply with recommendations from various government ministries. Selznick agreed, for example, that in the firing squad scene (when Rinaldi is shot) the riflemen should successfully complete the execution with one fussilade. Also, in keeping with a suggestion from the Defense Ministry, the movie would show fresh, young troops being advanced to the front after the retreat.[8] To make it very clear that the Italians did not lose the battle because they were cowards or weaker fighters, Hecht wrote a few lines for Frederic's commanding officer to say just before the Caporetto attack begins. The Italians have had to face the Germans alone, Major Stampi says. Even when America finally does send troops overseas, they will probably all go to the aid of the French. Frederic mentions that the Germans are "pretty good." Major Stampi shakes his head. No, the Germans are not better men. It is only that they have a better war machine, which they have been building for years while the Italians have been practicing civilization. "Now, of course," he shrugs, "civilization is not very useful."

With the preparation of the script of *For Whom the Bell Tolls* there was also a sensitive and complicated censorship issue vis-à-vis a foreign government—with this book, Spain. Because the picture was filmed in the time of war, there had to be serious regard for ideological and diplomatic interests.

In 1941, novelist Louis Bromfield, then working for Paramount, wrote the first script for that studio's version of *For Whom the Bell Tolls*. His version was almost totally without political character. There were no references to Fascists or Communists, Nationalists or Loyalists. Dialogue spoke vaguely of "the enemy" and "the cause." Bromfield, as he was pleased to explain to the press, had a classical conviction about the virtue of eliminating propaganda from art.[9]

Hollywood had a conviction about this as well. Lewis Jacobs in *The Rise of The American Film* identifies *Blockade* (1938) as the only "serious Hollywood film based on the war in Spain" until after that war. The fighting factions were not named in *Blockade*, though the movie's sympathy was with the Loyalists.[10]

Hemingway himself had said when he wrote the novel that he was through with the politics of the Spanish Civil War and that he was only trying to write the truth as he had seen it. Thus he had described Pablo's men seizing a village and ruthlessly murdering the Fascists and the Fascist sympathizers, though the scene reflected badly on the Loyalists. In this particular respect and several others, many people, including friends who had been so sure of his stand with them during the fight in Spain, thought the book was a betrayal. Hemingway admittedly felt the book was his break with "the ideology boys" on the Left.[11]

But when the movie came to be made—this has not been generally known—Hemingway's attitude radically changed. He *wanted* the movie to have the force of propaganda, even as *The Spanish Earth* had been a propaganda film. Everything was different after Pearl Harbor. In the spring of 1942 Dudley Nichols replaced Bromfield as script writer and was preparing a substantially different version. Hemingway wrote to his agent insisting that this new script could now be of use to the war effort, an asset of highest value in fighting the Fascists. He was not even sure anymore, though it was a wild delusion, that the conflict in Spain had been finally decided. By the time the picture would be released, Hemingway wrote, there was a real possibility that the country would have sent an expeditionary force for combat in Spain. It was not only that the movie had to say the word Fascist and speak of the Republic. It had also to show clearly why the ideal of the Republic was to be believed in and why men and women would die for it.[12]

Nichols seems to have been willing to follow Hemingway's line. Paramount was not. Controversy over the Spanish Civil War still existed in America with about equal American hatred for Fascists and for Communists. The final movie print included one speech—not in the novel—in which Robert Jordan explains that he is in Spain because the Nazis and Fascists are testing their war machinery against democracy in order to get the jump on England, France, and America before they are ready to defend themselves. The word Fascist was used only this one time. Maria speaks the Communist "Salud" once. Stalin is named once, though the line was edited out of some prints of the movie. In a review that satirized the censorship of the movie James Agee said, "There is a faint hint that Gary Cooper favors Russian cigarettes."[13]

Such faint traces of ideology were not likely to "make any trouble" for Paramount. It would be seen, commented Adolf Zukor, the chairman of the Board of Directors of Paramount, as a picture "without political significance." "It was not for or against anybody."[14]

The script was read by U.S. State Department officials who suggested revisions in keeping with the government's official position of neutrality towards Spain. The script was even read by the Spanish consul in San Francisco, who also suggested revisions, though the Franco government denied any intention to interfere or surpress.

The studio did not want to acknowledge any of this as censorship *per se,* and insisted the pressures had been disregarded. Rather, the changes represented an elimination of "Hemingway's confused political thinking."[15] To Hemingway it seemed Paramount was simply afraid of Franco.[16] It was probably no compensation to him at all that the movie title was used to advertise the sale of war bonds, when during theater intermissions a rousing march tune came over the loudspeakers, with the lyrics, "Your bonds buy bombs, For Whom the Bell Tolls!"

The politics of it aside, there were ways that *For Whom the Bell Tolls* clashed with public morality as described by the Motion Picture Code. For example, Robert Jordan shoots his comrade Kashkin after Kashkin is wounded and it is certain that he will be captured by the Fascists. Jordan's action could be understood as a mercy killing, which was expressly forbidden by the code: "Mercy killing shall never be made to seem right or permissible." Screen writer Dudley Nichols did not interpret the shooting as such; neither did the code administration, and the scene was retained in the movie.

In the novel, Pilar, with her gypsy superstition, tells Jordan that she knew Kashkin would die. He smelt of death, she says, and she describes the stench in repellent detail. The code cautioned that "the treatment of low, disgusting, unpleasant though not necessarily evil subjects should always be guided by the dictates of good taste and proper regard for the sensibilities of the audience." There was never any question of including the passage in the movie. For that matter, Maxwell Perkins and Charles Scribner, Hemingway's editor and publisher, were not sure it ought to be in the book.[17]

Pilar's description of the taking of the Fascist town one might suppose would have been an unsolvable censorship problem. "Excessive and inhuman acts of cruelty and brutality shall not be presented," the code stated. "This includes all detailed and protracted presentation of physical violence, torture, and abuse." Unlikely as it seems by that wording, the code administrators did allow the movie to show the vicious executions of Don Garcia, Don Faustino, and Don Guillermo, their passing through the gauntlet of flails and clubs to be thrown over the cliff to die on the rocks. Publicity urged the public to "SEE the Massacre at the Cliff. Incredible!" Then the sequence was drastically edited down by certain state and local censorship boards. It was cut almost entirely from prints for television release.

According to Pilar, the massacre became most savage when Pablo let the mob into the courthouse to murder the remaining prisoners. That scene was not filmed:

> I saw the hall full of men flailing away with clubs and striking with flails, and poking and striking and pushing and heaving against the people with the white wooden pitchforks that were now red and their tines broken and this was going on all over the room while Pablo sat in the big chair with his shotgun on his knees, watching, and they were shouting and clubbing and stabbing and men were screaming as horses scream in a fire.

There is a priest among the prisoners:

> And I saw the priest with his skirts tucked up scrambling over a bench and those after him were chopping at him with the sickles and the reaping hooks and then someone had hold of his robes and there was another scream and I saw two men chopping into his back with sickles while a third man held the skirt of his robe.

Later Pablo tells Pilar that he was disillusioned by the priest. He hated priests even more than he hated Fascists. It shamed him anyway that this priest had "little dignity," was "frightened," and "died badly." It was absolutely taboo that a movie should defame a priest that way, out of respect for the religious feelings of the audience quite apart from the violence of his death. Among the townspeople who are massacred in the movie there is no priest. Still, the Catholic Legion of Decency gave *For Whom the Bell Tolls* its "B" rating, largely because of the violence.

Producer Sam Wood's attitude toward the novel was essentially the same as Selznick's toward *A Farewell to Arms*. *For Whom the Bell Tolls* was more importantly about love than about war or politics. The Spanish Civil War was merely, first, the circumstance and, second, the background for the story of Jordan and Maria. "As I see it," Wood said, "it's simply the story of a man and woman frantically in love." Wood's problem was that Jordan and Maria are lovers before they are married. The novel and the movie both make it very clear that they intend to marry. That intention, as well as the fact that Jordan dies at the ending (thereby making it impossible for the audience to infer that the movie condoned fornication), had, as one movie reviewer put it, "an antiseptic effect on their relationship."[18] Nevertheless, the book contained far more explicit sex than could be permitted in the movie.

Much of the sex of the book is in Jordan's mind and in his sensations:

> Now as they lay all that before had been shielded was unshielded. Where there had been roughness of fabric all was smooth with a smoothness and firm round pressing and a long warm coolness, cool outside and warm within, long and light and close holding, closely held, lonely, hollow-making with contours, happy-making, young and loving and now all warmly smooth with a hollowing, chest-aching, tight-held loneliness that was such that Robert Jordan felt he could not stand it.

Such interior passages presented no difficulty; they were simply left out. Subjective narration does not translate readily into the objective medium of film anyway. Most passages of dialogue that referred to their sexual intimacy were not used.

Even Jordan and Maria's figurative way of speaking of the quasi-mystical orgasm they experienced—they felt the earth move—was not used in the script. (There was an allusion to the experience of feeling the earth move in the dreadful lyrics by Ned Washington for a love ballad adapted from one of Victor Young's musical themes for the soundtrack score. The ballad was called "A Love Like This," as in the words "A love like this is so great it moves the earth. All other loves just miss. Give me a love like this," and so on. The ballad was sold as sheet music in promotion of the picture but, thankfully, was not sung in the movie itself. Young's score for the picture did win an Academy Award, however.) Very possibly it is the most familiar line Hemingway wrote. A *Playboy* cartoonist draws a car overturned in Lovers' Lane: "I felt the earth move! I felt the earth move!" the girl is exclaiming. A sportscaster describes a dunk shot in the Washington Bullets championship game: "That's what you call a Hemingway basket. He slams it home and you feel the earth move!" A writer for *Ladies' Home Journal* offers advice about "Getting More Joy Out of Sex": "If you're working at having a better sex life, . . . and if you're disappointed because the earth doesn't move, . . . here's a sane look at what sexual pleasure is—and isn't." It must not have been the movies that made the line famous.

The dramatic action of the sleeping robe scenes was played in the movie, but with special discretion. In the novel, the first night Jordan is with the guerilla band, he sleeps outside their cave, as Pilar has directed him to do. Maria wakens him in the cold night. For a moment she is hesitant about getting into the robe with him, but she had come to be with him and had already taken her shoes off when she came from the cave, as she admits to Jordan. That first night they become lovers. Whereas Borzage and Selznick found the progression of the sexual relationship in *A Farewell to Arms* too slow, Sam Wood found it too fast in *For Whom the Bell Tolls*. In the movie, this first night Maria does come to Jordan, but only to warn him that Pablo may be dangerous. Pablo comes out from the cave to see to his horses, and Jordan quickly covers Maria with the blanket to hide her. Then Rafael comes out, too, and Jordan hides Maria again. Jordan goes off with Rafael to keep an eye on Pablo, and Maria runs away. She does not spend the night. There is no way of knowing where Maria sleeps the second night. The third morning Jordan is *alone* when he wakes (in the novel Maria is with him). Maria brings coffee out to him in a wifely way. It is certain in the movie only that the third night Maria sleeps with Jordan. With fading out and cutting away, the movie remains modest about that night, too.

Louis Bromfield's original script was even more delicate with the love scenes. The first night, for example, there is no lying down together, even to hide from Pablo. They sit leaning against a rock ledge, only to talk. Jordan arranges his sleeping robe as a cushion. Bromfield did venture a line about the earth moving, but it is simply a kiss, not orgasm, that has this seismic effect. "It is true, rabbit. When I kiss you it is as if the earth moves."

A kiss, of course, was the most ecstatic sexual moment you could show in the movies. Really, kissing is as much a thrill in Hemingway's book as in the movie. It is very exciting about Hemingway's Maria that she has never been kissed by any man before her Roberto, though terrible things had been done to her. One of Maria's most innocent expressions of passion comes when, in more than virginal anxiety, she timidly and boldly tells Jordan that she does not know how to kiss. "Where do the noses go? I always wondered where the noses go." The movie promoters picked up on that line. "GIRLS!" teased a publicity flyer, "MARIA WANTS TO KNOW WHERE THE NOSES GO WHEN YOU KISS!!!"

Hemingway had been urgently concerned about the way censorship had vitiated the force of the movie as propaganda, but he was good-humored about censorship of his love scene for decency's sake. He thought it was a joke on his friend Gary Cooper that with the chance to make love to Ingrid Bergman he had to keep his clothes on.[19]

Hemingway did become angry when the movie people vilified

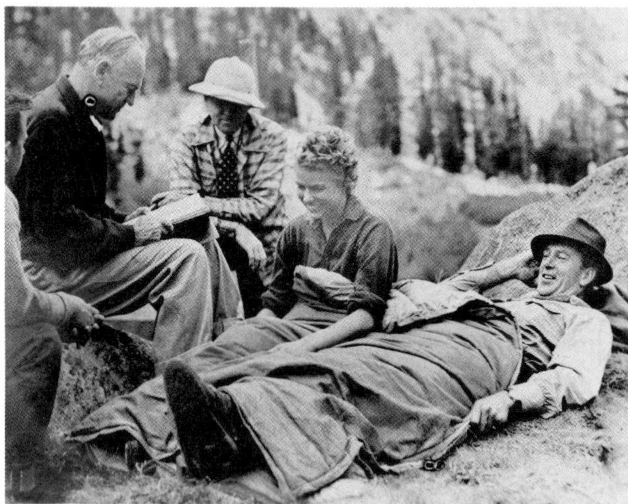

A moment of posed laughter during filming of *For Whom the Bell Tolls*. The publicity still shows that Gary Cooper at 6' 4" is too tall for the sleeping bag. Holding the script is Sam Wood. Publicity still courtesy of Paramount.

the morality of his novel in order to persuade the public how wholesome a movie could be: "('The Bells,') he [Wood] admits, is a dirty book, and he does not see why it should have been written as a dirty book. Maybe, he said yesterday, that sort of thing sells a few books. He feels that it has no place on the screen. He has always kept dirt out of his pictures."[20] Such remarks as these, and every mention in the press of the almost notorious sleeping bag passages, might have given the public rather exaggerated impressions of what Hemingway's writing was like. It was all like so much gossip, to the embarrassment if not shame of the book.

No producer of a Hemingway movie was more deferential to his audience's morals than Jerry Wald in the filming of *Hemingway's Adventures of a Young Man*. Wald, like Sam Wood, always kept dirt and controversy out of his pictures. Wald had produced *The Breaking Point*, it will be remembered, without any disturbing idea. Wald, like Selznick, was an adapter of "celebrated books." In 1957 Wald had produced *Peyton Place* (20th, 1957), a sexy book in those days, with such propriety that the movie was rated "A" by the Legion of Decency. The picture was profitable, too. Morality in movies, Wald believed, was what made you money afterwards. Every potential viewer kept away from the theater out of embarrassment was more profit lost. In the early Sixties, because of the tremendous overinvestment in *Cleopatra* (1963), Twentieth Century-Fox had to be certain of profits. Wald needed *Hemingway's Adventures of a Young Man* to be free from any controversy whatsoever.

Wald wanted a family picture. Adults would see it and approve it for young people. Nick Adams was to be a clean-cut, likely lad of solid American moral stock. The movie was to affirm the fundamental decency of America's youth. The character of Nick Adams represented, according to a studio press release, a "tribute to . . . young Americans of every age, . . . a rebuttal to the leather jacket–switchblade school." There was an irony to the casting. Richard Beymer, as Nick Adams, had last been seen on the screen being switch-bladed to death in *West Side Story* (UA, 1961).

Wald's moralistic attitude limited his choice of Nick Adams stories. He would not buy "The Light of the World," though Hemingway was willing to include it in the package. Among the characters of that story are five prostitutes and a homosexual. A. E. Hotchner, Wald's writer, had used "The Light of the World" in the television drama "The World of Nick Adams" without any trouble. But Wald thought it was totally inappropriate for a movie.

Wald did purchase but did not use "A Very Short Story," in which a young soldier returns to Chicago after the war. The nurse he intended eventually to marry writes him from Italy to say that she has fallen in love with an Italian major. Disillusioned with romance, the American boy picks up a salesgirl in a Loop department store and then picks up gonorrhea from her "while riding in a taxicab in Lincoln Park." It was an unpleasant, cynical story of moral squalor. It was not about Nick Adams anyway, but another young man.

The Nick Adams of the movie has a very pathetic love story, but a chaste one. Nick is wounded in Italy and falls in love with his nurse, Rosana Griffi. (The name was adapted from Count Greffi, the very old man in *A Farewell to Arms* who plays billiards with Frederic Henry.) A scene was filmed in which Rosana goes to

Lobby card for *Hemingway's Adventures of a Young Man.*

Nick's hospital room late at night. She sits on the edge of the bed to loosen the pins from her hair. The scene dissolves as they embrace. To see her sit on Nick's bed and let down her hair—even *that* was more sex than Wald wanted. These shots were cut in final editing. Nick visits Count Griffi to ask formally for Rosana's hand. The count, who is a forthright man, asks Nick if he and his daughter are already lovers. Nick frankly admits that they are. These lines were also edited out of the movie, and their love stayed perfectly pure.

What happened to the story "Indian Camp" in the movie is a very curious instance of censorship. As Hemingway wrote the story, Nick Adams as a little boy (young enough still to address Dr. Adams as "Daddy") goes with his father to the Indian camp across the lake where an Indian woman is reported to be very sick. Doctor Adams sees that she must have a Caesarian section immediately. He has neither anesthetic nor instruments, so he performs the operation with a jack-knife and sews up the incision with gut leader from his fishing tackle. Nick is in the cabin while the surgery takes place. After successfully delivering the baby, Dr. Adams discovers that the woman's husband, who apparently had been asleep in the upper bunk, has slashed his throat from ear to ear because he could not stand the woman's suffering.

Hemingway critics generally agree that "Indian Camp" has a significant theme. As Philip Young has said, it is "Nick's initiation to pain, and to the violence of birth and death."[21] It is the first of a series of events in Nick's life that dramatize a consciousness that is extremely sensitive to violence, and it is the first time that Nick learns, by the Indian's suicide, that there is such a thing as psychic pain more unendurable than physical pain.

The movie version loses all of this meaning. In the first place, Nick is nineteen years old in the screenplay (perhaps ten or twelve years older than he is in the story). Presumably his maturity makes him somewhat less vulnerable to the shock of the situation. Furthermore, the meaning of the story is lost because the agony of surgery is moderated. The code cautioned that scenes of childbirth must be handled with "discretion and restraint and within the limits of good taste." (Some reviewers of Selznick's *Farewell to*

*Arms* thought that that movie, with a protracted scene of Catherine in the delivery room, violated the code on this point.) Hotchner complied with the spirit of the code by having Dr. Adams use a hypodermic of anesthetic and real surgical instruments.

What worried Wald more was the husband's suicide—not only the grisly fact of his nearly severed head but the idea of suicide. Suicide was a very touchy topic. The code stated that "suicide, as a solution of problems occurring in the development of screen drama, is to be discouraged unless absolutely necessary for the development of the plot, and shall never be justified, or glorified, or used specifically to defeat the ends of justice." By this definition the suicide in "Indian Camp" was allowable. So was the eventuality of Dr. Adams's own suicide. Later in the screenplay it is learned that Dr. Adams has killed himself because of the intolerable situation of his married life. Wald thought that including two suicides in the movie was taking an unnecessary risk with the Catholic audience. One was enough. In Hotchner's preliminary script, the Indian husband runs from the cabin when the operation begins. His son follows him. After the operation, the Indian boy comes back to tell Dr. Adams that his father has had an "accident" and needs help. The film cuts to a shot of Nick and his father rowing back across the lake later, and the dialogue suggests that the husband *attempted* suicide but did not succeed. Wald decided even this version was too strong. In the release print, the Indian only runs away.

"A Pursuit Race" (not a Nick Adams story but used for the movie) also had to be fixed. The Bill Campbell of the story is an advance man for a touring burlesque show. His manager, Mr. Turner, finds him one morning in a Kansas City hotel room, apparently drunk. Turner has found him this way many times before. He is not drunk this time, Campbell insists, as he lies in bed with the covers pulled over his face. He has only been drinking a little to ward off the nausea that is the first symptom of withdrawal. There has been, as he calls it, a "new development." He is really "hopped to the eyes," and he shows his boss the puncture marks on his arm to prove it.

The line "hopped to the eyes" is included in the screenplay, and Campbell does show the hypodermic marks on his arm. Very likely, though, most of the audience missed the point of the line and of the gesture. In the preceding scenes it has been clearly established that Campbell is a lush. The audience is diverted into thinking that Campbell's problem is drink, not drugs. In his first appearance he is seen swilling from a bottle. He spends the night before Turner finds him clowning in the hotel bar guzzling glass after glass of whiskey. Only with great difficulty is Nick Adams, who for the purposes of the screenplay has been hired as his assistant, able to get him to bed. Campbell pulls the sheets over his face and falls immediately into a deep, drunken sleep. In the morning Nick finds him still dead asleep, and then Mr. Turner shows up. Therefore the revelation that Campbell is a drug addict makes no sense at all. When Turner advises Campbell to stay in Kansas City to take "the cure," it sounds like he means that Campbell should dry out. And at the end of this sequence of the picture, Nick meets Mr. Turner in New York and asks whatever happened to Billy Campbell. Turner says that he ran away from the hospital. "But he'll turn up again," Turner beams cheerfully; "you can count on that—wreathed in a halo of bourbon!"

Wald was attempting to pass over quickly the subject of narcotics. After 1956, when Otto Preminger produced *The Man with the Golden Arm* (UA), the code's stand on the appropriateness of drug addiction as a movie subject was liberalized, so in this respect there was nothing in Hemingway's material that violated censorship standards. Wald simply did not want Nick around drugs; better for Nick, and better for the audience, if Campbell is only a wild comic drunk. In remarks to a *Los Angeles Times* reporter, Hotchner quoted Hemingway as saying to him, "That Nick was a good boy."[22] Hemingway could have felt assured that with Wald as producer Nick was not going to be corrupted by the movies.

Each one of Hemingway's other novels and stories conflicted, at least in some passing way, with the industry's standards of morality and decency. And across the entire spectrum of Hemingway's writing, somewhere, there was probably a violation of nearly every article of the code. Thoreau once asked, "If you are acquainted with the principle, what do you care for a myriad instances and applications?"

Why were there different standards for books and for movies? A "theory" section of the code explained that the media were different; literature was less intense in its impressions than film. A book only described, reaching the mind through words "on a cold page." Film, on the other hand, vividly represented to the eyes and ears of the audience the "reproduction of actual events" involving "apparently living" people. Also, "the reaction of a reader to a book [depended] largely on the keenness of the reader's imagination, [whereas] the reaction of the film [depended] on the vividness of presentation."

No less important, it was a matter of different audiences, from two different classes of the culture, as described by the code. Books like Hemingway's were written for and appealed to, for the most part, a "mature," "selective," and "discerning" audience. Movies were made for and appealed to a larger audience that included both "the cultivated and the rude, the mature and the immature, the self-respecting and the criminal." Only in a censored version was a Hemingway movie advisable for all. Jerry Wald once described the class problem of censorship in rather similar terms: "The big problem is how not to offend the innocent and yet not antagonize the intelligent."[23] (And you would offend no one by calling the ignorant "innocent.") Still another way to mark the class difference would be between those who were Hemingway's readers and those who were innocent of his books.

CHAPTER VII

# Story, Movie, Film: "The Killers"

In a saloon in Lodgepole, Montana, two gunslingers are waiting to kill an Apache half-breed called Johnny Blue-Eyes. They know that Johnny always comes in for a drink after he drives the stagecoach in from Rock Springs. He is not coming in tonight, though. For a long time he has expected to be gunned down. There is an old score of a double-cross that has to be settled against him. Now he is resigned to his death, knowing that there is nothing he can do about it. He is in his room behind the livery stable, just waiting for the gunmen to find him there and shoot him.

This is the opening sequence for a movie that has never been filmed, *The Happy Death of Johnny Blue-Eyes*, a screenplay by Daniel Mainwaring, who wrote the script for *The Gun Runners*. It is a western version of Hemingway's famous short story "The Killers." Given the premise of the adaptation, the scenes and characters of the story and movie can all be matched. Summit, Illinois, in the 1920s is moved back to the Old West. Henry's diner and a room at a boardinghouse become the tavern and the livery stable. Al and Max, the professional killers sent down by the Chicago mob, are outlaws with six-guns. Ole Andreson, called the Swede, the ex-heavyweight fighter who got in wrong with the gangsters, is the title character of the movie. If one adds a bartender like George the counterman, and a greenhorn cowboy named Nick Adams, who would happen to be in the tavern when the killers stride through the swinging doors, then the cast of the story would be nearly complete. The movie could follow the action of the story, then (to complete the length of a feature) show in a series of flashbacks what Johnny Blue-Eyes had done to deserve this shooting.

It would be difficult to find Hemingway's meaning in such a movie as this. For example, Johnny Blue-Eyes and the Swede would have to have the same reasons for waiting so passively to be killed. In a western movie, Johnny's bravery might have something to do with his Indian heritage. The screenplay writer, Mainwaring, was not especially interested in the idea of the character except insofar as it offered an entrance to his own movie plot.

Jerry Wald once had the idea of remaking *For Whom the Bell Tolls* as a western, with Pablo's band as outlaws in the Wyoming Hills.[1] (One thinks that a Texan/Mexican war would have offered a more appropriate scene.) But no script was ever developed for that western epic. *Johnny Blue-Eyes*, too, will probably never be shot.

The two filmed versions of "The Killers" that have been produced represent the distant and near extremes of resemblance that a Hollywood movie might have to its source. The 1964 Universal *Killers* kept Hemingway's title and, of course, used Hemingway's name. Except for those promptings, even a reader who knows the story well might not see it at first in Gene L. Coon's "updated" screenplay. (Nick Adams will carry a cane.)

The movie opens with two men named Charlie and Lee (played by Lee Marvin and Clu Gulager) standing on the sidewalk outside the Sage Home for the Blind in Miami. They wear conservative business suits and have on dark glasses (for about the same reason that the killers in the story wear gloves). Charlie carries a briefcase. Blind children are playing in the yard; a man walks by with a seeing-eye dog. Charlie and Lee go to the administration office. They do not answer the receptionist, Miss Watson, when she asks if she can help them. Lee quietly pours water from a flower vase onto her desk. She does not react, so they know she cannot see them and later describe them to the police. Charlie now tells her they are looking for Jerry Nichols (played by John Cassavetes). Nichols is not blind, but he teaches a class in auto mechanics there, having learned about engines in his past years as a racing car driver. Miss Watson, being pleasant, explains that he has a class now, but, touching the raised dial on her watch, he will be able to see them in an hour and a half. "I'm sorry, lady," Charlie says, "we don't have the time." There is an edge in his voice that frightens her, and she cautiously reaches for a buzzer on her desk. Lee jerks out the cord, and Charlie grabs her throat and shoves her to the floor. They leave her there unconscious and tied up. They lock the office door behind them.

An old man with a white cane is coming down the stairs as Charlie and Lee go up. He is on his way to the office, but finding the office door locked, calls to Miss Watson, then goes around to another entrance.

Upstairs in his classroom Jerry Nichols and the men in his class are standing around an engine. The intercom phone rings, and Nichols answers. The old man has found Miss Watson and is calling to warn Nichols that two men are after him. Miss Watson thinks they are going to kill him. The old man asks if he should call the police to try to get help. Nichols is quiet for a moment, then says not to bother. He hangs up the receiver. He announces that class is dismissed, then shouts it angrily again when the class seems not to understand. The killers shove past the students crowding out the door. Standing behind the desk, Nichols only nods when Charlie says his name. Charlie takes a heavy gun with a silencer from the briefcase, and smoothly aims and fires. The camera shifts almost imperceptibly into slower motion as Nichols's body convulses with the impact of the slug. He slumps against the wall. Both killers are shooting, emptying their weapons. They run down the hallway and out.

Hemingway's material has already been used up in the movie in less than five minutes. The audience does not necessarily know that. The audience might not even know that "The Killers" was a short story rather than a novel, for if the audience has believed that this much of the movie represents Hemingway's writing, they could believe that the rest of the movie is Hemingway's material also.

In all their professional experience Charlie and Lee have never known a victim to be so calm about his death as Jerry Nichols. Charlie has the impression that he has seen him somewhere before, that he might be a racer from Miami named Johnny North, who was said to have been involved in a million dollar mail truck robbery in California some years before. The killers do not know who paid their $25,000 contract to kill him. It might be whoever master-minded that robbery, and if Charlie and Lee can find him, they might also find a way to extort a million dollars for themselves.

They start to track down some of the people who knew Johnny in the old days—the man who was his mechanic, then someone else who was supposed to be a member of the robbery gang. In a series of flashback sequences they find out about a girlfriend, Sheila Farr (played by Angie Dickinson), who had started to hang around the track where Johnny was racing. Everyone else knows that she is poison. She has to be around men who live dangerously. (The audience would recognize her as a type of Hemingway woman. Before Johnny there was a boxer whom she ruined. Before that there was a bullfighter.)

When Sheila meets Johnny she already belongs to a powerful gangster named Jack Browning (played by Ronald Reagan, in his last picture and in his only villain role). Sheila lets Johnny fall in love with her anyway; she and Browning need him for something.

Johnny starts talking about marrying Sheila, using as a nestegg the prize money from a big race that he knows he can win. But he

Lobby card for the 1946 version of *The Killers*. Burt Lancaster double-crosses the other members of the gang as they divide the money after the robbery.

has bad luck. In the race sequence of the movie Johnny blows a tire and rolls his car. He survives the crash, but his eyes are hurt permanently (something about peripheral vision), and his professional career is finished.

Sheila now tells Johnny about a spectacular mail robbery that Browning is planning. The gang needs an expert driver. Johnny agrees, thinking that with his cut of the take he can start a new life with Sheila.

Then just before the robbery Sheila lies to Johnny that the other gang members intend to cut him out of his share. What they should do, Sheila convinces him, is double-cross them first. Johnny will have the million dollars in his car; she will meet him, and they will run off with the money all for themselves.

The robbery goes perfectly. But Sheila has only been setting Johnny up for a murderous double-cross. Her loyalty all along has been to Browning. When Johnny meets her with all the money, she takes him to a remote motel where Browning is waiting to kill him.

Johnny escapes from Browning with only a wound. He is more nearly destroyed by Sheila's betrayal. Also, he knows that the other gang members, believing that he has the money, will be after him. They would kill him anyway for the double-cross he pulled. Browning will have killers after him, too—professionals like Charlie and Lee. The night at the motel Browning did get the money, but if he does not have Johnny killed before the gang finds him, Johnny might get a chance to explain how the double-cross really worked and say who has the money now. Johnny takes the name Jerry Nichols and tries to vanish in an identity as a teacher for the blind. All this has led to the opening sequence of the film.

Charlie and Lee know who their man is now. They think they can get to Browning through his woman and apparently succeed in threatening Sheila into betraying him. But Sheila and Browning are good at setting a trap, and Charlie and Lee walk into the aim of Browning's high-power rifle when they walk out of their hotel. Lee dies on the sidewalk; Charlic is badly wounded, just able to drag himself to his car.

Browning and Sheila know they have to clear out of the country now. They return to Browning's house to collect the million dollars from the wall safe. Though he is bleeding to death, Charlie follows them there and murders them. He staggers outside and collapses, dumping the money all over the lawn for the police to collect when the movie is over.

Originally this version of "The Killers" was planned as a television movie. When the script developed so violently, it was decided not to confront the issue of television censorship and to produce it as a theater feature instead. There is more violence than the plot summary has shown. Along with all the high caliber shootings are various other acts of brutality. For example, Charlie and Lee get one of the old gang members to talk by burning him in a steam bath. They get Sheila to talk when they start to throw her out the window of her high-rise apartment.

One reviewer described the movie as "93 minutes of sock-em-in-the-mouth rough stuff that beats the original story to a bloody pulp."[2] Violence, the critics agreed, was being done to Hemingway's reputation. Louis Chapin, writing for the *Christian Science Monitor*, was angry about the fraud of promoting such mayhem as authentically Hemingway's: "It seems that everybody's supposed to know who Hemingway is, but nobody's really expected to read him."[3] Eugene Archer, for the *New York Times*, wrote: "Hemingway is the victim in all of this. All that remains of his original story is the author's name, big and enticing in the advertisements, giving discredit where it is far from due."[4] But the movie brought no discredit to Hemingway in the eyes of those who liked violent movies. "Only Hemingway could have conceived it!" the movie publicity said. "Excitement, thrills, building to the impact of a forty-five slug!" The audience would more easily think that of Hemingway than suppose he imagined his story without any killing at all.

Some critics, Archer among them, were especially hard on the 1964 *Killers* because they remembered the first movie of *The Killers*, also a Universal picture, produced in 1946 by Mark Hellinger, directed by Robert Siodmak, with the screenplay by Anthony Veiller. In 1946 *The Killers* had not been an especially distinguished movie. Its only award was the Edgar Allan Poe Prize from the Guild of Mystery Writers of America. It was, though, the most prof-

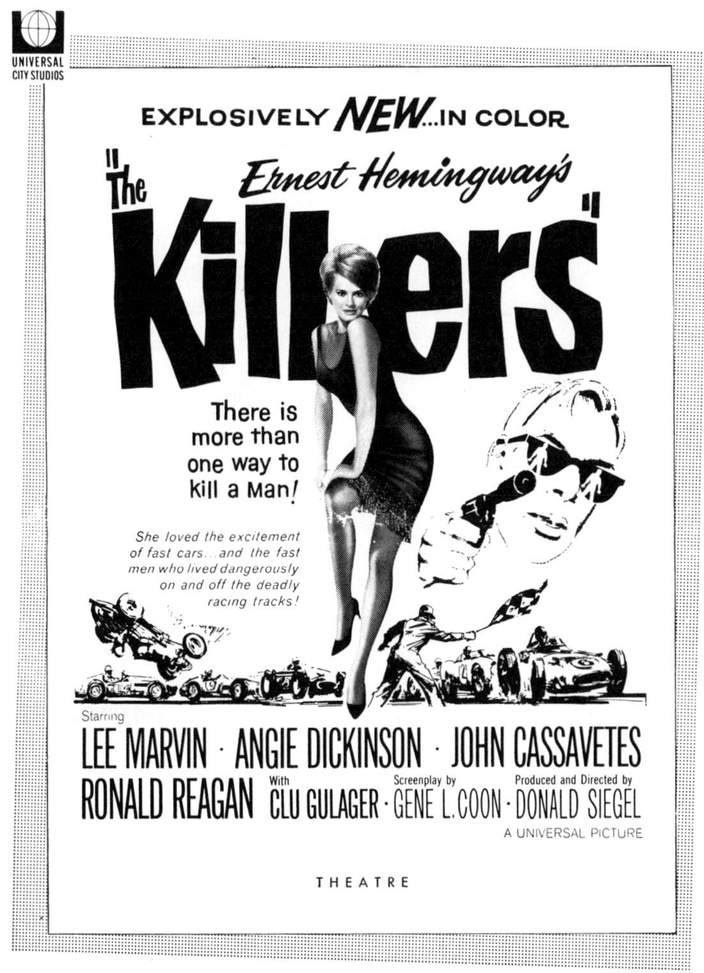


The 1964 and 1946 versions of *The Killers* as advertised in the newspapers.

itable gangster movie of the year, setting attendance records at the theater where it opened. And it came to have some minor fame because it was Burt Lancaster's first movie, in the role of the Swede, and also Ava Gardner's first major role, playing the girl whom Angie Dickinson played in the '64 remake. Thinking back on the first *Killers*, critics believed it was the best Hollywood treatment of Hemingway's material. (Hemingway once said, though, "Memory, of course, is never true.")

The first movie version of "The Killers" was a little longer (by ten minutes) and considerably more complicated in its turnings of plot. In the first movie it is an insurance investigator who does the tracing of the victim's past, not the killers themselves. Instead of a mail robbery, it is a quarter of a million dollar payroll robbery of the Prentiss hat factory in Hackensack, New Jersey. The double-crossings are about the same. It is all routine gangster melodrama—"factory made," as James Agee said in his review.[5] One sees it again in *Criss Cross* (Universal, 1959), also starring Burt Lancaster and directed by Robert Siodmak. That movie has an armored car robbery.

In its extension from Hemingway's short story beginning, the '46 *Killers* looked something like what Hemingway might have written. Anthony Veiller knew from the story, for example, that the killers' victim, the Swede, had once been a heavyweight fighter. In one of the flashbacks to the Swede's past, Veiller invented a boxing scene for the end of his career. He is brutally beaten, though fighting courageously with a broken hand. To the audience the entire movie might have had a Hemingway look. John McNulty, reviewing for the *New Yorker*, said, "Hollywood has so frequently botched a good story by extending it that this one instance of preserving the quality of the original is most cheering."[6]

A newspaper clipping listing the time and channel for a television showing of *The Killers* offers this synopsis: "Based on the best-selling novel by Ernest Hemingway, the story centers on an insurance investigator, probing the killing of a washed-up boxer." That was a mistake, calling it a novel. But the story is told that Hemingway joked about redoing "The Killers" as a full-length novel himself, so much did he like the movie.[7]

"Don't let us speak about the motion pictures based on Ernest's stories," Mrs. Hemingway once said in a published interview. "Of all of them, there was only one that he liked," this *Killers*.[8] Actually, he liked a few others too, but he did like this movie best. His old friend Mark Hellinger arranged a private screening at the Sun Valley Lodge before the premiere. Hemingway was delighted and called Hellinger the next day to say so.[9] Hellinger gave him the print, and in later years, Hemingway would haul out a projector and show *The Killers* to house guests at the Finca though falling asleep after the first reel.[10]

Probably Hemingway started to lose interest well before that. His story was over before ten minutes had run. Considering only the first sequence, it is easy to understand why Hemingway was pleased and impressed. The illusion that the movie is like the story is immediately convincing. Hemingway must not have cared—because the movie was fun—that Veiller's script and Siodmak's direction changed *many* important details of the story and disregarded its meaning. It was an excellent beginning for a movie, but what has come to be its reputation as a nearly perfect movie adaptation is hardly deserved, as a close comparison shows.

## The Story

Sitting at the counter of Henry's lunchroom is one customer. His name is Nick Adams. It is not said how old he is. At one point in the story, Sam, the cook, thinking Nick is about to do something foolish, disparagingly calls him a little boy. Apparently he is old enough to be out in the world on his own, as he is in this town of Summit (near Chicago) only for a short time before moving on. Nick has been talking to the counterman, George, who is probably about Nick's age—late teens or early twenties. Later one of the killers makes the wisecrack that, because George "can cook and everything," he will "make some girl a nice wife." The line was cut in the screenplay.

Outside it is getting dark. A streetlight turns on shortly after two men come in and sit down to look at the menu. Al and Max are dressed alike, wearing derbies, overcoats, silk mufflers, and gloves. Their coats seem tight because they are concealing sawed-off shotguns, though the reader does not know it for the time being. They leave their coats on, which might not be unusual in a short-order diner. They leave their gloves on, too. Fingerprints.

The Movie

A sedan cruises down the highway at nightfall. The headlights pick up a sign reading Brentwood, New Jersey (in reality, the sign would not name the state), which is the town that the killers are looking for, though it is not Hemingway's town. The titles are rolling as Al and Max drive into town and park the car. They look in at the gas station closed for the night. The diner across the street is brightly lighted through the night haze.

Al reaches his hand inside his coat to adjust his revolver. (The gun is not seen yet, but it is a handgun. Strictly interpreted, the Motion Picture Code forbade arming movie gangsters with illegal weapons such as sawed-off shotguns.)

Like Max, Al wears a soft felt hat in the style of the 1940s, but no scarf and, more interesting to note, no gloves. Veiller's script called for the killers to stop by a lamp post to draw on grey gloves—at that moment the street light would switch on. Unaccountably, that dramatic visual detail was not filmed.

Al and Max enter the diner by different doors. George, who looks to be about fifty years old or older, is serving a sandwich to a customer, Nick Adams. Nick looks about thirty.

The Story

Al and Max order the dinner specials on the menu, but, as George explains, the dinners will not be ready until six o'clock. It is only five o'clock now. The wall clock says twenty minutes past five, but it runs twenty minutes fast. To menace and intimidate George, the killers make some ugly remarks about the menu and the clock. They must know perfectly well what time it is and that the Swede will not be in for another hour. In the meanwhile they will have something to eat: "'I'll take ham and eggs,' the man called Al said. . . . 'Give me bacon and eggs,' said the other man."

Hemingway has made a mistake at this point. That's no way to order your eggs. You have to say what way you want them, over or up, scrambled or poached, and if you forget that, the waiter always asks you about it.

Some minutes must pass while Sam, out in the kitchen, fixes their orders. Hemingway does not account for all the time that passes in the story. The action is discontinuous. Al and Max talk about this hot town Summit, where you cannot get anything to drink and where nights folks come "to eat the big dinner." They call George "bright boy," which is another way of leaning on him a little.

George is uneasy watching them eat with their gloves on. Max asks him what he is looking at. George says "Nothing," and laughs nervously when Max presses him about it.

Perhaps a few minutes later Max tells Nick, the other bright boy, to get around to the other side of the counter. Then Al takes Nick back to the kitchen with Sam and ties them both up.

## The Movie

The dialogue is very nearly the same, and the voices of actors William Conrad and Charles McGraw (Max and Al) sound very like those of movie gangsters. The pace of the dialogue seems too fast, however, as if the characters were rushing their lines.

The clock runs differently in the movie—only ten minutes fast, George says, not twenty. The wall clock is only faintly seen, almost too briefly to be noticed; the hands read just before six. The movie killers enter the diner at about five minutes till six instead of five o'clock, as in the story. They have left themselves only a few minutes to set up the hit, and it hardly seems that they would think there is still time to eat, if the Swede comes in by six. Coffee maybe. But in the movie Sam is an incredibly fast cook. It takes him less than a minute to serve Al and Max their ham-and-eggs and bacon-and-eggs.

The movement of time is very different in the story and in the movie. There are blanks of time in the story, falling between lines of dialogue. The action is continuous in the movie, however, without interruptions for minutes of idle time-marking. Once the killers enter the diner the cameras keep rolling.

The Story

George wants to know what it's all about. Max says that they are going to kill the Swede, Ole Andreson, when he comes in for dinner. They have never actually seen the Swede themselves; they don't have anything against him personally. They are going to kill him "for a friend."

Al is guarding Sam and Nick in the kitchen. "You talk too much," Al complains to Max. "The nigger and my bright boy are amused by themselves. I got them tied up like a couple of girl friends in the convent." (For several obvious reasons that wisecrack was impermissible in the movie.) Max does not think it matters too much if George knows what is going on because there is nothing he can do to stop it, and afterwards he is going to be dead too, probably. Max does not want George thinking already that he is as sure as dead. In that case George might try something desperate. When George asks about "afterward," Max implies that that is something to be decided later, depending on how well George behaves.

If anyone other than the Swede comes in, Max tells him, George is to get rid of him, saying the cook is off. At five minutes till six (the line of the story says "quarter past six," but the reader knows that the clock is twenty minutes fast), a streetcar motorman walks in and asks if he can get supper. That seems a strange question to ask in a diner, but he must know that the dinner is usually not ready until six sharp. George says that Sam is out, and the motorman says that he will try the place up the street. Again the story notes the time: twenty past six, that it, six exactly. Hemingway is forcing the reader into an alertness about time. George, the killers, and the reader know that any moment now the Swede might come through the door and get blasted.

The Movie

Max explains to George that they are going to kill the Swede who works at the filling station across the street. (Nothing is said in the story about where he works.) That would be Pete Lunn, the name he goes by now. Later it is learned that his real name is Ole Anderson (with the spelling Americanized in the script). This is a sensible difference between the story and the movie. Hiding as he is, the Swede probably would take another name.

The action across these minutes of the movie is not significantly different from what it is in the story.

### The Story

There is another skip in time, to six fifty-five, really six thirty-five. In the meantime, two more customers have stopped in. Henry's place is not doing an especially good business, the reader might think. George says a couple of times that the Swede is not coming in tonight. Max says they will give him ten more minutes. When the ten minutes are up, Max is ready to go. Al says to wait five more. Another customer comes in and leaves angry when George tells him the cook is sick.

Now Al and Max have to decide what to do about George and the other two. Max says they are all right because he and Al are "through with it," meaning, presumably, that if they had killed the Swede they would have had to kill the witnesses as well, but now their assignment is over. Someone else will kill the Swede some other time. It does not matter if the Swede finds out what almost happened tonight. He might run, of course, but he will be found wherever he goes.

As a last word to the bright boy, Al tells him that he has a lot of luck. "That's the truth," Max agrees. "You ought to play the races, bright boy." They leave, having been in the diner about one hour and fifty-five minutes.

### The Movie

After the motorman comes in there is only one other customer—the angry man. But the time span of the story has been compressed for the movie. It is only a minute or two after six; the killers have been waiting about ten minutes. (It has not really been ten minutes as measured by any watch in the audience. The movie time is running somewhat faster than actual time.) George says that if the Swede is not there by six he's not coming at all. Max feels sure that the bright boy would know better than to try to fool them. As in the story, Al and Max decide it is safe to leave George alive. They want him to know that he has a lot of luck.

These killers are not "through with it," though. They are impatient waiting in the diner because they could be out looking for the Swede instead of waiting for him. So they cross the street to the station where the Swede pumps gas, figuring to find his address there.

Now the movie is not making very good sense. It is not especially professional of the killers to be improvising this way when the first plan does not work. It might very well be harder to kill the Swede at his rooming house. They could have difficulty in getting in. He might have his door locked. He might have a gun. There might be confusion in the hallway if boarders rush out at the sound of gunfire.

For that matter, Hemingway's plan for the killers to shoot the Swede in the diner does not seem especially smart either. Ordinarily they would want to avoid a situation where innocent bystanders might have to be murdered. Police are not so enthusiastic about solving gangster murders if it is only gangsters killing each other. The killers might have done better to wait in the car and drop the Swede on the sidewalk when he comes by.

Be that as it may, it is very hard to believe what happens in the movie, that Al and Max would take the risk of going to look for the Swede while George, unguarded, not even tied, might find the courage to try to interfere, say by getting the police. Even if George seems too frightened to get involved, they could not be very sure about the cook or Nick Adams.

The Story

George unties Sam and Nick and tells them that the men were going to kill the Swede. George thinks Nick should go to Hirsch's rooming house and let the Swede know.

It is not a long walk. The landlady lets Nick in and shows him up to the Swede's room. She calls to Mr. Andreson that there is someone to see him, and the Swede tells Nick to come in.

The Movie

They are all lucky to be alive, George says, as he frees Sam and

Nick. Nick has the very sensible idea to run for the police, but George tells him to warn the Swede first. It does not occur to George that he might go for the police himself, or send Sam, while Nick is on the way to the rooming house.

The camera follows Nick as he leaves by the rear door and runs down back streets. He bursts into the Swede's room.

## The Story

The Swede is lying on his bed looking at the wall. Hemingway mentions the wall five times in the scene—how the Swede is looking at it or turning toward it. In a simple way the wall is metaphoric. The Swede is a man up against the wall, or facing a future that is a blank wall. He is not interested in what Nick is telling him about the men who were at the diner to kill him. He does not want to know what they looked like and does not think it would do any good for Nick to notify the police. Nick will not let it alone, so the Swede goes on to say that he will not try to get out of town because he is through with all the running. He says there is no way to fix it because he "got in wrong."

There is something on the Swede's mind, seemingly trivial, besides the danger of the killers. He has been in his room all day trying to make up his mind whether to go outside or not. Mrs. Bell, the landlady, had talked to him earlier and urged him to go for a walk on this nice fall day, but he cannot decide. It is not that he has any fear of the killers being outside. There is no reason for the reader to suppose that he has had any warning or intuition that the killers would find him today. He is not inside to keep himself safer. The door was not locked when Nick let himself in. The Swede's problem, in one sense, is that he is so paralyzed with despair that he cannot will himself to do much of anything. The simplest decision—whether to go outside—has become very hard.

He understands that he is out of danger for the time being. He tells Nick after a time he will make up his mind to go out. He thanks Nick for coming around to tell him.

The story stays with Nick now. Downstairs on the way out he talks briefly with Mrs. Bell, who looks after the place for the owner Mr. Hirsch. Mrs. Bell tells Nick how nice Mr. Andreson is, and how gentle, even though, as they both know, he used to be a boxer. Nick says good-night to her and goes back to the diner to talk it over with George.

The Movie

The room is so dim that the Swede is barely visible lying on his bed next to the wall. Nick is a little out of breath trying to tell him what happened a few minutes ago. (The dialogue is similar to the story's, but there is no talk about taking a walk.) The Swede tells Nick that there is nothing to be done about the killers. The script has Nick ask directly why the killers are after him, to which the Swede replies, "I did something wrong—once." Then he thanks Nick for coming, and Nick goes away.

Remarkable about the conversation is that Nick does not tell the Swede that the killers are on their way to his room right now, that by now they probably have his address. Whereas in the story Nick comes to give the Swede a report about what has already happened, in the movie, with the plot changed, Nick comes to give the Swede a report about what is about to happen—then, unaccountably, does not give the warning. One would think that the warning would be the first thing Nick would say: "Swede! Two men with guns are after you! You've got to get out of here!" or words like that. Instead Nick wastes time asking questions like "Why do they want to kill you? He raced to the Swede's, but once there the desperation of situation seems out of his mind. There is no sign either that Nick is thinking how unlucky it will be for him still to be at the rooming house when Al and Max find the place.

The camera stays in the Swede's room when Nick leaves. There is no conversation with Mrs. Bell downstairs. (Much later in the screenplay Mrs. Hirsch appears briefly. One of the other members of the gang that robbed the hat factory has come looking for the Swede. The Swede is dead by this time, but "Dum-Dum" rents the room to search it for the $250,000 the gang thinks the Swede ran off with in the double-cross.)

Nick was lucky not to cross the killers on his way back to the diner because very soon the Swede, still lying on his bed, hears the front door squeak open, then hears footfalls on the steps and down the corridor. He raises up to watch his door, which he can just barely see from the edge of light around it. The killers listen for a few moments in the hallway. Swede sees the door open and the killers standing there with drawn guns, strongly silhouetted by the light behind him. As soon as they can see the Swede in the dim light, they start firing, the muzzle flashes brightening their faces. They empty their weapons (later the coroner's report says that eight slugs hit him) and are heard running down the hall. The camera in close-up shows the Swede's hand slide down the brass post of his bedstead and fall.

The Story

At the diner Nick tells George how the Swede reacted. Neither Nick nor George seems sure what to say about it. George offers the obvious opinion that "They'll kill him," not meaning Al and Max but whoever is behind it. Nick guesses so, too. George says, "It's a hell of a thing." Nick echoes him, saying, "It's an awful thing." There is a difference in what the lines suggest about a contrast between George and Nick. George has a formulaic, set way of saying how bad the situation is. He is not being insensitive, but he has the event in the right relation to himself. He can cope with it in his mind. Nick, on the other hand, as the last page of the story is showing, is being more sensitive than is safe and stable. For George the experience is over—wiped away, even as he is wiping off the counter with a towel. Nick cannot wipe it from his mind. He wonders aloud what the Swede did. George can account for that. He must have double-crossed somebody: "That's what they kill them for." Nick has an extraordinary next line. He says that he is going to get out of this town. The Swede, who has cause to be running, is going to stay. Nick, by ironic contrast, is going to get out of this town, as if it will be easier not to think about what happened tonight in some other place.

The Swede feels the hopelessness, but he is very stable, indeed almost inert, thinking about what is going to happen. Nick, however, "can't stand to think about him waiting in the room and knowing he's going to get it. It's too damn awful." "Well," George remarks in the last line of the story, "you better not think about it."

That is the standard, easy thing to say to someone whose mind is being disturbed by something. It is not worth much as advice, though; not if Nick is the sort of person who cannot help thinking about things like that which hurt him in his mind.

The story has a difficult pattern. It has three scenes, with transitions between (Nick going to the Swede's room and coming back). In the first scene it appears certain that the killers and what they are going to do are the major interest of the story. They are, after all, the title characters. But the first scene does not resolve the way one might likely predict. The killers merely go away, without killing anyone. The story goes on, setting itself up now, not as an action piece, but a character study and a dramatization of a condition of existential despair. The story might have ended after that second scene: "Nick went out. As he shut the door he saw Ole Andreson with all his clothes on, lying on the bed looking at the wall." This is not an exciting ending, but it would be a thoughtful one. It is true that the Swede is the central interest of the story, but in a positional sense, because his is the central of three parts. The story continues beyond, to observe Nick Adams and to think about the sensitivity of his consciousness. It is surprising to discover that in its resolution the story belongs to Nick, since in the beginning he seemed only accidentally present and in the middle part he seemed only a messenger. The story has a progression like one of the moves of a knight on a chess board: two squares in one direction, then a square to the side.

## The Movie

To readers not used to the way Hemingway sometimes structures stories, the last page could seem without purpose or anticlimactic. Even assuming that the movie-makers understood what Hemingway was doing, they did not want the sequence of the adaptation to land on the Nick Adams square. Nick Adams is not out of the script for good when he leaves the Swede's room. There is no scene back at the diner between Nick and George. The movie leaves out their conversation completely. But since Nick is about the only person in town who knew the Swede at all (from working with him at the gas station), he can try to answer some questions from the police and from an insurance investigator. (This insurance man, Reardon, turns out to be a major character in the movie. It is eventually Reardon who puts together the complete story of the Swede's past. When he starts the case, it is only as a routine search for the beneficiary of the Swede's small group policy as an employee of the gasoline company.) Nick takes the insurance man to the morgue so that he can look at the body. Nick remembers then that a black Cadillac with out-of-state plates came into the station the other day. The driver (Colfax, the leader of the robbery gang) and the Swede seemed to recognize each other. Right afterwards the Swede told Nick that he was feeling sick, left work early, and did not come out of his room again. Then Nick says to Reardon, "Look, mister, if you don't mind, I'm feeling kind of sick myself." That is Nick's exit line in the script. So he is a sensitive young man, too, though the movie audience understands that it is the corpse on the table that is making him queasy.

Anthony Veiller's responsibility was to make a popular entertainment out of a sophisticated story. It was natural to give the Swede the major role in the screenplay and let Nick Adams be a very minor part. Just as obvious is the reason why the Swede had to be killed in the movie. What kind of gangster movie would it be where the killers simply go away when their intended victim does not show up on time where he should be? You certainly could not call such a movie *The Killers*.

Possibly it did not so much seem to Anthony Veiller, Robert Siodmak, and Mark Hellinger that they were changing the nature of Hemingway's story as that they were *finishing* it for him. Many readers feel that the story is not finished. They feel this partly because the ending is rather subtle and difficult, and also because they wish for a very different kind of story than Hemingway intended. They are used to one kind of gangster story and do not readily imagine another kind.

The opinion that the story is incomplete may be illustrated by an editor's introduction to an obscure reprinting of "The Killers" in the June, 1947, number of *Ellery Queen's Mystery Magazine*. The editor identified the story as a classic, the winner of Second Prize among the *O. Henry Memorial Prize Stories of 1927*. Then the editor

Al and Max watch the diner from across the street at the filling station where the Swede works. They cross the street, enter, and place an order with George, "bright boy." At frame 5 Max makes a wisecrack about "the big dinner." George tells Sam to fix ham and eggs and bacon and eggs. Al orders Nick Adams, another "bright boy," around to the other side of the counter.

From the motion picture *The Killers* (1946). Courtesy Universal Pictures.

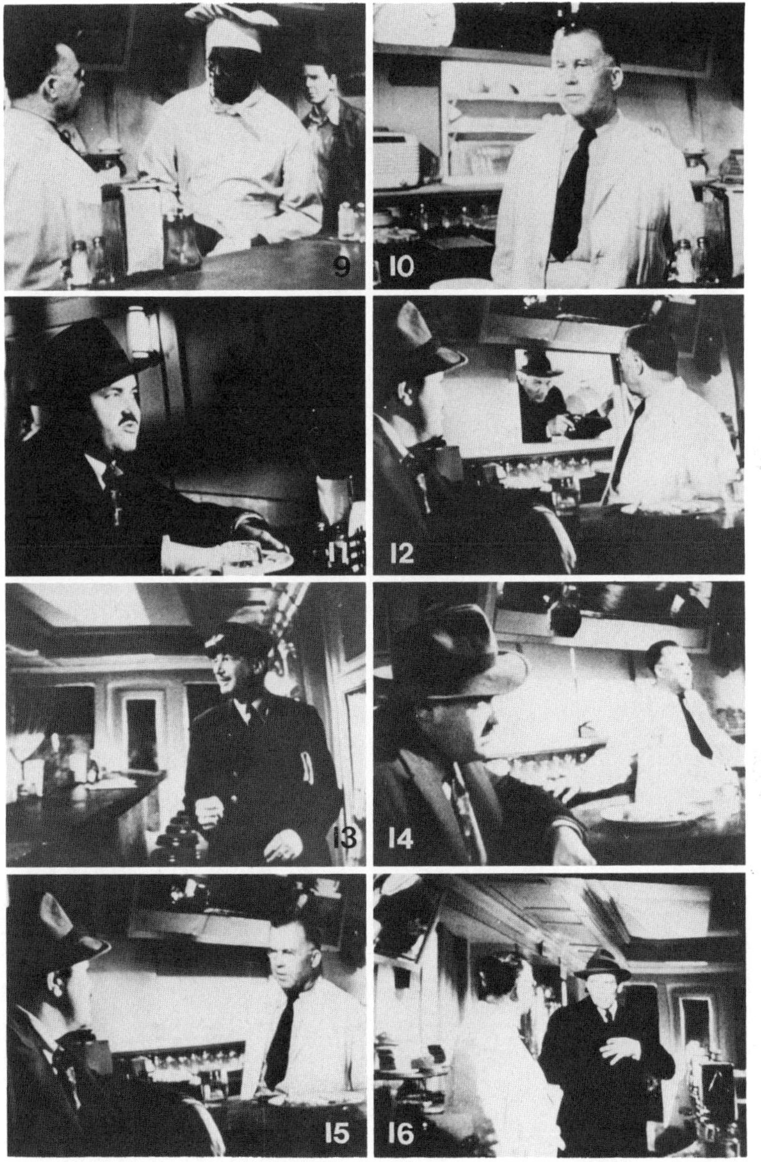

Sam and Nick will go back in the kitchen with Al. At frame 10, George wants to know what it's all about, and Max explains that they are going to kill the Swede, for a friend. Al has the place covered from the kitchen as a streetcar motorman comes in for supper. George explains that Sam has gone out, and at frame 15 Max tells George that was nice the way he got rid of him. In a few minutes the killers are ready to leave.

From the motion picture *The Killers* (1946). Courtesy Universal Pictures.

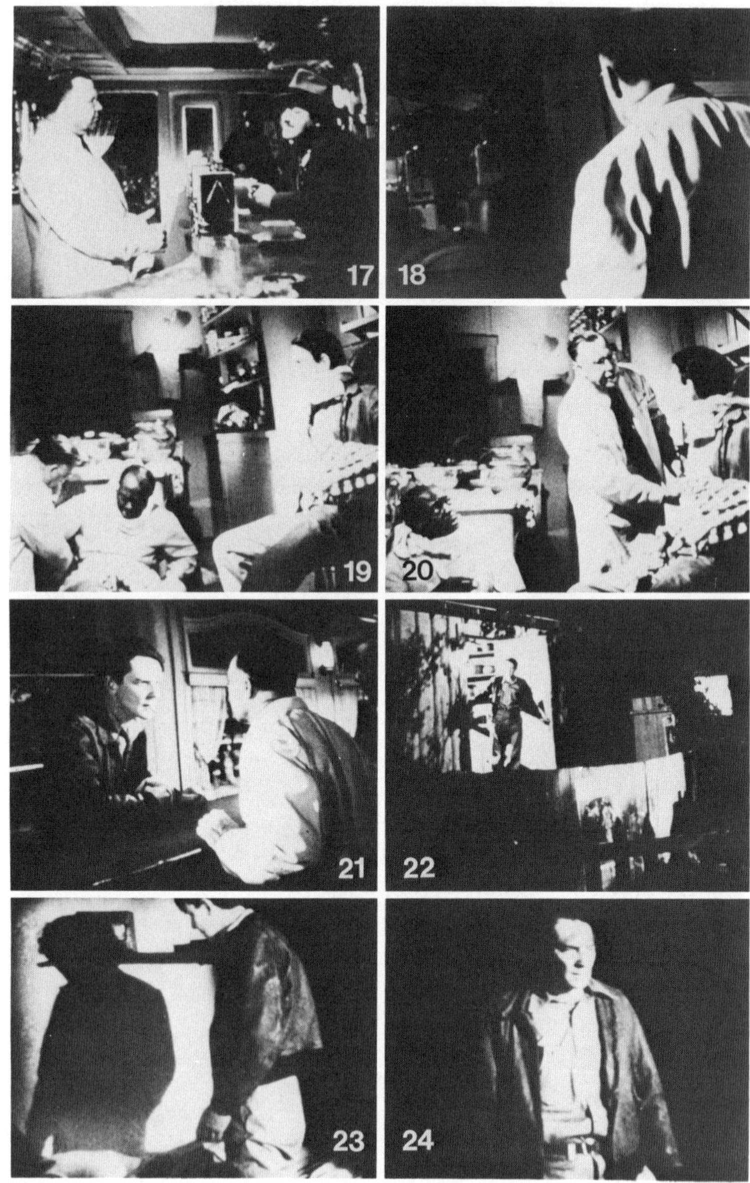


Max tells George he's got a lot of luck. George watches the killers leave, then unties Sam and Nick. Nick wants to go tell the Swede, and at frame 22 runs out from the diner down a back street. At his room at the boarding house the Swede just lies there as Nick tells him about the men who were going to kill him when he came in for supper. Nick leaves.

From the motion picture *The Killers* (1946). Courtesy Universal Pictures.

Moments later the Swede, played by Burt Lancaster, hears footsteps down the hallway. Of course it is the killers. They stand outside the Swede's door, listening cautiously. At frame 29 the Swede watches the door open, and the killers stand silhouetted in the doorway. They fire many times, the gun flash brightening their faces. The Swede's hand grips the brass bedpost, then falls out of the scene as he dies.

From the motion picture *The Killers* (1946). Courtesy Universal Pictures.

praised the Hollywood version from 1946, which almost all the magazine's readers would know. "The short story itself served merely as a springboard. . . . The finished product was an outstanding success, artistically and commercially, proving that Hollywood has the imagination and know-how to transform even an 'incomplete' short story into a gripping and cohesive motion picture."[11]

For comparison with "The Killers," *Ellery Queen's Mystery Magazine* paired with it W. R. Burnett's "Dressing Up," First Prize winner of the *O. Henry Memorial Award Prize Stories of 1930.* The editor felt they were stories that "cry out to be read together . . . a sort of double entry in the bookkeeping of butchery." The Burnett story has a professional killer called Blue spending money extravagantly in a swell Chicago department store. He buys lavender silk underwear, a dozen silk shirts, a gold collar pin, a dozen four-dollar neckties to go with his suit. He has come into a big wad of money gunning down the lieutenant of a rival gang. He has tickets for himself and his girl, Birdy, on the Twentieth-Century Limited to New York that night. A few hours before train time he gets hungry in his hide-out apartment and decides to run his lucky streak a little farther by going out for something to eat. He does not quite make it back. The story ends:

> Blue made a dash for the door, but across the street a Thompson gun began to spit. Blue stumbled, dropped his gun, and ran blindly out into the middle of the street; then he turned and ran blindly back toward the house. An iron fence caught him just below the belt and he doubled over it. Across the street a window slammed.

That is the kind of story ending that reads as if it were written for film—with violent action and climax, described almost as if by camera shots. This particular story was never filmed, but Burnett's novel *Little Caesar,* filmed in 1930, became one of the great gangster pictures of the early sound era.

In the spring of 1927 when "The Killers" was first published, Hemingway almost surely did not have ideas about selling the rights to the movies. Interestingly, however, the publication of "The Killers" falls at about the time when gangsters were more and more getting into the movies. (One may wonder why Hollywood did not buy the story sooner.) The *American Film Institute Catalogue* of motion pictures from 1921 to 1930 lists seventy-five movies under the subject heading "Gangsters." Most of these titles were released in the several years after "The Killers" was printed. (Josef von Sternberg's *Underworld* (Paramount) came out in the late summer of that year.) Summaries of the approximately twelve gangster movies that had been released before Hemingway completed his story in the spring of 1926 show no plot situations anything like that of "The Killers." None involves professional killers squaring a double-cross.

Besides, Hemingway was living abroad most of the time during his early career. He had probably seen very few gangster movies. Gangsters were also characters in popular fiction and popular theater (the "crook plays"). But Hemingway did not have to know about gangsters from such sources either. He had been a newspaper man. He was from Chicago. Presumably he was no more imitating the movies than he was writing "The Killers" for the movies.[12]

And yet the movies did cross Hemingway's mind while he was writing "The Killers," and he wrote the reference into the dialogue. When everything is set up for the killing, Max thinks he might as well talk to George about what is going to happen. Max says that they are going to kill the Swede when he comes in at six.

> "If he comes." [George said.]
> "We know all about that, bright boy," Max said. "Talk about something else. Ever go to the movies?"
> "Once in a while."
> "You ought to go to the movies more. The movies are fine for a bright boy like you."

This is another of Max's wisecracks. He does not really mean that the movies are fine any more than he means that George is bright. Max means they don't have to talk about the killing. For small talk they can discuss the movies, and that will be about George's speed.

In a well-known explication of the story in their book *Understanding Fiction*, Cleanth Brooks and Robert Penn Warren interpret the lines to mean more than this. Hemingway is telling the reader something. "In one sense, of course, the iterated remarks about the movies, coming just after the gangsters have made their arrangements in the lunchroom, serve as a kind of indirect exposition: the reader knows the standard reason and procedure for gang killings."[13] He knows, that is, because he has seen gang killings in the movies. Perhaps it is Max's indirect exposition, too (though this is not Brooks and Warren's point). Max has not changed the subject when he brings up the movies. He was explaining about the killing, and maybe he can make it simple for bright boy by letting him think it will all be like in the movies.

Hemingway could not have intended that meaning, nor could his readers in 1927 (nor George) have understood the lines that way, if it is true that the many movies about gangsters killing other gangsters had not yet been made. "New Critics" such as Brooks and Warren prefer not to make judgments about an author's intentions with a story or about the story's effect on its readers. Also, "New Critics" tend to disassociate a text from the historical context in which it used to be read in order to concentrate on an explication of the intrinsic and immediate meaning of the text as the critic discovers it to be now. The Brooks and Warren explication of the passage at hand illustrates what can be a failing of a particular approach, though on the other hand one would say that as the story continued to be read after the Twenties, their interpretation became very sound.

Brooks and Warren develop another point, which also came to be true as more gangster movies were made. The talk about the movies confirms the reader's sense of the story's reality; or more exactly, it makes the illusion of reality more convincing. The reader has to feel, if the story is to have all its effect, a quality of danger and fear more real than what in the movies is only pretending. It is as though Hemingway were deliberately contrasting the actuality of the situation in the diner with, as Brooks and Warren call it, "the artificial world" or "the unreal horror of the movie thriller."[14] George has to feel the difference, too. (Max isn't trying to make him feel better with the small talk. He wants him scared.) The Swede really is going to get killed. This isn't some kind of show.

There is another illustration of exactly the same point. *The Des-*

*perate Hours* (Paramount, 1955) is a movie in which Humphrey Bogart plays one of three escaped convicts who are terrorizing a suburban household until Bogart's woman can get there with the escape car and escape cash. Frederic March, the father, tries to impress on his family how real is their danger. "It's not like in the comic books or television. Those are real bullets." He could not say the line "It's not like in the comic books or in the *movies*." The audience would laugh at that wording, because of course it *is* only a movie. The line has purpose only if the situation on the screen seems more real than what is in comics or TV shows.

Max's lines about the movies were not used in the Hollywood version. They could not work in the film medium the same way that they do in print. The audience would likely laugh when, for a moment, the movie almost kids itself. Indeed, the lines would have the effect of reminding the audience that they *are* watching a movie, which would break down the illusion of reality. It would have been the same wrong effect in the story version if Hemingway had given Max the lines, "Ever read gangster stories? Gangster stories are fine for a bright boy like you."

One could try to make of this more than a question about the appropriateness of a passage of some twenty-five words. Is what is particularly true of these lines true of the entire story? Might it be that "The Killers" does not lend itself to movie adaptation at all, if as a movie it loses the convincing reality that it has as a story?

The question is somewhat more metaphysical than it is practical. The movies certainly can seem real when one is watching them, and stories also seem real. Whether the illusion of reality is more or less compelling in the movies than in gangster stories would be hard to say. "The Killers" itself, though it is only like a gangster story in some ways, is an illusion of reality. It is fiction, and not even as autobiographically true as many of the other Nick Adams stories. The impression of actuality it gives is not necessarily diminished simply by shifting it into the medium of film. One might tend to assume that the "fiction" represented by the movies is less significant than the fiction of a writer believed to be as meaningful as Hemingway, but that is a separate problem.

Questions about the differences between the media of literature and film are not necessarily abstract and remote. But there are so many different ways of presenting reality within either medium that it works very much better as a practical matter of criticism to limit the inquiry to a particular fiction with all its special stylistic characteristics as literature. (Fiction is only one mode of presenting reality even within literature, but the concern here is almost entirely with Hemingway's fiction.) Then one decides if these characteristics may be re-created or made equivalent in film. To the extent that these characteristics also exist in film, especially if they are important and distinctive characteristics, then one has a cinematic story, one that works well on film. If one has a highly cinematic story, then one's response to its effect, one's understanding of its meaning, and even one's perception and appreciation of its aesthetic character is essentially the same when the story is transferred onto film.

There should be distinctions made here. It is one thing to consider whether a story is good material for a Hollywood movie. It is another thing to consider whether it is good material for film. The first has to do with its potential as a certain kind of entertainment; the second has to do with its compatibility with the medium of film. The first consideration has more to do with the story; the second has more to do with style. To suggest one more distinction, in the making of a motion picture adaptation of a literary work, it is the screenwriter who has more to do with the story of the movie and the director who has more to do with the style of the film.

What, then, of "The Killers" considered in these two separate ways? The story had good potential for the movies that the screenwriter, Anthony Veiller, could bring out more. Did "The Killers" have a distinctive style that the director, Robert Siodmak, could film?

That might not be a right question, for it implies that a director ought to and would wish to transfer the style of the story onto the film. But a film director is not a music director, that is to say, not a conductor, whose commitment must be to complete the experience of the music with a performance appropriate to the composer's own style. We do not ordinarily think of a film director as a performing artist with someone else's composition. In any case, the conductor and the composer, or the dancer and the choreographer, also the stage director and the playwright, are within the same medium. The film director has a medium of his own, and to the extent that he is an artist he may have a style that is of his medium only. It happens that very many film directors do not display much of a distinctive style, just as very many ordinary authors do not. Hemingway, of course, did have style—very much, always. So did Robert Siodmak. That makes *The Killers* especially interesting to think about with regard to style in one medium and the other. Whereas some of the Hemingway films are without any remarkable style, *The Killers* is conspicuous among the others for its almost manneristic style.

*The Killers* is in the style of "Cinema Noir" (dark or grim, film), a term film historians use to classify ruthless melodramas of life in cities after dark.[15] "WHEN NIGHT FALLS OVER THE NAKED CITY, A KILLER STALKS HER SILENT STREETS!"—so read the movie-ad copy for *The Sleeping City* (Universal, 1950), another example of the genre and the other half of the double-feature bill when *The Killers* was re-released. Characteristically "Cinema Noir" had stark atmospheric effects of darkness and light. "ALL THE PASSIONS OF THE NIGHT AWAKE WHEN THE NAKED CITY DIMS HER LIGHTS!"

Robert Siodmak was very much a director in the tradition of "Cinema Noir." A movie's direction seemed most typically his when he played for strong, even garish effects of light within very dark scenes.[16] His use of light in the opening sequence of *The Killers* is especially striking. The headlights of the killers' sedan beam down the empty highway. The bright, hot lights of the diner glare through plateglass windows into the dark outside. Streetlamps cast angled patterns on the pavement. Picket fencing stands white down the dark back street to the Swede's place. All the lights are out in the Swede's room. Through the open door the bulb in the hallway throws Nick's shadow on the wall. The brass of the bed gleams with a dull sheen. The killers, outlined in light, stand in the angles of the door to the Swede's room—"framed á la Siodmak," the shooting script notes.

Such dramatic lighting is not derived from the story. Hemingway sometimes did write in a light-sensitive way—in the story "A

Clean, Well-Lighted Place," for example, where light has both a descriptive and a thematic use. In "The Killers" Hemingway happens to mention the street light four times, but it is not a meaningful detail. Otherwise the story does not mention light and dark at all. Thus it is not noted whether there is a light on in the Swede's room.

Light is the essence of the aesthetic and chemical properties of film, whereas light is only incidental to the descriptive and symbolic possibilities of literature, though the symbolic possibility is shared with film. Pictorial detail is another aspect of description, and in this way too Hemingway's style, in this story, is minimally descriptive. Hemingway notes only highly selective details about what characters, costume, and settings look like. All one sees about the Swede's room, for example, is that it has a bed (and, of course, a wall and a door). As much darkness as there is in the film, one sees much greater detail—for instance, the exact style of the brass bed. All the images of the story that the adaptation happens to include are rendered much more visually complete when they are photographed for the film.

Of course between story and film there is an essentially different way in which detail in light is perceived. Though the gleaming brass bed is only an illusory projection on a screen, without deep dimensionality, substance, or even color, it is still a bed that is actually seen, whereas in the story one only imagines the sight of a bed.

Is there an aspect of composition that film and this particular story have more in common? Film is a dramatic medium, and the narrative of Hemingway's story is highly dramatic. It reads very much like a script. Most of it is dialogue, along with simple notations as to which character is speaking—"Max said," "George said."

Almost everything in the text that is not dialogue is simple and direct observation, what a witness to the drama of the story would see. The door of the lunchroom opens and two men come in. They sit down at the counter. It is getting dark outside and the street light comes on. The two men read the menu. Nick Adams watches them. Except for a different tense and a slightly more involved syntax, the writing is about like that.

Not every observation is perfectly objective, as it is with the lens of a camera. A few comments are factual and reportorial, the kind of straightforward background material that a reporter might put into his story without editorializing any. For example, behind the counter is a long mirror left over from the time before Prohibition when the place was a saloon. The reader might not infer as much simply from seeing the mirror, but the story mentions it as a passing fact. "Henry's had been made over from a saloon into a lunch-counter." That is not an idea that a camera could easily show.

Also, there are a few statements of impression that break with the style of the rest of the story. For example, when Al and Max finally leave the diner the line reads, "In their tight overcoats and derby hats they looked like a vaudeville team." That is Hemingway's metaphoric impression; or perhaps it is George's, and Hemingway for an instant has violated his strict point of view and gone subjectively into George's mind.

> Nick stood up. He had never had a towel in his mouth before.
> "Say," he said. "What the hell?" He was trying to swagger it off.

At this one point of the story there are the reportorial fact and subjective impression in consecutive lines.

If Hemingway, writing from an omniscient point of view, had said very much about the thoughts and feeling of his characters, or if he had let Nick Adams tell the story in the first person as in some of the other Nick Adams stories, then the adaptation into film would not have been as convenient or as much the same. Because the story is dramatic and objective almost all the way through, however, the story does transfer easily and equivalently into film. For that matter, the story transfers into certain other visual, dramatic media just as easily. It could be a stage play or it could be a television play.[17] Therefore we have still not isolated a peculiarly cinematic aspect of Hemingway's style.

There is one. The most remarkably deft detail of the story is the clock, so compellingly real because it runs fast. And the most extraordinary aspect of the structural style of the story is its marking of time. "It was a quarter past six. . . . It was twenty minutes past six." Here the time is objectively shown as the fast clock face shows, not subjectively interpreted and adjusted to the actual time. Within this frame of time references takes place the dramatic action of perhaps fifteen seconds. A motorman walks in, asks a question, walks out. The rest of those five minutes is a space of blank time. Throughout the first scene of the story there are eight references to the clock in nearly two hours of time, most of it empty—not filmed, one could say. The best way to describe this is as a cinematic effect. (It is *not* accurately described as a dramatic effect; it cannot be realistically imitated on stage or before television cameras, though it does work on video tape, which is a species of film.) It is an editing of time movement, a cutting and splicing forward by repeatedly showing the clock.

A director could style the editing in one of several conventional, even old-fashioned ways. A close shot of the face of the clock, a cut to the action as the motorman enters and leaves, a fade-out/fade-in to another shot of the clock, the hands set a while later. Thus two hours of event could be edited to less than ten minutes of film. By another common film trick, the camera could show a close shot of the clock face. Then, as the film winds in time-lapse, the hands sweep past minutes like seconds, then stop for the next action in time so quickly advanced. It is as much a cinematic effect as Hemingway ever wrote in a story, yet Robert Siodmak ignored it in making his film. But then it is not really to be expected that Siodmak would look in the story for author's notes about how he should be directing his film.

A very similar clock effect, incidentally, is found in *For Whom the Bell Tolls*. It is very early in the morning before the dawn when Robert Jordan has to blow up the bridge. Maria is sleeping, but Jordan is thinking too hard to be sleeping. Chapter 35 ends, "He lay there holding her very lightly, feeling her breathe and feeling her heart beat, and keeping track of the time on his wrist watch." Chapter 36 follows the progress of Andres through enemy lines as he tries to take word to command headquarters that the attack must be cancelled. Chapter 37 comes back to Jordan. "Now Robert Jordan lay with the girl and he watched time passing on his wrist." Hemingway mentions the watch other times, too. When Louis Bromfield wrote the original movie script for *For Whom the Bell*

*Tolls*, he noticed some of Hemingway's cinematic effects. Over and again Bromfield focused on the watch dial, as in this striking dissolve.

| | |
|---|---|
| MARIA: | If it comes it will be soon: |
| JORDAN: | (Still regarding his watch, as if hypnotized): Yes—soon. (Maria leans against him fondly. We see again the face of the watch. It is now 4:27.) |
| *Dissolve to:* | (Through the face of the watch we dissolve to the face of a different watch. As the camera pulls back, we see a perfectly bare room with a table, two or three chairs, military maps on the wall. At the table sits [General] Golz in uniform. . . . He picks up the wristwatch that lies on the table before him. We see the dial. It is now 4:29.) |

Dudley Nichols rewrote the script and such shots were not used.

As Max commented when George explained that it was only five o'clock and not twenty minutes past, "Oh, to hell with the clock." In the major works, in sustained and important ways, did Hemingway write as for film, and did Hollywood care?

CHAPTER VIII

# Hemingway's Cinematic Style

Louella Parsons once praised Hemingway as "not only one of the greatest novelists of our era but one of the greatest screen writers as well."[1] The readers of her *Cosmopolitan* column, headed "Hemingway's Magic Touch," would have understood that Miss Parsons meant that his characters and what happened to them in his stories and all the powerful feelings they experienced made his material great for the movies. They would not have thought that she meant, and presumably she was not referring to, his way of writing. The style did not have much to do with the movies.

This is a version of the critical question about the writer as artist. Hemingway was a great artist for the aesthetic value of his style more than for the effect or significance of the content of his books, which made him a great writer. Of course these are not clearly divisible concepts. The style does affect the material even when the reader has slight regard for it. One may suppose, however, that most of Hemingway's readers respond to him as a writer rather than as an artist and are not especially appreciative of or attentive to the style, even when it is a very conspicuous style. Those who are very aware of the style tend to be critics, serious students and their serious teachers, and other writers. They might be screenplay writers, too. Whether of Hemingway's own generation or the next, some of his adapters admired his style extremely much, and their ambition, as writers, was to learn from him.

Ranald MacDougall, who wrote *The Breaking Point*, has said that studying *To Have and Have Not* as closely as he did then was the best discipline that he had ever undergone as a writer. He discovered that as an artist Hemingway was an extremely polished simplifier. MacDougall would have made the gesture to imitate the effect, but it was "like trying to copy Brancusi," and was not successful.

A. E. Hotchner, adapting the Nick Adams stories, talked over with Hemingway this same problem of finding an equation in film for the simplicity of style. They decided between themselves that the stories needed tight camera work, that they should be filmed without color and without wide-screen effect. It was not literally that Hemingway's writing was small-screen and black-and-white; the figure of speech only suggested an appropriateness of gesture towards a controlled, austere style.

Hotchner discussed the same ideas with his producer, Jerry Wald, and it seemed that Wald understood. In a 1960 press conference to announce the the production of *Hemingway's Adventures of a Young Man,* Wald insisted that the movie was going to be a small-scale production. The time for the epic movie was past. "Forget the big screen and get back to the story. It is with the works of literature that Hollywood can regain its lost audience."[2] Perhaps Wald was saying so because he doubted, at a time of tight money at Twentieth Century-Fox, that the production would be allowed very much of a budget. He would not want to admit that he was compelled to make a cheap movie. It turned out that he was later given the money for Cinemascope, which was the format in which his audience liked literature best. With a small screen and in black and white, his picture might have made no more money than a foreign film in a shabby art theater where college kids go.

As a young man, Denne Petitclerc, who wrote the screenplay for *Islands in the Stream,* copied out Hemingway's fiction in longhand in order to learn the style. It was the way students of a previous century had learned to write by copying extensive passages from Addison and Steele. But Petitclerc's respect did not mean that he could write Hemingway's style into a movie. What is written in the script is essentially dialogue, where the distinctive style is not found.

A film's style develops in the way that the cameras are directed within the scene and, afterwards, in the way that the film is edited. But Franklin Schaffner, who was attentive to every problem of montage as well as *mise en scène* in the production of *Islands in the Stream*, did not feel that his purpose was to discover Hemingway's style. His actor, George C. Scott, might think of himself as dramatizing a Hemingway character, but Schaffner himself would not pretend that he, as director, was playing the role of Hemingway as author. Indeed Schaffner would as soon not have known who had written the book, as if a consciousness of Hemingway's style might interfere with his sense of an appropriate style for the film.

Some sequences from a few of the Hemingway movies might seem like a close film translation from prose. When that happens, it is a lucky effect more accidental than sought. But it is no reason to be disappointed with the Hollywood versions of Hemingway because his style seldom was filmed. The style is Hemingway's peculiarly literary quality. Why would anyone expect to find it, even *wish* to find it, anywhere other than in the writing itself?

Yet because the media of literature and film are only different and not completely alien to each other, a valid and important critical question remains about the relation of Hemingway's style to the aesthetic theory of film. As a question having to do with Hollywood's Hemingway movies, it is hard to see any relevance to it. Nevertheless, as long as there has been critical intellection about the arts, critics have found it very natural and illuminating to think in the comparatist's way, their appreciation of one art informing their appreciation of a different art.

Though he did not want to sound like a professor or critic, Hemingway easily thought as a comparatist. He once said that Melville was like a left-handed pitcher without control anymore, though he was still very good for having played with so many clubs and learned all the tricks.[3] One may feel sure that Hemingway was very pleased with himself for having understood this, even if he was making a joke.

Hemingway knew that bullfighting was a very serious art. Across the following paragraph of *Death in the Afternoon* Hemingway passes at several comparisons to other arts and to sports:

> When I first saw bullfights the only part I did not like was the banderillas. They seemed to make such a great and cruel change in the bull. . . . When the banderillas are in he is done for. They are the sen-

> tencing. The first act is the trial, the second act is the sentencing and the third the execution. But afterwards when I learned how much more dangerous the bull becomes as he goes on the defensive, how, after the banderillas have sobered him and his speed of foot has been cut he aims every horn stroke, as a hunter aims at an individual bird in a covey rather than shooting at them all and missing, and finally, when I learned the things that can be done with him as an artistic property when he is properly slowed and still has kept his bravery and his strength I kept my admiration for him always, but felt no more sympathy for him than for a canvas or the marble a sculpture cuts or the dry powder snow your skies cut through.
>
> I know no modern sculpture, except Brancusi's, that is in any way the equal of the sculpture of modern bullfighting.

In another passage from *Death in the Afternoon* Hemingway described the technique of a matador he especially admired:

> The fact is that the gypsy, Cagancho, can sometimes, through the marvellous wrists that he has, perform the usual movements of bullfighting so slowly that they become, to old-time bullfighting, as the slow motion picture is to the ordinary motion picture. It is as though a diver could control his speed in the air and prolong the vision of a swan dive, which is a jerk in actual life, although in photographs it seems a long glide, to make it a long glide like the dives and leaps we sometimes take in dreams.

It is a provocative comparison, because of the suggestion that the perception of film, our subconscious reception of film, is like the surreal projection of dream. This might be Hemingway's only comparative reference to film.

Though Hemingway's own critical writing does not show that this is true, film winds and rewinds through the critical awareness of his generation and the next. Many critics writing about Hemingway develop the idea more or less successfully that his writing is like film.

W. H. Frohock, in his 1947 essay "Violence and Discipline," argues that *A Farewell to Arms* is not a very substantial novel in the conventional sense of the term.

> Few books are made of less material. Hemingway depends almost entirely on the trained and disciplined eye, and the carefully accurate report on the emotions. The end product may be—and I believe it is—closer to a good movie script than to a conventional novel. . . .
>
> I do not mean that Hemingway was working on this book . . . with Hollywood production . . . in mind. I do mean that in large portions

> of the book his eye is working as the camera works when it is responsible to a good director.

Frohock then ennumerates the ways:

> Time is relentlessly foreshortened: chapter one takes you through a whole fall and part of a winter of a war, in a series of impressions briefly sketched, one flowing into another, by a sort of selection very much like that of the narrating lens. . . . By the end of chapter three you have Henry back from his winter leave and spring coming on; what has intervened amounts to nothing—you know this from the stream-of-memory stuff, the familiar flashback technique which was probably an even more common device in the day of silent film than it is now.[4]

It may be doubted that the flashback technique really was more common in silent film than in film of the 1940s. Even if it were so, the fact would not support the idea that Frohock almost explicitly says, that Hemingway learned the technique—that if narrative can go forward it can also go back—from the movies. Writing about the epic quality of *For Whom the Bell Tolls*, Carlos Baker remarks that "Homer knew and used (if indeed he did not invent) the device of flashback."[5] Baker does not suggest Hemingway learned the device from reading Homer.

Frohock's point about the sequence of impressions in the opening passage, like camera shots selected by "the narrating lens," is more pertinent to the question of Hemingway's renowned style. Frohock selects another passage for quotation and analysis in support of the same point. In chapter 8 the description of Frederic's ambulance climbing to the mountain front is "handled as if the camera were mounted on the truck."

> We were in the foot-hills on the near side of the river and as the road mounted there were high mountains off the north with snow still on the tops. I looked back and saw the three cars all climbing, spaced by the intervals of their dust. We passed a long column of loaded mules, the drivers walking along beside the mules wearing red fezzes. They were bersaglieri.

Frohock continues the illustration for one more paragraph, then comments: "This is straight movie script, complete with everything but the shooting directions, the lens being permitted to pick up more or less, and to hold it longer or shorter times, according to the mood of Frederic Henry."[6] This is to say that the narration is like a strip of film that Frederic Henry directs from his point of view. The comment "They were bersaglieri" is not cinematic because it is interpretive. The pronouns "I" and "We" give a subjectivity to the passage that would disappear in the mechanism of the camera. But the progression of discrete images does seem very much like a series of shots edited into the continuum of film. If one thought it worthwhile, in a mountain location with ambulances, drivers, and mules, one could shoot the passage so that it shows what Frederic says that he sees. What one could *not* do successfully, though, is film the way that he writes it, with the same diction, grammar, syntax, and cadence.

Let such an experiment be imagined. Project a film clip such as this passage describes for a perceptive, literate viewer who does not have the book. As the film runs and reruns, have him write down what he sees. It is unlikely that the descriptive style would match Hemingway's own. The lines in question happen to be written in a simple way that is not especially interesting for its style. If one were to try with the wonderful opening pages of *A Farewell to Arms*, one could not possibly make a film that would adequately stand for the style, even if it included everything shown on the page.

> In the late summer of that year we lived in a house in a village that looked across the river and the plain to the mountains. In the bed of the river there were pebbles and boulders, dry and white in the sun, and the water was clear and swiftly moving and blue in the channels. Troops went by the house and down the road and the dust they raised powdered the leaves of the trees. The trunks of the trees too were dusty and the leaves fell early that year and we saw the troops marching along the road and the dust rising and leaves, stirred by the breeze, falling and the soldiers marching and afterward the road bare and white except for the leaves.
>
> The plain was rich with crops; there were many orchards and fruit trees and beyond the plain the mountains were brown and bare. There was fighting in the mountains and at night we could see the flashes from the artillery. In the dark it was like summer lightning, but the nights were cool and there was not the feeling of a storm coming.

Ford Madox Ford described his response when he read the novel's beginning:

> I experienced a singular sensation on reading the first sentence of *A Farewell to Arms*. There are sensations you cannot describe. You may know what causes them but you cannot tell what portions of your mind they affect nor yet, possibly, what parts of your physical entity. I can only say that it was as if I had found at last again something shining after a long delving amongst dust. I daresay prospectors after gold or diamonds feel something like that.[7]

Sometimes it truly is this exciting to respond to Hemingway's discovery of possibilities for the art of a written language—seemingly simple possibilities about the coordination of images by conjunction and cadence—such as perhaps had never been read like this anywhere else. It is an art in writing that is untranslatable into a language of film.

It was just as well, then, that Frank Borzage simply ignored the opening pages of *A Farewell to Arms* in making his film. His opening shot lasts for about fifteen seconds of film. A blank screen after the titles: then the camera holds for a moment on a vista of mountain peaks, snow-covered, next to clouds, on a further range. Then the camera angles down to the left and moves past the face of a soldier lying dead next to the root of a tree. The camera pans slowly over his body to a long shot of ambulances in convoy climbing the road. Borzage's meaning with the shot, that in the beauty of this mountain scene there is the dying of war, and Borzage's effect, as we are startled to see the corpse there, are not the same as Hemingway's thought and emotion. But Borzage's possibilities with a style are simply and properly for film. The shot is the movement, selection, and discovery which a camera does well. The effect of the shot is not purely photographic. Without the soundtrack—a light melody in woodwinds giving over to the deep minor notes of a grim fanfare in brass—one might think for a moment that a man is taking a nap. But sound, too, is a possibility of film that is not shared with writing.

One expects any medium to seek its own style. This is the opening of a radio adaptation of *A Farewell to Arms*. A host for the program has set the scene for the play, said who is in it, playing what characters, from whose novel, where and when the story takes place. An orchestra overture introduces Frederic March speaking in Frederic Henry's voice:

> (*Music down*) In the summer of 1916 the Italian front wasn't so bad. We had Austrians across the line. They weren't looking for any trouble 'n neither were we. Every once in a while some brass would show up from the general staff and then there'd be a few artillery shells tossed back and forth—not much. In the night there was fighting in the hills. We could see the flashes from the big guns.
>
> (*Italian street music up, then to fade*) The company was quartered in the small village at the foot of the big mountain. The wine wasn't bad and the roof didn't leak, so we were satisfied. We were an ambulance company, but there wasn't much doing. . . .

Of course this is not the actual speech as the character says it. This is only a written transcript of it, and one does not hear the very casual tone and all the easy conversational features of speech, which the style of the written version, as by its contractions, incompletely suggests. It might be a stupid reduction of Hemingway's content: "The wine wasn't bad, and the roof didn't leak." It is, however, the obviously appropriate style for a radio show because it is so talky. One also notices by the comparison how different is Hemingway's writing from the mannerisms of conversational speech.

Marshall McLuhan offers a strong proposition about the relation of media to each other. He demonstrates the proposition first with a light bulb, which he uses as an example of "a medium without a message, as it were, unless it is used to spell out some verbal message or name." The light has a use but no content of its own until it is used as a sign to make print. This, McLuhan says, is comprehensively true:

> This fact, characteristic of all media, means that the content of any medium is always another medium. The content of writing is speech, just as the written word is the content of the telegraph. If it is asked, "What is the content of speech?" it is necessary to say, "It is the actual process of thought, which is itself nonverbal."[8]

If McLuhan is correct in this, adaptations, such as between literature and film, ought to be excellent illustrations of his idea.

What, according to McLuhan, is the content of film? What would one wish it to be for the discussion at hand: the content of film is the novel.

> The close relation . . . between the reel world of film and the private fantasy experience of the printed word is indispensable to our West-

> ern experience of the film form. Even the film industry regards all of its greatest achievements as derived from novels, nor is this unreasonable. Film, both in its reel form and in its scenario or script form, is completely involved with book culture.[9]

McLuhan's point is not refuted simply by reference to footage of any Hemingway movie that seems far less than "completely involved" with Hemingway's book. The difference only means that the adapters have departed from the content of *Hemingway's* novel to favor some alternative idea of a novel which they have come up with themselves. The opening shot of Borzage's *A Farewell to Arms* is in fact a fragment of narrative about a soldier found dead in a remote place. The premise is not developed into a story, but one knows there are possibilities there, as in the Middle English narrative poem about the corbies that find a new slain knight.

Graham Greene's *The Third Man* became an adaptation by a unusual turn. In his preface to the novel Greene explains that he was invited to write an original film, but that before he could do the screenplay his imagination had to create a novel.

> To me it is almost impossible to write a film play without first writing a story. Even a film depends on more than plot, on a certain measure of characterization, on mood and atmosphere; and these seem to me almost impossible to capture for the first time in the dull shorthand of a script. One can reproduce an effect caught in another medium, but one cannot make the first act of creation in script form. One must have the sense of more material than one needs to draw on. *The Third Man*, therefore, though never intended for publication, had to start as a story before it began those apparently interminable transformations from one treatment to another.

Thus *The Third Man* was an odd book in that it was "never written to be read but only to be seen."

Of course fine films are often made from original scripts for which a novel never exists; indeed, there does not even have to be so much as a script. It happens that Greene's experience with *The Third Man* agrees with McLuhan's proposition. Whether one wishes to controvert their position or not, both McLuhan and Greene are talking about man's extension of meaning, or content, from one medium to another. They are not talking about the expression of art. Even when Greene mentions such abstract qualities as mood and atmosphere, or "*effect* caught in another medium," he is referring to content. However, for its *style*, as distinct from its content, film extends its own capabilities as a medium. The style of film may be contiguous at some points with the style of the novel. But the art of the film is not derived from the art of a novel insofar as it is a written arrangement of words.

When the style of novel and film at all seem the same, critics want to conclude that one imitates the other. It might have been nearly futile, this discussion has shown, for film to attempt to imitate the great and essential ways of Hemingway's style. To turn the question around: if only in inessential ways, was Hemingway's style imitative of film, as is often said? Frank D. McConnell, for example, quotes the first paragraph of *A Farewell to Arms* to show how the style is symptomatic of Frederic Henry's mind as it is disillusioned with a romantic vision of the world. Feeling as he does, his language is remote from the view it describes in the way that a lens is objectively disinterested in all that it sees. "This is language," McConnell says, "imitating the supposed impartiality of the camera."[10]

McConnell's idea may be only figuratively instructive. It is true that certain writers have created a style in imitation of film. Alain Robbe-Grillet, "new wave" French novelist and film director, is sometimes an extreme instance of this.[11] And American writers of Hemingway's generation have been keenly interested in learning from film in one way or another—Dos Passos, Farrell, and various others. It was simply not an interest that Hemingway shared. In the famous *Paris Review* interview Hemingway tried to answer what he called George Plimpton's "very good but solemn question" about his "literary forebears." Trying not to be solemn, Hemingway named many writers, many painters (Tintoretto, Bosch, Bruegel, and others including impressionists), and two composers (Bach and Mozart) as well who had influenced him.[12] Probably it would not have occurred to him to classify film directors with writers, painters, and composers. And it may be wondered whether he really knew that there was a way creatively to study film, even though he did know wonderfully well the interrelation of arts.

Edward Murray is sure that Hemingway did have a "cinematic

imagination" (which expression is the title of Murray's book, one chapter of which is given over to Hemingway), but not until the mid-Thirties, after *A Farewell to Arms*. "Ernest Hemingway has often been called a cinematic writer; but it is only in his fiction of his middle period that we find him imitating motion picture construction." (In the word "construction" one sees that Murray is considering a larger structure of style than the cadenced arrangement of words.) Except to imply that the production of two Spanish Civil War documentary films might have had something to do with it, Murray concedes that "it is not easy to say why Hemingway was drawn to cinematic form in the thirties."[13] Nevertheless, Murray argues that such a story as "The Capital of the World," published in 1936, shows Hemingway consciously employing "a filmic crosscutting technique."

In "The Capital of the World" a boy, Paco, playing at matador, bleeds to death from a "goring," an artery severed by one of the butcher knives wrapped to the legs of the chair his friend Enrique has been charging at him, as if a bull. Near the end of the story:

> As the doctor from the first-aid station came up the stairs accompanied by a policeman who held on to Enrique by the arm, the two sisters of Paco were still in the moving picture palace of the Gran Via, where they were intensely disappointed in the Garbo film, which showed the great star in miserable low surroundings when they had been accustomed to see her surrounded by great luxury and brilliance. The audience disliked the film thoroughly and were protesting by whistling and stamping their feet. All the other people from the hotel were doing almost what they had been doing when the accident happened, except that the two priests had finished their devotions and were preparing for sleep, and the gray-haired picador had moved his drink over to the table with the two houseworn prostitutes. A little later he went out of the cafe with one of them. It was the one for whom the matador who had lost his nerve had been buying drinks.

The passage is indeed like crosscutting from one scene to another taking place at the same time, or a little later. Not all of the story is like this: the strange next paragraph is purely subjective, Hemingway saying what the boy Paco is not thinking about now, since he is dead. But there are other paragraphs which show the same construction. To Murray it seems important that in the paragraph quoted Hemingway alludes to a movie—*Anna Christie* (MGM, 1930), with Greta Garbo. "It is interesting to note," Murray says, "that Hemingway's 'Capital of the World' . . . borrows filmic techniques for material that deals with motion pictures."[14] That strengthens Murray's argument, but there is mention of movies in "The Killers," too, which is a cinematic story in some ways, and that story dates from ten years before Murray marks the beginning of Hemingway's cinematic period.

The following passage is from the story "Up in Michigan," which Murray does not discuss:

> Jim began to feel great. He loved the taste and the feel of whiskey. He was glad to be back to a comfortable bed and warm food and the shop. He had another drink. The men came in to supper feeling hilarious but acting very respectable. Liz sat at the table after she put the food on and ate with the family. It was a good dinner. The men ate seriously. After supper they went into the front room again and Liz cleaned off with Mrs. Smith. Then Mrs. Smith went upstairs and pretty soon Smith came out and went upstairs too. Jim and Charley were still in the front room. Liz was in the kitchen next to the stove pretending to read a book and thinking about Jim. She didn't want to go to bed yet because she knew Jim would be coming out and she wanted to see him as he went out so she could take the way he looked up to bed with her.

There is more crosscutting here than in "The Capital of the World," but "Up in Michigan," from 1923, was in Hemingway's first book, *Three Stories & Ten Poems*. We may metaphorically call it crosscutting, but cannot suppose that he learned it from movies or was imitating the construction of film. It might be an equally interesting argument that he learned this technique of his structure from Bach's counterpoint. Quoting again from the *Paris Review* interview: "I should think what one learns from composers and from the study of harmony and counterpoint would be obvious."[15]

Of Hemingway's novels it is *For Whom the Bell Tolls* that seems most obviously cinematic. "With the publication of *For Whom the Bell Tolls* at the end of the decade," to quote Murray, "the cinematic tendencies of Hemingway's fiction of the middle period finally become unmistakable."[16]

It is very easy to go to this book to find where Hemingway shifts point of view rapidly and cleanly, as if a film were cutting from one shot to the next. In chapter 15, Anselmo is watching on the road to keep mark of enemy troop movement:

> As he crouched . . . he heard a motorcar on the road. It had on chains and one link of the chain was slapping and, as he watched, it came up over the snow covered road, green and brown painted, in broken patches of daubed color, the windows blued over so that you could not see in, with only a half circle left clean in the blue for the occupants to look out through.

Then the narration cuts back to Anselmo's point of view:"The car passed in the snow directly below him. Anselmo saw the chauffeur, red-faced and steel-helmeted."

Chapters are intercut with each other. The night before the attack Robert Jordan sends Andres to pass through enemy lines with a message for General Golz to cancel everything because apparently the Fascists have learned their plans. The narrative structure across chapters 33–42 is like a cinematic editing between scenes of Jordan in the sleeping robe with Maria and later with the guerilla band preparing for the demolition of the bridge (chapters 33, 35, 37–39, 41) and scenes on the Republican side of the lines as Andres tries to get through to headquarters (chapters 34, 36, 40, 42).

There are many flashback passages, if one will call them that. The novel opens with Robert Jordan and Anselmo on the mountain slope looking down in the distance toward the bridge that must be exploded. Three pages later there is a flashback in Jordan's memory to the night-before-last meeting with General Golz when the orders were given. Not only does Jordan often remember, as in flashback, so do other characters, too. In flashback Rafael tells the story of the blowing of the Fascist train. That was when the band of Pablo rescued Maria. Late in the novel Maria tells the story of the Fascist atrocities against her. The most vivid horror of the novel is Pilar's telling of the day when Pablo led the capture of the Fascist town and the atrocities then.

There are other cinematic qualities to the book besides that of its construction. It is sometimes written in intensely visual description, as with the sharp, hard focus of a lens. On the opening page, for example:

> The young man who was studying the country, took his glasses from the pocket of his faded, khaki flannel shirt, wiped the lenses with a handkerchief, screwed the eyepieces around until the boards of the mill showed suddenly clearly and he saw the wooden bench beside the door; the huge pile of sawdust that rose behind the open shed where the circular saw was, and a stretch of the flume that brought the logs down from the mountainside on the other bank of the stream. The stream showed clear and smooth-looking in the glasses.

One has seen this simple optic effect in the movies often enough. A character looks through binoculars; the far view blurs into focus through a masked frame. The trick was *not* used in the movie of *For Whom the Bell Tolls*, by the way.

In some descriptive passages there is a sense of, one might say, camera placement, field of view, and range, as when a weapon, or a camera, is aimed. In chapter 21 Robert Jordan wakens in danger:

> . . . and then he saw the horseman coming through the trees. He crouched now in the robe and holding the pistol in both hands aimed it at the man as he rode toward him. He had never seen this man before.
>
> The horseman was almost opposite him now. He was riding a big gray gelding and he wore a khaki beret, a blanket cape like a pancho, and heavy black boots. From the scabbard on the right of the saddle projected the stock and the long oblong clip of a short automatic rifle. He had a young, hard face and at this moment he saw Robert Jordan.
>
> He reached his hand down toward the scabbard and as he swung low, turning and jerking at the scabbard, Robert Jordan saw the scarlet of the formalized device he wore on the left breast of his khaki blanket cape.
>
> Aiming at the center of his chest, a little lower than the device, Robert Jordan fired.

One may compare this with the sequence of shots in the Hollywood version of the same action.

> *Long shot* Jordan and Maria in f.g. [foreground] looking off.
> *Medium long shot* Jordan and Maria by rock in f.g.—trooper entering in b.g.
> *Medium long shot* trooper looking off. He reaches for gun.
> *Closeup* Jordan turning around; Maria tipped in.

> *Medium long shot* trooper. He pulls gun.
> *Medium long shot* Jordan and Maria. Maria ducks down as Jordan draws gun.
> *Medium shot* trooper. He aims gun.
> *Medium long shot* Jordan. He fires off.
> *Medium shot* trooper. He gets shot, starts to fall from horse.
> *Close shot* feet and legs of horse. Gun falls into scene.
> *Long shot (high angle)* trooper on horse. Horse starts away, rears up, throwing trooper out of scene.
> *Medium long shot* Jordan rises, runs out. Maria enters around rock, looks off. Pablo enters in b.g.
> *Long shot* horse runs in, dragging trooper.
> *Camera pans.* Trooper's foot breaks loose from stirrup and he falls to ground. Horse runs out.

The approximate effect of Hemingway's shifting point of view can be suggested by film, even though in the film there are more cuts at a faster pace than the passage directs. One effect of Hemingway's editing has to be lost. That is the strong way that he shifts point of view between clauses, counter to a stylistic convention of unity. "He had a young, hard face and at this moment he saw Robert Jordan." The same effect is in the next sentence. Also, Jordan's way of seeing is not exactly like a camera's. His mind sees very particular details—the ammunition clip, the insigne—in a way that a camera at this distance could not select.

There are other great paragraphs where a character aims (all of them anticipating Jordan's target on the last page of the book). In his important essay "Observations on the Style of Ernest Hemingway," Harry Levin quotes another passage that aims at a target. El Sordo, trapped on top of the hill, lying perfectly still and pretending he's dead, waits gleefully for an officer with more bravado than sense to walk up the hill and take count of the bodies. There is a satisfaction for El Sordo that he will take someone with him in dying.

> Come on, Comrade Voyager. . . . Keep on coming with your eyes forward . . . Look. With a red face and blond hair and blue eyes. With no cap on and his moustache is yellow. With blue eyes. With pale blue eyes. With pale blue eyes with something wrong with them. With pale blue eyes that don't focus. Close enough. Too close. Yes, Comrade Voyager. Take it, Comrade Voyager.

Levin comments on this.

> Prose gets as near as it can to physical conflict here. The figure enlarges as it advances, the quickening impression grows clear and sharp and almost unbearable, whereupon it is blackened out by El Sordo's rifle. Each clipped sentence, each prepositional phrase, is like a new frame in a strip of film; indeed the whole passage, like so many others, might have been filmed by the camera and projected on the screen.[17]

The film metaphor has a limited success here. The view of the enemy officer is not really enlarging and clearing in focus. Rather, this is El Sordo's awareness searching out details. The fragments of sentences do not really move as a film moves steadily through a projector. The movement is more like the way that a film strip, not a movie, is geared through a projector with stops. The effect could be suggested by a series of shots, to the face of the enemy captain: a long shot, to a medium long, to a close shot. But in the film as was made of the passage, the shots of the captain were intercut with shots of El Sordo in the rhythm of alternation as in the sequence before when the horseman was killed.

| | |
|---|---|
| *Close shot* El Sordo behind body of horse. He slips down behind it, sights along gun. | CAPTAIN: (*calling indistinctly—off*) |
| *Long shot (high angle)* Captain coming up steep mountainside, waving gun. | EL SORDO: Now, comrade voyager! Close enough, comrade voyager! |
| *Medium long shot (high angle)* Captain coming forward. | CAPTAIN: Can you hear me coming?! |
| *Closeup* El Sordo squinting along Lewis gun's sights. | CAPTAIN: No, you can't hear me coming! |
| El Sordo fires gun. | CAPTAIN: (*off*) I am going to spit— |
| *Close shot* Captain. He gets shot, falls to ground. | CAPTAIN: —right— |
| *Long shot (high angle)* Captain rolling down side of mountain—butt of machine gun visible in f.g. | |
| *Closeup* El Sordo firing gun and laughing. | |

Some of the content of El Sordo's voice-over is carried across from the book. In the way of seeing what happens in the passage, however, it does not seem that the film is adapted from what Levin calls Hemingway's "cinematographic" prose style.[18]

Both classical and romantic critics wondered about the way that a poem should be like or is like a picture. For ages and ages this was an important critical theme. In this century critics will speak of how a novel could be like or is like a motion picture. For most of this century everyone of our culture has had an awareness of film, and as writers are in advance of the critics, they might have felt the influence of film before it was analyzed for them.

Gertrude Stein had a wonderfully simple understanding of this. In her lecture "Portraits and Repetition" she explained how she wanted to represent reality as it *is, not* as it is remembered, not as it *was*. "Funnily enough," Gertrude Stein said, "the cinema has offered a solution of this thing. By a continuously moving picture of any one there is no memory of any other thing and there is that thing existing." By her style of advancing an almost the same statement or image over and over again, she tried to give an impression of an experience of reality that is happening now.

But no, she further explained, she was not actually thinking of film while she was making this style. "I of course did not think of it in terms of the cinema, in fact I doubt whether at that time I had ever seen a cinema but, and I cannot repeat this too often any one is of one's period and this our period was undoubtedly the period of cinema and series production. And each of us in our own way are bound to express what the world in which we are living is doing."[19]

CHAPTER IX

# The Hemingway Hero as Hollywood Star

In one of the letters Hemingway wrote to his Hollywood agent Donald Friede in the spring of 1942, he discussed the Hollywood star system and what effect it would have on the success of *For Whom the Bell Tolls* as a picture. Some people, Hemingway said, went to the movies from habit and because they had nothing else to do. Others went to the movies not so much to see the picture as to see the stars playing in it. When it happened that a truly great movie also had great stars, untold numbers of people would see it.[1] When that letter was written, Hemingway still was not sure who the players in *For Whom the Bell Tolls* would be. The script was coming around, Friede had told him. Now everything depended on the cast.

Whenever it was that Hemingway began to be sure that *For Whom the Bell Tolls* was a book for the movies, that early he probably began to think about the casting. It is often supposed that Hemingway wrote the book thinking of Gary Cooper as Robert Jordan and Ingrid Bergman as Maria.[2] (If that were true, Hemingway should have won some brassy Academy Award.) Cooper had played Frederic Henry in *A Farewell to Arms*, the only Hemingway movie before *For Whom the Bell Tolls*. At a private screening arranged for him at Sun Valley, Hemingway had seen Ingrid Bergman in *Intermezzo* (UA), her first American picture, in 1939. Hemingway must have been impressed with her as much and for the same reasons as almost everyone else who saw *Intermezzo*. Later the press would report that he decided right then that she would be Maria if a movie were made.[3] Probably many novelists were thinking it would be nice to watch Ingrid Bergman as heroine of their works-in-progress.

Hemingway met Gary Cooper for the first time on September

28, 1940, at Sun Valley. The novel was finished by then, and during the times they spent hunting together, the strong friendship began. It obviously did not matter that Hemingway had had black thoughts about the movie version of *A Farewell to Arms*. He talked with Cooper as if he should play Jordan, and he gave him a copy of the new novel to read in galleys.

In Hollywood, Donald Friede was bargaining hard with RKO, MGM, and Twentieth-Century Fox, as well as Paramount. It might have been Cooper's influence that tilted the sale to Paramount. Cooper asked Cecil B. DeMille to read a prepublication copy; DeMille told Frank Freeman, production head at Paramount, that they ought to buy it.[4] The contract with Paramount was signed on October 25, 1940. Hemingway might have said something then about how it would be good and very suitable to him if Cooper and Bergman were signed for the leads. However, it seems he did not feel it was his place to be really insistent about the casting "in the face of such a hell of a deal" Paramount had given him with money that would run to about $150,000.[5]

Actually, there was nothing Hemingway could insist upon. It could not work so simply, that Paramount would name Hemingway's ideal cast. Cooper was under exclusive contract to Samuel Goldwyn; Bergman was under contract to David O. Selznick. Stars could be "loaned" from studio to studio, at very high prices and only after complicated negotiations. That would take a while.

Paramount was not in a rush to settle the casting anyway. The studio would let there be another great, nationally publicized "talent search"—like Selznick's search to cast the role of Scarlett O'Hara. That was an excellent way to excite the public's interest in the production. By December, Paramount had sent out a questionnaire to 150 book reviewers around the country, asking their advice. The newspapers would write about that, though one can imagine how little attention Paramount executives and producer Sam Wood would pay to those suggestions.[6] Movie fans began sending in letters, thousands of them during the next year. As if to do *Gone With the Wind* again, Clark Gable and Vivien Leigh were often nominated. Among other actors were Tyrone Power and Errol Flynn. Actresses included Barbara Stanwyck, Katharine Hepburn, Ida Lupino, Paulette Goddard, and Frances Farmer. (Frances Farmer was a blonde that Hemingway liked to look at, and he had wanted her for the lead in the 1939 Theatre Guild production of *The Fifth Column*, though Katherine Locke got the part.) Leading the public opinion sampling were the names of Cooper and Bergman, possibly because the press had let the public understand that they were Hemingway's preferences.[7]

National coverage was given to Hemingway's first meeting with Ingrid Bergman on January 30, 1941. Hemingway and his wife were in San Francisco preparing to embark for China. It was arranged for Ingrid Bergman to come from Nevada, where she was vacationing, to have lunch with them. *Life* ran pictures of the event. The accompanying article noted that "exacting author Hemingway was obviously pleased with Miss Bergman, discussed the role at great length with her over a salad and dry white wine. He explained that in the movie she would have to wear her hair cut short and laughingly asked to see her ears to judge their photogenic qualities." Hemingway was quoted as saying, "If you don't act in this picture, Ingrid, I won't work on it."[8] He was kidding about that. There had never been any idea that he would work on the picture.

Hemingway got to know Ingrid Bergman much better during the fall of 1941 when she and her husband vacationed in Sun Valley. By this time he was calling her "daughter." Why he should have been so fond of her is easily understandable. In his memoir of his father, Gregory Hemingway describes him as having been rather foolishly infatuated with her that season (which he misremembers as 1940 instead of 1941, as it was).[9] Perhaps it was an exaggerated impression; Gregory was only ten years old at the time. Whatever was the quality of Hemingway's affection for her, he could see her as Maria very clearly. Long before the casting was decided, he sent her a copy of *For Whom the Bell Tolls* inscribed, "To Ingrid Bergman, who is the Maria of this story."[10]

During 1941 Paramount was making hundreds of screen tests for the principal and secondary characters. Among those tested or considered for Jordan were MacDonald Carey, Rod Cameron, Robert Preston, Sterling Hayden, and Ray Milland. Among the many actresses tested for Maria were Susan Hayward, Barbara Britton, and Betty Field. Hemingway did understand that Bergman could not automatically be given the part. By one newspaper report, Hemingway put forward two other names that would be acceptable to him: Annabella, the French actress who was Tyrone Power's wife, and Miceala Taranda, a Cuban actress.[11]

By November, 1941, only one major role had been cast, Joseph Calleia as El Sordo. The first shooting of the film, the major El Sordo sequence, was done very late that month, on location in the Sierra Nevada mountains. The day the cameras were to film the bombing of El Sordo's band at the hilltop, the Japanese attacked Pearl Harbor.

In the spring Katina Paxinou was signed to play Pilar. (Nazimova had also been tested; movie fans had recommended Gloria Swanson, Pola Negri, Ethel Barrymore, Katherine Cornell, and Norma Talmadge.) Katina Paxinou would be the only cast member to win an Academy Award. Akim Tamiroff was signed as Pablo. (Lee J. Cobb had also been tested; fans had recommended Wallace Beery, Charles Laughton, and Edward G. Robinson.) Both the *New York Times* and the *Herald Tribune*, incidentally, had reported Hemingway himself to be among those being considered for Pablo's role. By one version of the rumor—without valid foundation—Hemingway had nominated himself.[12]

On March 6, 1942, Paramount signed Cooper to a contract to play Jordan, an arrangement having been made with Samuel Goldwyn whereby Cooper could do this movie for Paramount if Sam Wood would direct Cooper in *Pride of the Yankees* (1942), which was Sam Goldwyn's RKO movie about Lou Gehrig. To play Maria, Paramount signed Vera Zorina.

She was not an unknown, Vera Zorina. Movie audiences knew her as a wonderful dancer with gorgeous legs whose stage name seemed to place her in the line of the great Russian ballerinas. (Her real name was Eva Hartwig, and she was born in 1917 in Berlin, where she was trained.) Her American success began, naturally, in the New York dance world. Her first movie was *The Goldwyn Follies of 1938* (UA), a variety show which, for class, offered the audience interludes of elite culture lavishly filmed. *The*

Vera Zorina, who was originally cast as Maria in *For Whom the Bell Tolls*. She was replaced by Ingrid Bergman after one week of shooting. Courtesy of Mrs. Goddard Lieberson.

*Goldwyn Follies* featured George and Ira Gershwin songs, and also arias from *La Traviata*. It had Edgar Bergen and Charlie McCarthy in their vaudeville turn, and also a water-nymph ballet choreographed by George Balanchine for Zorina, his wife, and the American Ballet Company of the Metropolitan Opera. Zorina was an elegant success with all the critics. Then in 1939 Zorina starred in the Warner Brothers production of *On Your Toes*, the Rodgers and Hart musical. In 1940, in the Twentieth Century-Fox picture *I Was an Adventuress*, for the first time Zorina did more acting than dancing. The critics were less excited about her. The reviewer for the *New York Times* wrote, "On her toes—where she belongs—Zorina is a thing of beauty, but when she comes down to the level of ordinary folk, she is just another mediocre actress."[13] The next year, 1941, Zorina came to Paramount, and in B. G. DeSylva's production of *Louisiana Purchase* she showed that she could play comedy well. Bosley Crowther wrote, "You will see nothing lovelier, we assure you, than Zorina in Technicolor, and, to top it, she can play comedy with an airy and winning grace."[14]

It was during the filming of *Louisiana Purchase* that Buddy DeSylva asked her to do a screen test with Gary Cooper for *For Whom the Bell Tolls*. She did not expect that anything would come of it because so many actresses were being tested. Some who were being talked about most she considered to be much more gifted dramatic actresses than herself. When DeSylva told her that she had the part, she knew it must have been because DeSylva, as production head at Paramount, had decided to promote the stardom of one of Paramount's actresses rather than to negotiate longer for one of Selznick's stars. It was an extraordinarily fortunate opportunity for her.

But almost as soon as she joined the company on location, Zorina was able to sense that producer Sam Wood was resisting DeSylva's choice. The first week at the Sonora Pass in the mountains she did almost nothing except sit around in the long peasant skirt and full-sleeved blouse which seemed to her a foolish costume for a girl who was living with mountain fighters. Her hair was cut very short. She walked in front of the camera for only the briefest possible time, down from the mouth of the cave to say "Hello"—that one word only—to Robert Jordan.

At the end of the week it was explained to her that Sam Wood was worried about her smile, and that she should return to Los Angeles in order to consult with a dentist about having her teeth capped. Back in Los Angeles, before there was any dental work done, she was telephoned to be told that she was being replaced.

The studio would say to the press, vaguely, that Zorina had been found "inadequate" for the role. There was nothing that Zorina could do to protest the damaging, nearly disgracing publicity without jeopardizing her future at Paramount. (As it turned out, she would make several more musicals before retiring from the movies.)

What had happened, Zorina understood, was that by such rough play of power as typified Hollywood politics, both Sam Wood and Gary Cooper had threatened to walk off the picture if Zorina stayed. DeSylva capitulated to that pressure, and Paramount agreed to pay Selznick $120,000—almost as much as Hemingway had been paid for the rights to the story—for the privilege of "borrowing" Ingrid Bergman.

On Ingrid Bergman's side, she had been wishing for the part since her name had first been mentioned as Hemingway's Maria. She was on the set of *Casablanca* now, and during a break in the shooting she was called to the phone to be told that she had taken over the part for Zorina. It was a triumphant moment for her.

Bergman made her screen test on July 31, 1942—merely a formality—and was in the mountains one week later ready for shooting. The week after that, on August 13, at the Finca in Cuba, Hemingway received the letter from his agent Donald Friede saying that Zorina had been replaced by Ingrid after all. Hemingway had not seen the news in the papers and was almost afraid to believe it because it could be one of those things that were so good and yet not true. It was bad enough, he said, to have in Sam Wood a director who would not listen to suggestions as to what the movie should really look like. Now at least Zorina would not be spoiling the picture. He thought she had legs like Pavlova's, and her figure was all right. But he did not think she had the face for Maria. (His description for Friede was like a cartoon.) He told Friede to send him a confirmation with details. Once in Valencia Hemingway had spent what he thought were lottery winnings before the official winners were posted. He did not want it to be that way again.[16]

Ingrid Bergman was Hollywood's most photographed actress between that summer and the next, when the movie was released. She was on the covers of *Screen Guide, Ladies' Home Journal, Movie Show, Look, Motion Picture, Modern Screen, Movies, Movie Life, Cue* (twice), *Movie Story, Photoplay, Screenland,* and *Time.*

In the newspapers there were cute columns about her costume, about how there was some difficulty deciding whether her trouser legs were to be rolled to the knee or left down. Finally they were left down, and the movie would not show her calf. And the man's pants had to be tucked at the waist and the man's shirt had to be pinned inside the trousers to fit her snugly.[17]

The women's columnists wrote at length about her hair-style:

The collage of magazine covers is reproduced from the pressbook for *For Whom the Bell Tolls.*

Ingrid Bergman shows the "Maria" hair style made popular by the movie. Courtesy of Ingrid Bergman.

> Seven experts were consulted before Miss Bergman's ash-blond tresses were snipped to meet Hemingway's description. Then, Miss Bergman had an idea. To make it alluring, she said it should have a curl. As a permanent was impossible, bobby pins were put to work each morning to produce a slightly curled effect. Soon this treatment eliminated the "porcupine" appearance and the curls were alluring, feminine and very, very exciting, everybody agreed.[18]

(Perhaps this did not need to be explained in a column for women readers, but a permanent was impossible because her hair was too short to wind around curlers.) She was photographed and illustrated so often with that hairstyle that it became known as "the Maria look." Beauty shops all over the country promoted it: "The 'Maria'—Irresistible Hair-Do! As Pretty for Evening as It's Practical For Busy Days!" For women working in war industries the Paramount people wanted it known that there was "danger in long hair around moving machinery."

Hemingway would not have had the woman's interest in the fussing with Maria's hairstyle. On the other hand, it was very much like Hemingway to notice his heroine's hair. Maria's hair is described in the book as "a golden brown of a grain field that had been burned dark in the sun but it was cut short all over her head so that it was but little longer than the fur on a beaver pelt. . . . She has a beautiful face, Robert Jordan thought. She'd be beautiful if they hadn't cropped her hair." No mention is made of alluring curls. It is almost directly said that Maria is *not* beautiful with her hair the way it is (whereas Ingrid Bergman was beautiful with her hair the way it was). Maria would be beautiful because she has a beautiful face, although the reader cannot vividly imagine a detailed image of her beauty. In other lines Hemingway does say that she has high cheekbones and full lips, but these are features of most beautiful women.

Even less is said by way of particular details of description about Robert Jordan. He is a "young man, who was tall and thin, with sunstreaked fair hair, and a wind- and sun-burned face." With respect to specifics, it was a little silly, therefore, for the press to rave about the perfect comparison between characters as described in the novel and the appearance of Cooper and Bergman.

> Everything had to be exactly right, Mr. Wood explained [in a newspaper interview at the time of the premiere]. The casting was of major importance. Ernest Hemingway had described in detail the characters in *For Whom the Bell Tolls*. . . . "Hemingway wrote that book as though he had the screen in mind," Mr. Wood remarked. . . . "Those characters are described as though it were a picture. That helped, of course, in many ways. But if we didn't get those characters exactly right, all the values were gone. Hemingway must have had Gary Cooper and Ingrid Bergman in mind when he was writing."[19]

One might suppose that something similar would have been said if a different actor and actress had finally been cast—Tyrone Power, even Zorina. One does not have to mistrust Wood's sincerity, though. Wood might have believed in the star value of Cooper and Bergman that much. From the point of view of a Hemingway critic it seems to demean the novel by saying that without them "all the values were gone." But from the point of view of a Hollywood producer, it might have been the highest tribute to a novel to say that it was written "with the screen in mind."

A few movie critics thought that Wood did not have the casting quite right after all. One critic commented that Gary Cooper was somewhat unbelievable because having "played a shy, retiring man in so many pictures" (excluding *A Farewell to Arms*, one would have to say), he seemed to lack "the magnetism and strength" that guerilla fighters would have to see in a leader.[20] (Hemingway himself expected Cooper's acting in the picture to be good enough to make up for a script which, in the love scenes at least, tried to make him the shy dope of Hollywood cliché.)[21] Most other reviewers seemed to think that Cooper was right and comfortable in his flannel shirt image of the Hemingwayesque hero in war and the movies.

More than Cooper, it was Ingrid Bergman who raised objections from the realists. The reviewers did not seem to mind her accent not being Spanish (there was a clutter of accents in the movie anyway). But reviewers did think she looked "unbelievably lovely," given the war story.[22] It was difficult to believe in both the atrocity of war and a character who looked this good. Ingrid Bergman was "much too beautiful, healthy, and serene looking for the troubled girl whose innocent eyes had beheld indescribable horrors and whose tender flesh had been ravaged by beasts."[23] A British reviewer said, "Ingrid Bergman weeps convincingly, but after nine months in a mountain cave looks as if she had just been voted the prettiest polo player in Pennsylvania."[24]

Many literary critics made the same objections to the novel. Alfred Kazin said that Maria was "totally unreal."[25] Maxwell Geismar found her "more theatrical than substantial," and felt that "the central love affair was impossible except for the movies."[26] The British reviewer Edward Sackville-West spoke of "the exasperating falsity of what I can only describe as the sex interest (one eye firmly on Hollywood)." Malcolm Cowley felt that Maria was "more of a dream than . . . a woman."[28] Edmund Wilson found that the Maria material "lent itself all too readily to the movies." "This love affair with a woman in a sleeping bag," Wilson continued, "has the all too perfect felicity of a youthful erotic dream."[29] (To Wilson's opinion, Hemingway made the remark, "I have not only met more people than Edmund Wilson, but I also know a good deal more about the pleasures of sexual intercourse.")

The way in which reactions to the novel so closely match impressions from seeing the movie would seem to indicate that Ingrid Bergman was playing the image as it had been created. For even as producer Sam Wood said, Hemingway was imagining the screen in some passages of his characterization. Robert Jordan himself thinks of Maria as a star. He wishes for her to be just like he had known her in the movies:

> Maybe it is like those dreams you have when someone you have seen in the cinema comes to your bed at night and is so kind and lovely. He'd slept with them all that way when he was asleep in bed. He could remember Garbo still, and Harlow. Yes, Harlow many times. Maybe it was like those dreams.
>
> But he could still remember the time Garbo came to his bed the night before the attack at Pozoblanco and she was wearing a soft silky wool sweater when he put his arm around her and when she leaned forward her hair swept forward and over his face and she said why had he never told her that he loved her when she had loved him all this time? She was not shy, nor cold, nor distant. She was just lovely to hold and kind and lovely and like the old days with Jack Gilbert and it was as true as though it happened and he loved her much more than Harlow though Garbo was only there once while Harlow—maybe this was like those dreams.

He has to take the risk of finding out that she is not "like those dreams." He touches Maria's arm and speaks to her:

> "Hello, *Ingles*," she answered and he saw her tawny brown face and the yellow-gray eyes and the full lips smiling and the cropped sunburned hair and she lifted her face at him and smiled in his eyes. It was true all right.

And now he believes in her as much as in the night he believed in those dreams.

Two hundred pages later, the night before the assault on the bridge, Jordan and Maria are lying together, not making love right now because it would be painful for her. It is one of the times when fantasy is preferable to actuality, so they talk and lose themselves in pretending. Maria has somehow intuited what image of her most excites Jordan. Jordan asks about her hair:

> "How long will it take it to grow long?"
> "Really long?"
> "No, I mean to thy shoulders. It is thus I would have thee wear it."
> "As Garbo in the cinema?"
> "Yes," he said thickly.
> Now the making believe was coming back in a great rush and he would take it all to him. It had him now, and again he surrendered.

This dialogue was not used in the movie. Ingrid Bergman wishing to look like Greta Garbo, also Swedish, who was in retirement by then, would have sounded like a joke. Indeed, sometimes when David O. Selznick wanted to say something teasing about Ingrid Bergman he would call her "the Palmolive Garbo."

Ingrid Bergman did not have the heavily passionate mystique of Garbo or Harlow; hers was a sensuality of a different style. Yet for as many years as Garbo and Harlow, Ingrid Bergman would come into the American dreams of someone seen in the movies. Nothing Hemingway wrote about Maria was as strong an excitement as she was on the screen. Movies were more exciting than books, even more exciting than calendars.

The audience's memory for that movie seems indefinitely long. It may be said that the images of the movies are like the images of dream, but dreams are seldom so clearly remembered. Images from the movie screen can be remembered as perfectly as images of friends, or at least the snapshots of friends. In an image so bright in the darkened theater, in a close-up so huge on the screen, Ingrid Bergman—as Maria realizes what Jordan is meaning to say to her, that he will die and she will have to live her life for both of them—wept some of the most glisteningly sad tears in the history of movies. If one reads the book later, it is still Ingrid Bergman one sees.

And who is it the audience really cares about? Ingrid Bergman or the character that she plays? Gertrude Stein held that the novel was not a successful form in the twentieth century, because char-

Another publicity still the pose of which emphasizes Gary Cooper's size compared to Ingrid Bergman's.

acters in most novels did not stand out enough and did not seem important. She cited Hemingway, along with Fitzgerald and Sherwood Anderson, in demonstration of this. Readers cared about the titles of their novels, and about the form of their novels, but not about the characters in their novels. It was not this way in the century before, she continued: "You realize how they did in the Nineteenth Century. People really worried about and felt for these characters. Now, you see, even the cinema doesn't do it for them. A few actors or actresses do, but not the characters they portray." And then she asks, "Can you imagine anyone today weeping over a character? They get excited about the book but not the character."[30]

*For Whom the Bell Tolls* might be a book to use in argument with Gertrude Stein on this point. Certainly Gary Cooper and Ingrid Bergman were among the actors and actresses that people really did care about. But then people wept about Jordan and Maria before the movie was made. Still, if Gertrude Stein is at all right in this, we have another way of knowing why it is a very interesting experience, and maybe very fortunate for the novel, if a character in a book comes to exist as a character in a movie, if played by one of the actors or actresses people do care about. On the other hand, if people do care more about a few actors and actresses than they care about characters in novels, then it would seem to be an unfortunate thing for an author if the movie star is contrary to his imagination and his wish.

Catherine Barkley in *A Farewell to Arms* is a romantic idealization of the girl who in real life was Agnes Von Kurowsky. Agnes was a twenty-six-year-old American girl, one of the nurses at the hospital in Milan where Hemingway, nineteen years old, was recuperating from war wounds. Descriptions and photographs of Agnes show her as a tall brunette, attractive, but not a wonderful beauty at all. Frederic Henry describes Catherine as being "quite tall," blonde, with grey eyes and tawny skin: "I thought she was very beautiful." The book does not mention how old are Frederic and Catherine. It does not seem in any way that Frederic is younger than she is. Catherine might be in her mid-twenties. She meets Frederic in the spring of 1917. The summer before her fiancé had been killed in the Battle of the Somme. She had been engaged to him for eight years, though of course she might have been engaged very young.

As Hollywood's first Catherine, Helen Hayes was thirty-two years old, one year older than Gary Cooper as Frederic. She was not tall and slender; she was only slightly over five feet tall. Her short hair was curly brown. She was a pretty Catherine but not beautiful in the way that Hemingway was fantasizing. If she was not glamorous, however, she was certainly an excellent actress who would be able to play realistically even the most extravagantly sentimental passages of the script. Understandably, she took it amiss when she heard that Hemingway was making faintly insulting remarks about her having been given the role, calling her "the peanut," and complaining that Paramount should have cast a taller, sexier star. Hemingway was saying that Claudette Colbert should have played Catherine. Hemingway's other choice, though he did not yet know her and was several years away from becoming her very close friend, was Marlene Dietrich.

Perhaps this is not exactly what one would have expected. Colbert and Dietrich were fine actresses, but Hemingway was excited about them because they projected themselves more sensually than did Helen Hayes. Hollywood is often ridiculed for promoting the sensual image, as in lines of Karl Shapiro's poem "Hollywood": "Here all superlatives come true / And beauty is marketed like basic food." It is interesting to see in this instance of casting how taken was Hemingway himself by the glamour of stars.

Hemingway was outraged by the casting of Catherine for Selznick's remake of *A Farewell to Arms*. He was not impressed with Selznick's reputation for having a kind of genius for casting, and he did not appreciate, if he knew about, how much thought Selznick gave to some of the parts in *A Farewell to Arms*. There was, for example, the part of the ancient Count Greffi, who plays billiards with Frederic in the hotel at Stresa. Among the people Selznick wanted for the Count were John Gielgud, Alfred Lunt, Jean Cocteau, Noel Coward, Leopold Stowkowski, Frank Lloyd Wright, and

Bertrand Russell! When they were all unavailable or uninterested, Selznick decided that he would rather not use the character at all.[31] Though he had this much imagination for players, Selznick never had any other intention than to use *A Farewell to Arms* as a vehicle for his wife, Jennifer Jones. It is not known if Hemingway had some other actress in mind. (Would he have been pleased with the idea of Grace Kelly appearing as Catherine?) Hemingway was simply sore because Jennifer Jones was far too old for the part. She was thirty-eight, and Hemingway's impression was that she was even a few years older than that. According to Selznick's biographer, when Selznick offered to give Hemingway $50,000 from the movie's profits, Hemingway sent back a message expressing doubt that there would be any profits with a forty-one-year-old actress (Hemingway's wrong guess at her age) playing a twenty-four-year-old Catherine. If by some miracle the movie did show a profit, Hemingway wished that Selznick would take $50,000 in change and just shove it.[32]

Hemingway was not alone in thinking that Jennifer Jones was miscast because of her age. Hollis Alpert, for the *Saturday Review*, tried to say it kindly: "Miss Jones has a good deal of skill as an actress, but she's a fairly mature woman now, the mother of children, and that big movie screen has gruesome ways of revealing the disparity between what might be termed screen age and actual age."[33]

Her age showed up all the more because she was playing opposite Rock Hudson, who was eight years younger than she.[34] Rock Hudson's image was that of a massively handsome fraternity man, or cadet, whom the girls dreamed about for his shoulders and wavy hair. (Selznick refused to let Hudson's hair be styled for a 1917 drama because an old-fashioned haircut might ruin his image.)[35] Some of the fatuous lines which the script (not the novel) gave Rock Hudson to speak made his romance with Jennifer Jones seem nearly grotesque. For example, a surgeon asks Frederic if Catherine is his "girl." "I'm her fellah," he says bashfully and grins at her like a proud fool.

Holden Caulfield, in *Catcher in the Rye*, did not even like Frederic Henry as he acted in Hemingway's novel. Holden's brother got him to read it:

> What gets me about D. B., though, he hated the war so much, and yet he got me to read this book *A Farewell to Arms* last summer. He said it was so terrific. That's what I can't understand. It had this guy named Lieutenant Henry that was supposed to be a nice guy and all. I don't see how D. B. could hate the Army and war and all so much and still like a phony like that.

Holden should have seen Lieutenant Henry in the movie.

And yet Rock Hudson was the most popular male star in the country when the movie was made. He was not a great actor; but then it was not really a subtle enough script to need a great actor.

Selznick did attend to details of Hudson's acting, trying to make it as convincing as possible. And Selznick did give Hudson as much encouragement as he could coming into the shooting of the heavy dramatic scenes, wanting him to believe that his stature as an actor very much depended on his success with the tragic material.[36]

At the same time Selznick believed that the role of Catherine would dominate the picture, if his wife were allowed to express her interpretation freely. He especially wanted Vidor to allow her first to play a scene as she saw it: "If you direct her before getting her conceptions, I am fearful that you will lose the benefits of the intense and very lengthy study that she always gives to her roles and has given particularly to this role."[37]

Jennifer Jones might have been making it a more difficult role than it needed to be. Was there really so much for her to study? "You're a fine simple girl," Frederic says to Catherine. "I am a simple girl. No one ever understood it except you." If she is only a simple girl, perhaps she is not so interesting or challenging a character for an actress to play. Catherine actually tries to efface her own distinctive identity in order to love Frederic more perfectly. It is an idea (not a good one) that she has, that Hemingway has, about what a woman must do for her love. "There isn't any me," she tells Frederic; "I'm you. Don't make up a separate me." She gets the notion that she should have her hair cut and Frederic should let his hair grow a little longer: "Then we'd both be alike. Oh, darling, I want you so much I want to be you too." The actress who plays Catherine accurately might have to style her as vapid.

There is one way that Catherine is a little complicated. Sometimes she is, as she says, a little "gone off." Before she loves Frederic as Frederic she almost believes that he is her fiancé come back. Also, she has certain fears, including a fear that she will die in the rain.

Helen Hayes played Catherine as cheerful and stable, not at all "off." But Jennifer Jones played Catherine as a twitchy neurotic. It was an interpretation that Selznick encouraged, as is seen in a note that he sent to his composer Mario Nascimbene trying to describe Catherine as she should be suggested by a musical theme. The melody should have a little madness to it: "She is a little fey and certainly neurotic. There should be a little discord in the melody."[38] Selznick seems to have been looking for virtuosic passages for his wife to play out—mad scenes. As a consequence, Jennifer Jones wildly overacted the role.

Jennifer Jones had expected to play Lady Brett Ashley in Zanuck's movie of *The Sun Also Rises*. One can imagine that she would have also have exaggerated this role toward the psychotic, for Brett may be the most "disturbed" of Hemingway's women—unhappy in marriages and successive affairs, frustrated, compulsive, distressed sometimes with guilt. Jennifer Jones did hold the contract, then let it lapse when the production was delayed. Selznick's explanation was that she read the script and agreed with him that it was "completely terrible," "appalling." Though disappointed in one way, in another she thought herself lucky to get out of the part.[39]

Hemingway probably thought it extremely lucky that the part went to Ava Gardner instead, though she too seems to have thought at first that the screenplay was awful.[40] Ava Gardner was another of Hemingway's favorites. He thought that she had had a very tough life and admired her for that. He felt that their personalities went along with each other perfectly well.[41]

*The Sun Also Rises* was not Ava Gardner's first Hemingway movie. She had been the *femme fatale* in the 1946 *Killers*, the picture Hemingway liked so well. In Zanuck's version of *The Snows of Kilimanjaro* (1952) she had played Cynthia Street, a character not from the story but adapted quite freely from Lady Brett. Zanuck told his biographer that Hemingway had telephoned him personally from Cuba to urge him to give Ava Gardner the part in *The Snows of Kilimanjaro*.[42]

Ava Gardner certainly had the image of Brett, as Hemingway described her: "Brett was damned good-looking. She wore a slip-over jersey sweater and tweed skirt, and her hair brushed back like a boy's. She started all that. She was built with curves like the hull of a racing yacht, and you missed none of that with that wool jersey." So that "you missed none of that" in the movies, Ava Gardner wore red. To Hemingway she might have seemed a perfectly acceptable fantasy based on Duff Twysden, who had been the basis for his creation of Brett. Agnes had not had the blonde beauty of Catherine, and Duff had not had the voluptuous figure of Brett.[43]

Even the style of Ava Gardner's life as a celebrity was a little like an impression of Brett. In the decade before the release of *The Sun Also Rises* the movie magazines had given her Brett's reputation. For every reader of the novel who had ever styled her fantasy life after Brett's, it might have seemed that Ava Gardner had best succeeded. For every movie fan who took vicarious pleasure in the gossip and scandal of a movie star's publicly intimate life, there was a knowledge that Ava Gardner, even as Brett, had shared a great passion with a matador, Domingúin.

Zanuck had no Domingúin for his movie. Zanuck had cast Robert Evans as the bullfighter for his matinee good-looks. *The Sun Also Rises* was only Evans's second picture. (Eventually Evans would become head of the Paramount studio.) Hemingway had never heard of him, but he had heard that they had found someone absolutely awful to play Romero.[44] Before his career in Hollywood, Evans had been in women's fashions, with Evan-Picone of New York. In connection with the picture's release, his company promoted the Diva line of tailored sportswear featuring "dramatic debonair casual Taper Pants [toreador pants as the style was commonly called], inspired by the matador's decoratively trimmed garb." To prepare himself for the role of Romero, Evans "trained for months with top Mexican and Spanish matadors," publicity stories claimed. He supposedly read twenty books on bullfighting. If true, it was certainly an excessive amount of reading, since his time on film seeming to fight a bull was brief. For the purpose of the movie, it was far less important that Evans have the movements of a bullfighter than that he should have an image as elegant as Valentino's when in *Blood and Sand* (Paramount, 1922) he dedicated the bull to Nita Naldi "and all the beautiful ladies of Spain."

By one or two of those associations that give a superficial coherence to the history of movies, in 1941 Darryl F. Zanuck remade *Blood and Sand* (20th). This time the bullfighter Juan Gallardo, Valentino's role, was played by Tyrone Power. Very possibly Zanuck thought of *The Sun Also Rises* as about the same kind of story. Anyway, Tyrone Power was cast as Jake Barnes. That was one of the unkind ironies of becoming older as an actor: the bullfighter now "impotent," only an aficionado of bulls.

Zanuck and Fox were proud of their cast for *The Sun Also Rises*. Except for Robert Evans, there were many "veteran players," all stars. "The Cast That Took Two Years To Assemble!" the posters announced (each actor being two years older by the time shooting began): Ava Gardner, Tyrone Power, Eddie Albert, Mel Ferrer, Errol Flynn, and, to quote the publicity, "many other fine gems of characterization." Hemingway seems to have wisecracked to a number of people that a movie with Errol Flynn its best actor was a bad movie. His acting aside, for Flynn as for Tyrone Power, *The Sun Also Rises* seemed on the screen a decadent romance. An audience that knew Flynn's legendary reputation as a swashbuckling hero might have seen in Hemingway's Mike Campbell a little of Robin Hood or Captain Blood sadly aging, and now playing the fool.

One reads a novel and imagines a character directly. One sees a movie and usually recognizes an actor whom he already knows. This recognition might distract from a perception of that original character whom the actor pretends he should be. Most of Hemingway's characters were confounded by a famous actor's identity. That was a consequence of the way the star system worked. Stanley Kauffmann once wrote that this was the main reason that most

Hemingway movies were failures. Kauffmann cited Jennifer Jones and Rock Hudson, also Ava Gardner and Tyrone Power, as actors who "sound like movie stars, no matter how earnestly they try to act." Spencer Tracy was a more extreme instance still, as Kauffmann objected in his review of *The Old Man and the Sea*. "As the Old Man, his hair has been clipped and dyed white, he has put on pajamalike Cuban clothes, and he walks about barefoot, but he carries with him always fifty films in which he tipped his fedora back and was urbanely sage."[45] What was worse, Kauffmann doubted that Tracy was very able or even very earnestly trying to act. He was a performer with only his own personality to project.

In a recent television biography about Hemingway, the playwright imagines a conversation between Papa and a rather vacant girl. She wants him to know how terribly much she admires his work, though it seems she hasn't read much. *The Old Man and the Sea* she thought was wonderful. "I've always loved Spencer Tracy."[46]

Which of Hemingway's heroes might John Wayne have played? One of Hemingway's hunters one might imagine, but it really would make little difference since his mannerisms would have cancelled what lines of detail Hemingway had drawn. Wayne had in fact been asked by Warner Brothers to play Harry Morgan in *The Breaking Point* remake of *To Have and Have Not*. Wayne turned down the part because, it is said, he felt that *To Have and Have Not* was a dirty book.

In *To Have and Have Not* Hemingway wrote lines for a Mrs. Laughton. She is a tourist, a vulgar woman. She sees Morgan in a bar and gets excited looking at him. She wants to talk about it to Freddy, the bartender:

> "Gee, he's beautiful," the wife [Mrs. Laughton] said.
>
> Freddy laughed. "I heard him called a lot of things but I never heard him called that."
>
> "Don't you think he has a beautiful face?"
>
> "Take it easy, lady," Freddy told her. "He's got a face like a ham with a broken nose on it."
>
> "My, men are stupid," the wife said. "He's my dream man."

Those could be the lines of a movie fan under the dryer in a beauty salon talking about Humphrey Bogart. In the movie *Sirocco* (Columbia, 1951) Bogart's lover says to him: "You're so ugly. You really are. How can a man so ugly be so handsome?"

Bogart's image was appropriate enough for the Hemingway part; his screen personality one could say, too. It was a lucky circumstance that sometimes happens in movies. What one could not expect was for an actor of Bogart's recognition to suppress his own character as a hero in order to build a character (in Stanislavski's sense of the phrase) that belonged in some Hemingway book. Some years after *To Have and Have Not*, Bogart played in a radio serial called *Bold Venture*, about the adventures of a tough guy named Slade Shannon, who pilots his boat through trouble in Caribbean waters. Shannon's "mate" was called Sailor Duval, played, naturally, by Lauren Bacall. Slade Shannon, even as only a radio voice and Harry Morgan of the movies are of course the same man because they were both only Bogart. A movie star of a certain magnitude has to dramatize only himself.

The Hemingway movies created the reputation of only one new Hollywood star, Lauren Bacall. Her photo became as important as Bogart's in ads. Just as all movie fans knew what she looked like, they knew how she talked. "If you want anything, Mister, just whistle!' What was supposed to have been her most notorious line was quoted on posters and lobbycards. (In fact she did not say that exactly. In the movie she said, "You don't have to do anything. Not a thing. Oh, maybe just whistle. You know how to whistle, don't you, Steve? You just put your lips together and blow." And movie fans knew how Howard Hawks had had her yell herself hoarse in order to give the husky delivery for her every line of innuendo.

Now Lauren Bacall's admirers have her autobiography to read, *Lauren Bacall By Myself*. But when *To Have and Have Not* was a new movie, her fans knew about her "discovery" from what the movie magazines wrote. Lauren Bacall had been "discovered," which was the most exciting possible beginning for a star's career. Howard Hawks had flown her out from New York for a screen test after he had seen her on the cover of *Harper's Bazaar* for March, 1943. An anonymous mannequin, she was posed in a setting with a war theme—in front of a white door with a pebbled glass panel lettered American Red Cross Blood Donor System. She wore a black suit with flared lines and a high-peaked collar like a cape. She was (as if Raymond Chandler had described her for one of his tough novels) an image of Catherine Barkley as vamp for a lurid nurse's-night-off.

Catherine Barkley really was more Hemingway's style. The sleek model with dangerous nerve was never a character Hemingway described in a book, though the movie audiences would not have known that. But another aspect of Lauren Bacall as Marie is also important in that it reflects on the public's impression of Hemingway's women, pictured as "hard" in a few of the movies but not in the books. It was different with Maria in *For Whom the Bell Tolls* who had had "things done to" her within the atrocity of war. Marie (Lauren Bacall) of *To Have and Have Not* has been slapped around, and, as it is not so with Maria, she is used to it now and can take it. During interrogation, Marie is slapped by one of Renard's thugs. She does not even flinch. Later Morgan (Bogart) tells her he has a pretty fair idea of what her life story must be like.

MORGAN: That slap in the face you took. . . . You hardly blinked an eye. That takes a lot of practice. Yeah, I know a lot about you, Slim.

MARIE: Hm-m. Next time I get slapped I better do something about it.

It is very difficult to imagine that Catherine Barkley has ever been slapped. She slaps Frederic once, in a clumsy way, probably never having done it before, and Frederic's eyes tear from the sting. Of course Catherine never has any reason to be dangerous to a man.

Angie Dickinson, as Sheila Farr in the 1964 *Killers*, was of the same character type as Lauren Bacall—the girl who is roughly manhandled. (*The Killers* publicity claimed that Angie Dickinson was also, like Lauren Bacall, a Howard Hawks discovery for *Rio Bravo* (WB) in 1959. Actually she had her first part in pictures five years before that.) One of the publicity stills captioned for newspaper release showed her recoiling from being slammed in the face: "Ronald Reagan, in a fit of violence learns that Angie Dickinson is two-timing him, slaps her viciously in Ernest Hemingway's 'The Killers,' a furious melodrama in color from Universal." Reagan "takes real joy in slapping around his girlfriend, Angie Dickinson," an advance story read. "In fact, just for good measure, he slugs her not once but twice!" But Angie Dickinson herself represents the threat of sexual violence and revenge. For posters she posed in a clinging black cocktail dress and black stockings. "There is more than one way to kill a man!" the posters said, as if that were a theme of Hemingway's story.

In the 1976 Paramount release *Lipstick*, cover-girl Margaux Hemingway, Hemingway's granddaughter, made her movie debut. Margaux's character in the movie, Chrisie, also a model, is viciously raped by a sodomist. At his trial, the rapist is acquitted. Soon afterwards, he rapes Chrisie's fourteen-year-old sister. As an avenging angel in a glittering scarlet, high-fashion gown, Chrisie slams him on the pavement of a parking lot, firing shell after shell at close range from a .358 Weatherby Magnum. She aims at the groin, mutilating the body. The audience cheers. It is the promise kept of what Lauren Bacall warned in *To Have and Have Not*: "Next time I get slapped I better do something about it."

The reviewer for *Time* wrote: "There she is, Papa's granddaughter, a rifle tucked coolly, familiarly against her shoulder, blasting away expertly, thereby calling up the memories of machismo associated in the popular mind with the Hemingway name."[47]

"Machismo" is a word that has a popular currency, especially in the mass media, where it more often describes actors and movies than authors and books. It is partly because Hemingway is so often represented in the mass media that the word machismo is now often associated with him. From the books it would be as likely that he would be remembered for his dutiful romanticism, for his idealism, or even his cynicism and despair. Instead the public imagines it remembers him for such masculine violence as is expressed with almost expletive directness by the term "macho." Hemingway's manliness had more sensitivity and grace than the words macho or machismo connote. But the movies tend to intensify the perception of violence and sex.

"Of arms and a man" is the opening theme of Virgil's *Æneid*. In what is "macho" is that classic ideal now made crude. It is true,

Publicity still of John Garfield as Dan Butler in *Under My Skin*, adapted from "My Old Man."

One-sheet poster for *The Sun Also Rises*. In full color, the poster has the stars' names in scarlet, matching Ava Gardner's gown. From the author's collection.

however, that the mightiest of mythic heroes are known by their armaments. For a mythic impression of Hemingway, the public has vaguely known about Hemingway's own guns—the shotguns with which he shattered skeet, the hunting rifles with which he killed timid kudu, the tommy gun he kept on board the *Pilar* in order to splash up water, make fearful noises, and scare off the sharks, and all his other guns including the weapon with which he ended his life. (A. E. Hotchner catalogued some of these weapons in "The Guns of Hemingway," for the magazine *True*. This was meaningful journalism in terms of the myth.[48]) But the public knows better the guns of Hemingway's heroes, which by transference were Hemingway's own.

Frederic Henry is not one of Hemingway's macho heroes, neither with his women nor his guns, not even in the movies. He does not arm himself easily and naturally. He is not even in the real army, but only, as he says, the ambulance corps. Even in the ambulance, because he is an officer he must carry a pistol or be subject to arrest. He says that he felt like a gunman until he practiced firing. He could hardly hit anything; the pistol itself was no good. "Then the ridiculousness of carrying a pistol at all came over me and I soon forgot it and carried it flopping against the small of my back with no feeling at all except a vague sense of shame."

Robert Jordan has no sense of shame at all about the potency of his gun, "the big automatic pistol" that is out of its holster when he beds down in the sleeping robe, tied to his wrist by a lanyard, even as he makes love. The barrel of the gun is a shamelessly erotic image the night that Maria first comes to him. He had been asleep; then in his sleep had rolled over and been awakened by the hard feel of the pistol. He shifts the pistol from under his side and settles happily back into sleep and such dreams as he might be lucky to have. Reflexively he grips the pistol when Maria touches his arm and wakes him again. He releases the pistol and reaches for her:

> "Get in, little rabbit," he said and kissed her on the back of the neck.
> "I am afraid."
> "No. Do not be afraid. Get in."
> "How?"

> "Just slip in. There is much room. Do you want me to help you?"
> "No," she said and then she was in the robe and he was holding her tight to him and trying to kiss her lips and she was pressing her face against the pillow of clothing but holding her arms close around his neck. Then he felt her arms relax and she was shivering again as he held her.

She feels the pistol and is frightened by the sexual thrust.

> "No," he said and laughed. "Do not be afraid. That is the pistol."
> He lifted it and slipped it behind him.

He will tease her lightly, but he does no violence to her. Even the last night they have together, he does not make love to her until she assures him there will be no profound pain.

There is another heavier weapon by which Jordan is armed—the Lewis machine gun, which Maria, her fear all gone, had imagined she would hold firm and steady when Jordan would fire. Of course the movie did not much touch such intimate matters of guns except subliminally. Posters and billboards for *For Whom the Bell Tolls* showed Maria and Jordan lying innocently together in the heather field: a blue sky, purple mountains, the barrel of the Lewis gun, tripod erect, thrusting at a masculine angle beside them.

After *For Whom the Bell Tolls* there is an arsenal of weapons in the Hemingway movies: heavy handguns, rifles, shotguns, automatic weapons, belonging to gangsters, adventurers, soldiers, and hunters. The guns in the hands of the hunters have a simple sexual meaning. When Richard Beymer as Nick Adams in *Hemingway's Adventures of a Young Man* and the boy in *The Snows of Kilimanjaro* are given their guns, it represents their coming to manhood. Now they ought to be ready for sex.

*The Macomber Affair* was a vicious styling of the sex of the Hemingway hunter. It was a perverse sales pitch. As the pressbook announced, "Only once in a great while so compelling a selling angle—that Mmm . . . Mmm . . . Hemingway kind of campaign." The movie-going public knew Hemingway as the author of "The Killers." *The Macomber Affair* was written "with all the fierce, frank power that he put into the love story of 'The Killers.'" A promotional article in *Parade* magazine identified him as "the leading proponent of the contemporary hairy-chested school of writing."

This newspaper ad, here photographed from the pressbook, matches the design for the one-sheet poster for *The Snows of Kilimanjaro*. The background color for the poster is blue, with the title in pale yellow.

His broad-shouldered hero for this movie was Gregory Peck. "Gregory Peck," read the newspaper ads, "After the biggest game of ALL . . . a Woman! On the hunt he took things as they came . . . the charge of a snarling lion . . . the fury of a fear-crazed coward . . . the lips of a love-crazed woman!" For the publicity campaign at the national level, United Artists placed full-page advertisements in twenty-five different magazines—ads which would be noticed, the promoters estimated, 217 million times. The ads used the slogan "GREGORY PECK MAKES THAT HEMINGWAY KIND OF LOVE TO JOAN BENNETT." Other slogans in newspaper ads, posters, and in radio spots described the sado-masochistic quality of "that Hemingway kind of love." Gregory Peck and Joan Bennett were "as primitive in their emotions as the beasts they hunted!" "Cruelty and yearning . . . of such things was their love made." "They loved as dangerously as they lived . . . HEMINGWAY STYLE!" Theirs was "LOVE LIKE THE LASH OF A WHIP—HEMINGWAY STYLE!"

*The Macomber Affair* was what the publicists called a "HOT FROM HEMINGWAY" movie. It was "Hemingway at his ruthless best!" *The Gun Runners* was also that style of exploitation of the macho Hemingway hero. It starred Audie Murphy, who came to Hollywood after the war that he survived as the most decorated American solider. (His war memoir *To Hell and Back* was a book Hemingway admired.[49]) The movie publicity described the violence and sex of cheap thrills in Hemingway. "HE RAMMED A STEEL FIST INTO THE HELL PORTS OF CUBA! THAT HEMINGWAY KIND OF EXCITEMENT" A newspaper ad showed Audie Murphy nuzzling Patricia Owens in a shortie nightgown: "Running a hot cargo by day and loving a warm woman by night." Another ad showed Murphy, his teeth clenched, stripped to the waist, wearing khakis and a yachting cap, swinging the butt of a carbine: "A guy who had nothing to peddle but guts in an explosive HEMINGWAY-HOT ADVENTURE!" The movie seemed like an adaptation of a story from some barbershop pulp magazine: HEMINGWAY SAGA or HEMINGWAY MALE.

There was one other war hero as star of the Hemingway movies. This was George C. Scott, Patton of the movies, with his ivory-handled .45 Colt "Peacemaker" and Smith & Wesson .357 Magnum, playing Thomas Hudson of *Islands in the Stream*, with his

25 WORDS

ANNOUNCER: Watch out for "The Macomber Affair," Ernest Hemingway's gripping drama starring Gregory Peck and Joan Bennett. It opens ........ at the ....... Theatre.

50 WORDS

ANNOUNCER: She wanted her husband to die! She hated him! A bullet from her gun killed him! Was it murder or accident? Gregory Peck, Joan Bennett and Robert Preston unfold the most gripping tale Ernest Hemingway ever wrote in "The Macomber Affair," a Benedict Bogeaus picture coming next.... to the ....... Theatre.

75 WORDS

ANNOUNCER: It's another Ernest Hemingway hit! The man who wrote ""For Whom The Bell Tolls'' and "The Killers" is the author of this electrifying drama, "THE MACOMBER AFFAIR" coming to the ....... Theatre next ..... It's the story of a woman who hated . . . . . . hated enough to kill! Was it murder or accident? Gregory Peck, Joan Bennett and Robert Preston unfold the strangest tale ever written by Ernest Hemingway. Don't miss the sensational opening next ........

100 WORDS

ANNOUNCER: "The Macomber Affair" is coming to the ........ . Theatre...! "The Macomber Affair"...Ernest Hemingway's latest triumph told by the man whose genius gave you "For Whom The Bell Tolls" and "The Killers." It's the story of a love that destoyed three people ...Francis Macomber, who was despised by the woman he loved... Margaret Macomber, who paid the penalty for loving and hating too fiercely...and Robert Wilson who fell desperately in love with Margaret--and found he couldn't have her. See "The Macomber Affair," Benedict Bogeaus' production starring Gregory Peck, Joan Bennett and Robert Preston at the ....... Theatre tomorrow.

Suggested radio advertising, here photographed from a page of the pressbook for *The Macomber Affair.*

Newspaper ad for *The Macomber Affair.*

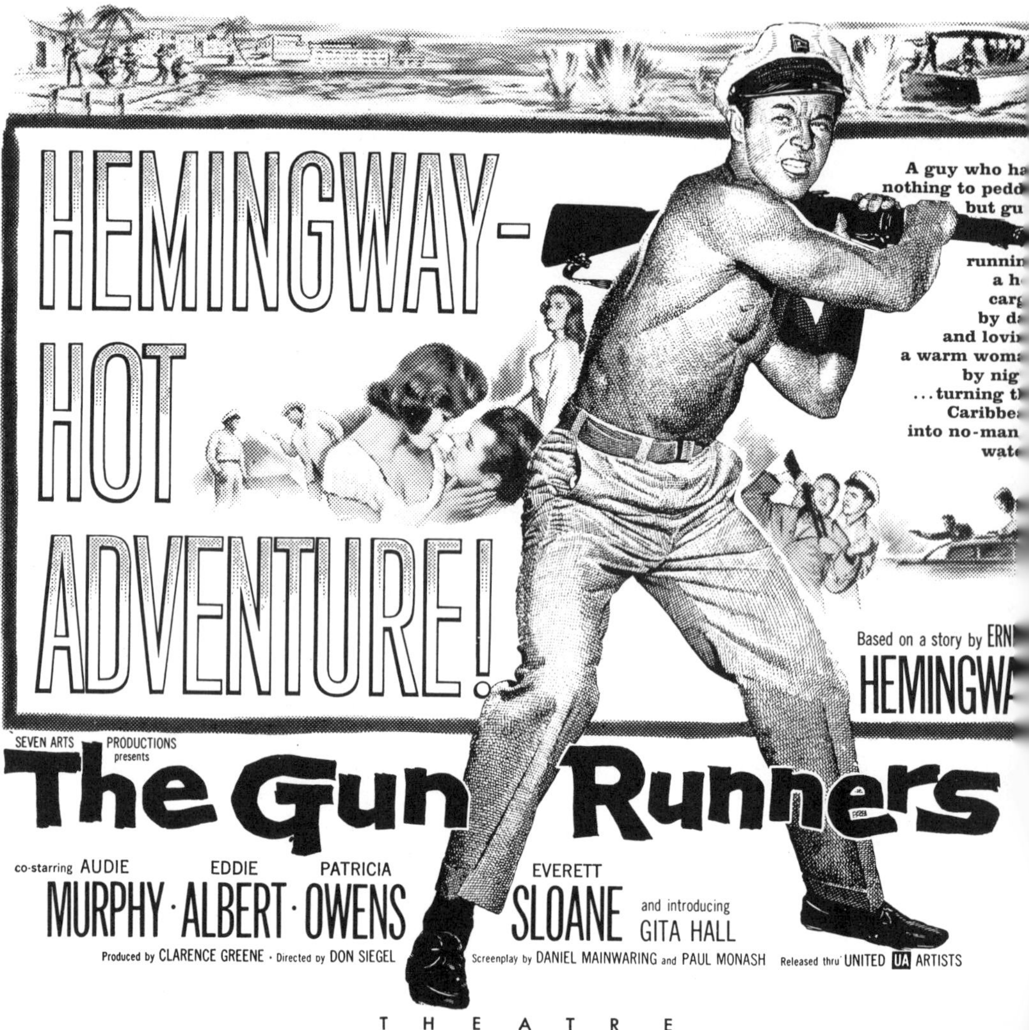


Newspaper ad for *The Gun Runners*, the 1958 version of *To Have and Have Not*.

Verey pistol and Mannlicher Schoenauer. It was a little like the machismo of weapons in movies before. It had been thought to illustrate the advertising for *Islands in the Stream* with a drawing of Scott, his naked torso criss-crossed with bandoliers. The image was rejected as being without enough dignity for a movie that expected prestige.

Hudson, of course, is not a professional soldier but a professional artist. He is a painter in the novel, a sculptor in the movie, burning and hammering metal. (If he were a hero of purer legend than is either movie or novel, Hudson might forge his own heroic weapons of steel in a mythic tradition.) The movie critic for *Newsweek* guessed why the hero is no longer a painter: "Hudson is now a sculptor, a good change, although it was probably done because Scott wielding a blow-torch is a more macho image than Scott wielding a bitty effete brush."[50] Perhaps then it was even easier for the audience to recognize Hudson as Hemingway.

*Islands in the Stream* was not the first movie in which the hero seemed a faint projection of Hemingway himself. Indeed, most of the movies confirmed the public's expectation that the writer as hero ought to have lived as manly a romantic life as did the heroes whose adventures he wrote. In some of the movies, Hemingway was his most extravagant fiction and his most coveted role.

CHAPTER X

# The Ernest Hemingway Story

It is evidence of the profound vitality of the Hemingway story that versions of his life are written not only in different styles of narration but also for audiences with different levels of appreciation. There are histories and interpretations of his life by professors and critics, memoirs by his family and his friends. Some of these books are read mostly by academic people, though some have wider appeal, even as book-club selections. Many other pages of Hemingway's life story are printed on cheaper paper stock, the biographies of our popular culture.

In 1961 Kurt Singer wrote *Hemingway: Life and Death of a Giant* as a 60-cent paperback for Holloway House.[1] The cover describes it as "the incredible story of Hemingway the man, a hard-drinking, thrill-seeking adventurer; bold, virile, and violent in life, death and love—a creative genius." This must be the most lurid of the Hemingway books. In this account, for example, with his friend Pablo, Hemingway hurls Molotov cocktails (his own empty Scotch and wine bottles) at Fascist trains. A twelve-year-old from the Madrid slums, Rosita, spends the night with Hemingway and nurses him through a violent, vomiting illness. She vanishes in the morning, leaving a love note for her "Generalissimo." And so on, for thirteen other chapters.

In 1968 Irwin R. Blacker published his novel *Standing On a Drum*: a *roman à clef* Hemingway, one could call it. The jacket blurb describes the writer hero:

> Wade Tyree, this novel's central character, is an original, a flamboyant man from Ohio, a world-famous writer, who is obsessed with Women, War, and Writing. . . . Under fire, on the battlefield, he finds his own bitter kind of truth. Rough, charming, irresistible, and often hateful, Wade has an insatiable appetite for women, among whom

> are a dancer, an actress, and a photographer. *Standing On a Drum* is the story of a man of our time, whose literary genius, whose prowess at fishing, hunting, drinking, and loving, earn for him world-wide adulation. Then comes empty desperation, and one of the most shattering climaxes in contemporary fiction.

The novel opens in a night scene of "Big Sur Country, California, 1949." There are no stars as Tyree walks on the beach down from his house. He is thinking about what his life has come to now; about the woman who is with him now, although she is asleep at the house; about his other women and friends; and battles. One thing he is sorry about is that there are no stars out this night.

> Somehow, the night was the final betrayal. All of his years he had loved the sky—black, expansive, and kind, and if not kind, at least the one neutral observer to the long struggle.
>
> And now with the clouds between, he could not see the sky.

Since there will not be any stars, he walks back to the house, where there is a single light on. He looks at the shelf of his books and touches them, then walks to his study and closes the door.

> The shot rang through the house and the woman upstairs sat upright in her bed. Beyond was the window and beyond that the night where the wind washing the darkness revealed a single star.[2]

Such extravagant fictions as these by Singer and Blacker are not valid in the sense that history requires. There might even be some question whether they are decent and respectful. But if one wonders about the mythology of it rather than the history, there are other questions about such legends besides "Are they appropriate?" and "Are they true?" One also asks "Are they worthy?" and "Are they believed?"

In *The Moon and Sixpence*, which is fiction suggested by the life of Paul Gauguin, Somerset Maugham describes the romantic principle of the process by which a man's history is transformed into myth:

> The faculty for myth is innate in the human race. It seizes with avidity upon any incidents, surprising or mysterious, in the career of those who have at all distinguished themselves from their fellows, and invents a legend to which it then attaches a fanatical belief. It is the protest of romance against the commonplace of life. The incidents of the legend become the hero's surest passport to immortality.

A moderated statement of this serves better for the understanding of the process of the Hemingway myth, which has to do with the American consciousness. Even within this culture not all the people have the same imagination for myth; it may be that intellectuals have it less than the mass audience. Usually the attitude toward the Hemingway myth was more casual than avid and fanatical. Before trying to imagine the immortality of the myth, one should grasp the myth as it has already happened.

Often the origins of myths are remote and obscure. But the Hemingway myth is recent and of a comprehensible scale; therefore one sometimes can know when and by whom the actuality of his life was made into legend. Hollywood was an important agent in this.

Let us go back to the time before Hemingway the hero was known. Already by the early 1930s—having written two conspicuously great novels, the best of his stories (not counting the two good African stories), and the bullfighting book—Hemingway was recognized as a major writer, maybe the best, by many critics. But his recognition and admiration by the public-at-large was still a lapse of time distant. In 1932 when Paramount made the first Hemingway movie he was not a celebrity yet. That was not especially a disadvantage for the studio publicists who had to turn out promotional copy about him. They could make him a star without his being asked.

First the copywriters had to have basic information about him. Some of the background in standard sources was very superficial. Hemingway's entry in *Who's Who*, for example, listed only his date and place of birth, his parents' names, and the titles of his books. Also, his publisher did not have a Hemingway profile for release, for when *A Farewell to Arms* was published, Hemingway had asked Scribner's not to publicize his personal life. Hemingway was sensitive about this for several reasons (as Michael Reynolds discovered in his research about the making of *A Farewell to Arms*). With the last novel Hemingway had not liked the talk about his relationship with the characters of *The Sun Also Rises*. He did not want *A Farewell to Arms* to be read as an autobiography, especially if it would seem to glorify his role in the war. Also, Scribner's had unintentionally released some misinformation about him; Hemingway wanted that not to happen again.[3] In short, Hemingway was probably using sensible judgment in trying to diminish the personal publicity that might come to him.

The process of myth, as Maugham explained it, "seizes with avidity upon any incidents, surprising or mysterious," and invents a legend about them. A 1932 publicity piece is headlined "SHUNS LIMELIGHT: HEMINGWAY MOST MODEST AMERICAN AUTHOR." The article claimed that Hemingway "avoided publicity like the owl shuns daylight," citing the thin *Who's Who* list and the agreement with his publisher as evidence of his near mania on the point. The movie publicity went so far as to suggest that Hemingway's secrecy was intended to cover something that he did not want coming out in the paper. Thus a Paramount publicity photo of the author carried the caption: "Won't Say a Word—That Personifies Ernest Hemingway . . . and it's earned him the reputation of 'the bad boy of American literature.'"

Other movie publicity for *A Farewell to Arms* tried to dispel any notion the public might hold that authors were bookish weaklings. "No demure, anemic fellow" was Hemingway. That he was over six feet tall (actually, he was just six feet tall) and weighed more than two hundred pounds proved he was manly. And he had done "the sort of improbable things that are more expected of a college football hero than an author." He was said to have won "a minor degree of fame as a football player."

Also, Hemingway was a fisherman, a bullfighter, and a boxer. An article headlined "Packs Punch" was about his prowess as a fighter: "At a middleweight boxing championship bout in Paris a few years ago, for example, he became incensed when the champion struck one foul after another at his opponent. Abandoning his ringside seat, Hemingway climbed into the ring, took a single sock at the champion, and knocked him out cold." This must have been a certain amateur, not professional, fight in Key West, not Paris, in 1929. Hemingway saw that the fight was rigged and stopped it, though without swinging and without knocking anyone out. It was one of the tall tales about Hemingway that was told many times in one exaggerated version or another.

Hemingway read the fight story the movie people put out and was sore. He composed a statement of denial, with a faint attempt at humor. "Any sane person knows that writers do not knock out middle-weight champions, unless the writer's name happens to be Gene Tunney." He concluded, "While Mr. Hemingway appreciates the publicity attempts to build him into a glamorous personality like Floyd Gibbons or Tom Mix's horse, Tony, he deprecates it and asks the motion picture people to leave his private life alone."[4] It seems Hemingway thought better of sending the message to the Paramount people. They might have published it to show it was just as they said about how modest he was, and how distressed by publicity.

Another theme to the Paramount publicity for *A Farewell to Arms* might have embarrassed Hemingway. The studio knew the public liked to think its romantic fantasies might be true. One biographical article was headlined "Like Story-Book Hero." Hemingway and Frederic Henry were both war heroes, wounded and decorated. "Like the hero of his *A Farewell to Arms* [Hemingway] was seriously injured in action. He still carries a silver plate in place of a bit of bone in one shoulder as a result of these injuries." Actually, Hemingway's serious wound was to his legs, not his shoulder. There was no silver plate. It was glamorous to say so, however. One is reminded of the way Catherine Barkley in the novel had hoped her fiancé would come home from the war with a romantic sabre wound. "Or shot through the shoulder. Something picturesque."

The movie publicity did not enumerate many other ways that Hemingway's hero was based on his own life. But neither did the publicity in any way limit or restrict the identification. No explanation was given that, for whatever the biographical relevance of the book, the resemblance between the book and the film was only slight. Therefore the audience could interpret a headline like "Lived Story" as broadly as it pleased. Any particular assumption about the way Gary Cooper might be dramatizing Hemingway's own life during the war years would seem about as valid as any other.

Paramount avoided saying anything about Hemingway's romantic life—no mention of wives, no hint of lovers. There was no direct suggestion that there had been a girl in Italy who corresponded to Catherine in the novel (though if the audience wanted a "storybook," they would wish to believe in the girl).

Publicists for Selznick's remake of *A Farewell to Arms* twenty-five years later, however, did lead the audience to believe in the girl. The souvenir program for the Selznick picture contained an article which offered the facts about Hemingway's having been wounded in the war, and offered, too, a simplified version of the critical thesis about the psychologically traumatizing effect of this wound and how it is a central fact in the understanding of Hemingway's writing. Then the article speculated that there must have been an even deeper psychic wound—the result of an unhappy love affair.

> Yet he calls this work his "Romeo and Juliet," nor is it strange that this story which comes directly out of battle, out of the Big Wound, should be a love story. With the young, the great theme of war has always been inseparable from the greater theme of love. And it is always love that leaves the Biggest Wound.
>
> Like his hero, he was an ambulance driver on the Italian front, and his hero too is wounded and feels that he dies. But Frederic Henry's Big Wound is a love wound. And so really is it all set down that we too feel it and are left wondering about the original of Catherine Barkley, whom critics have called "Hemingway's ideal woman."

There had been an "original of Catherine Barkley," Agnes Von Kurowsky, the nurse at the hospital in Milan where Hemingway recovered from wounds. Of course one is curious to know about her, but when one reads the true story, it turns out to be very ordinary, in almost every respect.[5] They were not equally in love. Hemingway was hurt when she broke off the relationship, but he got over it soon enough. It could hardly have been the "Biggest Wound" of his life. Almost everyone knows a more passionate and sadder love story than that. Those who read the program notes and saw the Selznick movie might have imagined otherwise, though. Even if the audience did not suppose that the movie was point for point true through to Catherine's pathetic death, they might have believed that some love affair of Hemingway's past must have been wonderfully romantic and sad for him to be able to write a love story like this.

Hollywood's suggestions that *A Farewell to Arms* was a biographical story were relatively slight, a few column inches of press release material and only a page in a souvenir program. No changes were made in the adaptations themselves to make them seem to match with his life, except that in the Selznick movie, Frederic Henry, instead of being a student of architecture, is an aspiring writer.

In strong contrast to *A Farewell to Arms*, two other Hemingway movies—*The Snows of Kilimanjaro* and *Hemingway's Adventures of a Young Man*—did try to persuade the public that they were showing their writer's life on the screen. These two movies misrepresented Hemingway's life quite as much as they misrepresented his writing. They were both low treatments of biographical material such as their producers thought the public would like, so that if these movies were believed at all, they had a special importance in creating a mythical Hemingway author.

I was nine years old when in 1952 I first saw *The Snows of Kilimanjaro* at the Mt. Lookout Theater in Cincinnati. I remember that it seemed a good movie—for all the African animals it seemed like a zoo—though it was not as exciting and frightening as *King Solomon's Mines* (MGM, 1950). But I was not quite old enough for this movie, not yet going to movies with girls, and this was billed as "Hemingway's Greatest Love Story."

The photo ads in the newspapers introduced Gregory Peck as "The Man who loved HEMINGWAY'S WOMEN!" Gregory Peck's picture ran on Monday, then each day for the rest of the week a pin-up picture of another of "Hemingway's Women" was featured. Susan Hayward was Tuesday: "This is Helen, equally alluring at a wild party or hunting wild game, who knew how to trap Harry Street even if it meant a thousand miles of safari to THE SNOWS OF KILIMANJARO." Ava Gardner was Wednesday: "This is Cynthia from

**HEMINGWAY'S WOMEN!...**

This is Liz, a Countess, who was all female with eyes that lured with subtle promise, but who tantalized Harry Street with a coldness like...

*Hildegarde Neff as "Countess Liz"*

*Gregory Peck as "Harry Street"*

THE SNOWS of KILIMANJARO

TECHNICOLOR

ERNEST HEMINGWAY'S GREATEST LOVE STORY

starring GREGORY PECK · SUSAN HAYWARD · AVA GARDNER

Produced by DARRYL F. ZANUCK Directed by HENRY KING Screen Play by CASEY ROBINSON

S I G N A T U R E

**HEMINGWAY'S WOMEN!...**

This is Cynthia from Montparnasse, a model with green-grey eyes and legs like a colt, who lit a fire in Harry Street that could only be quenched by...

*Ava Gardner as "Cynthia"*

*Gregory Peck as "Harry Street"*

THE SNOWS of KILIMANJARO

TECHNICOLOR

ERNEST HEMINGWAY'S GREATEST LOVE STORY

starring GREGORY PECK · SUSAN HAYWARD · AVA GARDNER

Produced by DARRYL F. ZANUCK Directed by HENRY KING Screen Play by CASEY ROBINSON

S I G N A T U R E

**HEMINGWAY'S WOMEN!...**

This is Helen, equally alluring at a wild party or hunting wild game, who knew how to trap Harry Street even if it meant a thousand miles of safari to...

*Susan Hayward as "Helen"*

*Gregory Peck as "Harry Street"*

THE SNOWS of KILIMANJARO

TECHNICOLOR

ERNEST HEMINGWAY'S GREATEST LOVE STORY

starring GREGORY PECK · SUSAN HAYWARD · AVA GARDNER

Produced by DARRYL F. ZANUCK Directed by HENRY KING Screen Play by CASEY ROBINSON

S I G N A T U R E

**HEMINGWAY'S WOMEN!...**

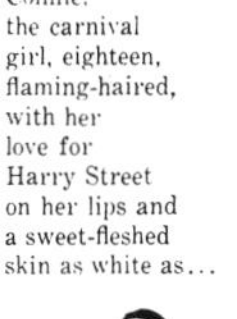

This is Connie, the carnival girl, eighteen, flaming-haired, with her love for Harry Street on her lips and a sweet-fleshed skin as white as...

*Helene Stanley as "Connie"*

*Gregory Peck as "Harry Street"*

THE SNOWS of KILIMANJARO

TECHNICOLOR

ERNEST HEMINGWAY'S GREATEST LOVE STORY

starring GREGORY PECK · SUSAN HAYWARD · AVA GARDNER

Produced by DARRYL F. ZANUCK Directed by HENRY KING Screen Play by CASEY ROBINSON

S I G N A T U R E

A series of newspaper ads, four days in succession, showing "Hemingway's Women" in *The Snows of Kilimanjaro*. The first ad in the teaser set showed Gregory Peck alone.

Montparnasse, a model with green-gray eyes and legs like a colt, who lit a fire in Harry Street that could only be quenched by THE SNOWS OF KILIMANJARO." Hildegarde Neff was Thursday: "This is Liz, a Countess, who was all female with eyes that lured with subtle promise, but who tantalized Harry Street with a coldness like THE SNOWS OF KILIMANJARO." And Helene Stanley was Friday: "This is Connie, the carnival girl, eighteen, flaming-haired, with her love for Harry Street on her lips and a sweet-fleshed skin as white as THE SNOWS OF KILIMANJARO." All this was faintly sexy, about in the same way as the idea of ladies' underwear in a different color and a different embroidery for each day of the week.

Only the first of these women was based directly on a character from the story. Hemingway's protagonist (whose name in the story is given only as Harry, not Harry Street) does remember other women as he lies dying, badly, on the plain beneath Mt. Kilimanjaro. In the story Harry believes that the women have had much to do with the destruction of his talent as a writer. He had loved too many times, quarreled and burned out the love then found another woman so that it all started again. The women were sensual pleasure, and also, because each next woman had more wealth than the last, they represented security and comfort, and it became more and more easy not to write well.

Carlos Baker has said that the story was written with a "good many personal memories" and "lay close to Hemingway's artistic conscience."[6] But essentially the story dramatized a style of life that Hemingway had declined. He had not let his life be like Harry's, "whose life, as his loves," as the newspaper ad said, "had been a sin." The movie audience might be tantalized by the scandal of sin, as if *The Snows of Kilimanjaro* were a *cinema à clef* based on Hemingway's own loves for a socialite, a model, a countess, and a carnival girl.

The movie is structured into four major flashback sequences in Harry's memory of old loves. The first of "Hemingway's Women" is Connie, the carnival girl.

In the first flashback, Harry is just seventeen. (He is too young to be acted by Gregory Peck, so the young actor's face is always shadowed or angled away from the camera in this scene. But Gregory Peck read the lines on the soundtrack, his voice sounding amazingly, comically bass for a kid.) Harry remembers the rustic house in the Michigan lake country where he lived after his parents were killed. His Uncle Bill (played by Leo G. Carroll) is the governing influence over Harry's values. Apparently in his sixties, Uncle Bill is a quiet, scholarly man who writes books on ancient history. He is also a world traveler and a great sportsman. It is from him that Harry learns the love of adventure and hunting and fishing. On this day in the movie, Harry is one week away from his eighteenth birthday, in 1917. Uncle Bill gives him his gift early, his first rifle, a Springfield.

Uncle Bill understands Harry's ambition to be a great novelist. As a writer himself, though not of fiction, Uncle Bill has the wisdom to know how difficult it will be to realize this ambition. Harry should be old enough now to appreciate some advice about writing, real writing. Writing is like a hunt, Uncle Bill says, with the writer pitted against evil and ignorance. It is a lonely safari all his life long. His quarry is a truth worth writing about, "something worth spilling his guts about which he has tracked down himself." Uncle Bill cannot be sure whether his nephew has the fortitude "to follow the spoor no matter where it leads, through what pain and suffering, though hell and high water." But Uncle Bill can wish him God's help and God's pity, and good luck. Young Harry does not seem especially attentive to any of this. Uncle Bill is being a bore somewhat in the way that Polonius is a bore. Still, the audience might take this speech to be Hemingway's creed as a writer. The audience would know that Hemingway was a hunter. The metaphor of the safari might sound like Hemingway's expression of what writing is like.

Uncle Bill has a warning for his nephew, too. He could destroy his career even this early, by loading himself down with "excess baggage." Uncle Bill is referring to a gorgeous redhead Harry's age who works at the carnival across the lake. Harry is sure that he loves her and wants to marry her. Despite his uncle's warning that she will distract him from his quest, that night Harry goes to claim his girl. She is not his lover only, however. She has already run away with a circus man from St. Louis. His pride wounded, Harry cannot return to Uncle Bill's. He runs away to Chicago and takes a place as a copy boy with the *Chicago Tribune*. That is the Hollywood version of how Hemingway began his career as a newspaperman.

The audience might well have sensed some recognition of the second of "Hemingway's" women, for Hemingway wrote a famous book about her in which he called her Brett Ashley. The scene of this second flashback sequence is Paris in the Twenties. Harry Street has given up his job as foreign correspondent for the *Tribune* (several years of promotions past copy boy) and is struggling to write his first novel. He has fallen in love with Cynthia Greene, as in green eyes. Like the famous Kiki, Cynthia is a nude model for painters in the Montparnasse quarter. She spends most of her time enjoying herself with abandon. She falls seriously in love with Harry the night that she meets him and directly agrees to his suggestion that she become "Harry's lady." The screenplay is deliberately vague about what that means. For the purpose of explanation to a censorship board, it would mean that she becomes Harry's wife. However that may be, they move into a little flat on the West Bank, where Harry finishes his book, "not knowing at the time how much it was about my Cynthia."

The audience reads a sample of Harry's dialogue in the typescript, as it if were authentic Hemingway idiom: "'You're everything', I thought. 'Everything. *On wheels*!'" The camera shows the book as it is published. The cover design is the Eiffel Tower and a tilting champagne glass. The title is *The Lost Generation*.

With the royalties from its successful publication, Harry takes Cynthia on a safari in Africa. In scenes based on material from "The Short Happy Life of Francis Macomber" (the audience might remember that Gregory Peck had played the white hunter Wilson in the movie *The Macomber Affair*), Harry discovers the virile excitement of big-game hunting. Someday, he decides, he will write a book about it.

They return to Paris, but soon Harry is restless. He wants to discover Spain and the Pamplona fiesta. As he explains to Cynthia: "I'm trying to become a writer, and it is the business of a writer to buzz around and find out things for himself and not sit on his can in a comfortable chair and reach for the bookcase for something he can crib from."

Cynthia does not want to go to Spain; she wants to settle in Paris. She is afraid to tell Harry that she is expecting a baby, for then he would be tied down and his career ruined. To avoid that, regardless of her own suffering, she deliberately tumbles downstairs and induces a miscarriage. After her recovery, they travel again.

Harry loves the bullfights, and he can write a book about that now. But no sooner is he happy in one place than he wants to be somewhere else. He is offered an assignment to report on the civil war in Damascus. Despairing that she can ever hold him, Cynthia runs off with a flamenco dancer, as Brett ran off with a bullfighter—if the movie audience imagines that Hemingway based his novel on events now more truly being shown on the screen.

The screenplay skips years. Harry has followed each successful book with another: *The Red Hat* ("Hollywood wants it. They want to put Garbo in it."), *Shadows of Things Past*, and *The Road to Rouen*. The latter is a war novel presumably matching *A Farewell to Arms*, and becomes very famous.

Success corrupts Harry. He trifles with his talent, selling hack stories to popular magazines, and writing interviews with himself for more sophisticated ones. The reputation is important to him because it might bring Cynthia back. In the meanwhile Harry lives on the Riveria in something like royal comfort as the "fiancé" of a countess. One day a letter arrives from Cynthia. The countess, sensing another woman in his past, destroys it before he can read it. But he has seen the envelope was mailed from The Hotel Florinda (*sic*) in Madrid. He abandons the countess to find Cynthia again if he can.

The Spanish Civil War has started, and he cannot find Cynthia in Madrid. Harry joins the infantry of the Loyalist army. By Hollywood's most curious variation on *A Farewell to Arms*, Cynthia is a volunteer ambulance driver for the Loyalists. She and Harry are on the same battlefield during a retreat. A shell hits Cynthia's ambulance, and she is fatally wounded. Harry finds her minutes before she dies, and they forgive each other their pasts.

After the war, in the final flashback sequence, Harry returns to Paris believing that he is condemned to being a famous writer but not a great one. He goes to see his Uncle Bill, who is now curator of a Paris museum. Uncle Bill has followed his nephew's career, and he understands that Harry has not achieved the goal he wanted for himself. He gives Harry an envelope, which he says is his only legacy to him. It is not money, but a curious riddle to which he does not know the answer himself. If Harry can answer it, he might save his career. The note in the envelope reads: "Kilimanjaro is a snow covered mountain 19,710 feet high, and is said to be the highest mountain in Africa. Its western summit is called the Masai 'Ngàje Ngài,' the House of God. Close to the western summit there is the dried and frozen carcass of a leopard. No one has explained what the leopard was seeking at that altitude."

Some exhibitors of the movie sponsored a riddle contest that invited townspeople to submit answers in a hundred words or less to explain what the leopard was searching for—winners receiving free tickets. All entrants should come to the movie to learn Hemingway's answer.

Harry Street understands that the leopard got lost following the wrong trail and the wrong scent. It is an allegory about his failed life. By his despondent interpretation, Harry understands that he is lost and will die now, too. The screenplay faintly suggests suicide. Very drunk, Harry wanders through Paris. At a bridge over the Seine, he stares down at the dark "inviting" water (as the script notes), "entertains the notion," then changes his mind. He lights a smoke.

Someone else is there on the bridge with him. She asks for a light from his match. At first Harry thinks in his stupor that it is Cynthia returned. But this woman is Helen, who has a Long Island fortune, who sometimes drinks very heavily, and who is bored with her lovers.

When Helen falls in love with him, Harry begins to remember

his lofty ambition of those early days in Africa with Cynthia. He will not be like the leopard who never found his way back to the path. He returns to Africa with Helen to find a new beginning in the same place it had been good once. Then the accident happened, with the infection, and the gangrene. "I might have made it," he thinks, if "two weeks ago a thorn hadn't needled me."

In the movie version, Harry is rescued before the gangrene kills him. It is clear at the end of the movie that he has learned a profound moral lesson. His life has been saved, as he has saved his own soul as a writer. The audience may assume he will have later great years as a writer when he will write the great and good books, perhaps like *The Old Man and the Sea*, which, as it happened, was published only two weeks before the release of this movie. The best-seller success of *The Old Man and the Sea* was excellent promotion for an obliquely biographical movie like this.

Gradually it became a grim, mortal decade for Hemingway, these last years that began with the success of *The Old Man and the Sea*. But there were other triumphs as well—the prizes that he won, the plane crashes that he survived; everywhere the prestige. The movie version of *The Snows of Kilimanjaro* looked forward to a wonderful future for Hemingway. The same script would not be written ten years later, after his death, when Hollywood made its next version of the Ernest Hemingway story. It became a different picture after he died.

*Hemingway's Adventures of a Young Man* was selected as the American entry for an international film festival in Czechoslovakia in 1962. By critical standards, it was a poor movie. But the State Department made the selection on the basis of two other factors. First, it was a suitable reflection of "the American way of life" to be shown in an Iron Curtain country. Second, it could be represented as a biographical tribute to America's most famous modern author. Senator Everett Dirksen, representing Hemingway's home state of Illinois, read a long, proud statement into the *Congressional Record* about the movie's selection. He said in part:

> This motion picture is based on the author's short stories involving perhaps the truest Hemingway hero of all, Nick Adams, because these stories were based intimately on his own early experiences as a

> young man growing up in the Middle West and encountering his first taste of war as an ambulance driver in Italy during World War I. . . .
>
> A. E. Hotchner received Hemingway's approval of the chore before his death and we therefore know that it is truly as the author would have wanted it. It is very sad that he did not live to see this most personal of his works brought to life on the screen.
>
> As a literary work these stories have revealed to thousands of readers the experiences that molded the youthful Hemingway into a great writer and a remarkable human being. Now, as a motion picture, . . . the work will reach an even greater world audience, a fine tribute indeed to this great artist.[7]

It was as if the senator were delivering a eulogy. His respect for Hemingway not withstanding, he need not have been saddened because Hemingway would not see the movie.

Hemingway had not read Hotchner's final script for the movie. He did know Hotchner's 1957 television play from five stories, *The World of Nick Adams*, which had been perfectly satisfactory—without biographical slant and, therefore, without embarrassment at all. Nevertheless, while talking with Hotchner about plans for a new script, Hemingway worried that the movie might seem biographical.[8] Hemingway had been distressed by the biographical, psychoanalytical studies of the Nick Adams stories—notably Philip Young's book.[9] Young's thesis about the biographical relevance of the character of Nick Adams was not familiar to the general public, however. As far as that goes, the Nick Adams stories themselves were not well-known, so there was not a great risk the audience would know they were watching a movie in any private way about Hemingway—unless Hollywood encouraged the idea.

All things considered, and because Hotchner was doing the script, Hemingway liked the idea of the movie. It seems that he even agreed to read a voice-over Prologue and Afterword—passages adapted from the Introduction to *Men at War*—for the movie soundtrack. He probably would have done that only for friendship's sake; it was almost like working for the movies again, which he had vowed never do to.

The production had not started when Hemingway shot himself in July, 1961. "Hotchner and I were in Rome [selecting locations] when we got word that Hemingway was dead," Jerry Wald said to the press. "That broke us up. Now we'll just be having an actor do the narration."[10]

The sensational fact of his death gave the production an entirely different value. There had been great public interest in Hemingway's life the year of the Nobel Prize, but it was nothing approaching the curiosity after his death. All the magazine covers and feature stories and the new biographies and memoirs that came out after the suicide were promotion for the new picture. The public might expect to see a biographical movie quite soon.

Jerry Wald decided that the picture should have its premiere in Chicago, Hemingway's first city, so that there might be extra coverage in the Chicago papers. Wald set July 18 as an opening date, which must have been as close as he could arrange to Hemingway's birthday, July 21. For the preliminary scripts Hotchner had used the working title "Young Man" or "Adventures of a Young Man" (which was also the title of a John Dos Passos novel). By the time of the premiere the title had been expanded to *Hemingway's Adventures of a Young Man.* It was a clumsy title, but it was an obvious try at meaning Hemingway's adventures *as* a young man.

It was an advantage, furthermore, that the title did not refer to any of Hemingway's works. It was not clear that the movie was an adaptation of fiction; it might just as easily seem a movie adapted from Hemingway's life. A disclaimer was printed in miniature letters on one newspaper ad: "This motion picture has a fictionalized story of a fictionalized character named Nick Adams and the story is not biographical in any way." No one need see that notice except lawyers (though the studio must have made very sure that no living person was even faintly represented in the movie). The public was expected to notice such a conspicuous ad slogan as "Nick Adams, or Ernest Hemingway—One Begins Where the Other Leaves Off!"

If by chance some of the audience had missed that slogan in the papers, the first image on the screen made the same statement visually: Hemingway's portrait, the famous Karsh image, staring out at the audience, then fading into the title. It seemed Hemingway's faraway gaze into the time of his youth.

When the production had first been announced, Jerry Wald pro-

"In the beginning, when you first ran away it was only to escape. And you finally stopped running. Tomorrow you will try again. The difference is that this time you are not running away—you're running toward something."

—NICK ADAMS. OR ERNEST HEMINGWAY...
ONE BEGINS WHERE THE OTHER LEAVES OFF.

Newspaper ad for *Hemingway's Adventures of a Young Man* promoted the idea that the picture was a Hollywood version of Hemingway's life.

fessed his belief that the star did not matter too much for this picture. "If you wait for Brando, you'll never get the picture done," he was quoted as saying.[11] Hotchner agreed with him on that point, and he recommended that Wald should cast Keir Dullea as Nick, since Dullea had played the part very credibly in Hotchner's television version of the same material. Wald would not choose Dullea, however. Because he could not wait for Brando did not mean that he had to take someone unknown in the movies. So Wald chose Richard Beymer instead, currently starring in the Hollywood version of *West Side Story*. It had not really been Richard Beymer in his own voice who had done Tony's wonderful singing, but the music, on the record album as well as on the movie soundtrack, had made him a star to a certain age group.

The movie is about Nick Adams's, or Ernest Hemingway's, nineteenth year, which the script represents as having been the crucial year in his life, when he broke away from his home and all that was disturbing him there. That was the year (as if the movie were true) of his first war, his first love, and his first real writing job.

Dr. Adams (played by Arthur Kennedy) is very close to his son. (Jerry Wald had very much wished that Gary Cooper would play Dr. Adams, but Cooper had died of cancer before the production began.) Dr. Adams and Nick seem to have the ideal relationship between father and son. The movie shows their times hunting and fishing together—like some image on a Father's Day card.

Mrs. Adams (played by Jessica Tandy) is extremely jealous of Nick's love for his father. Her own love for Nick is frustrated by his growing older. She still seems to want to touch and fondle him as if he were a very little boy. She still calls him Nickie.

She is not loving toward Dr. Adams at all, because he stands between her and Nick. She is cool, nearly contemptuous toward him. To damage the ideal that the father represents to the son, she is continually trying to humiliate him, with Nick there to listen. Time and again Nick has suffered for his father as he hears them argue about his lack of ambition to be a prominent doctor and what a failure he is.

Although it seems a psychological contradiction in the screenplay, Mrs. Adams, possessive though she is, wants Nick to marry.

She does not know that Nick has already broken up with his girlfriend Caroline (named Marjorie in the story "Three-Day Blow") in an earlier sequence of the movie. Perhaps his mother's approval of her has spoiled Nick's first love affair, or he has come to fear that his own marriage would turn out very like his parents'. Beyond this, Mrs. Adams's ambitions for her son are not expressly stated. Vaguely they have something to do with Nick's music lessons, though it would be silly for her to imagine that a nineteen-year-old who hates the viola, rarely practices, and studies in Sidess, Michigan, has any promising future as a musician. To Mrs. Adams, his music represents refinement and culture, if not specifically a career in the arts. To the audience, the music represents feminine values as opposed to the masculine values of his father's hunting and fishing—viola vs. shotgun.

All these tensions line themselves out in an early scene of the screenplay. Mrs. Adams observes to Nickie that she has not heard him practicing the viola today. Won't he do that now, she means. Nick objects that he and his father were about to go hunting, to try out the new shotgun that his father has just given him for his nineteenth birthday. Dr. Adams tries to support Nick in this, but that makes him vulnerable to his wife's attack. Dr. Adams says that he was the same way when he was Nick's age; he didn't want to practice, either. "You're different," Mrs. Adams replies. "You don't have that kind of ambition. Why else would you have taken up practice in Sidess?" Mrs. Adams demands that there be no interference between her and Nick. Dr. Adams capitulates as he invariably does and suggests to Nick that he practice now. They will go hunting some other day. The doctor is not a weak man, but he wants quiet, and cannot stand the fighting.

NICK: (to Dr. Adams) You really want me to practice?
MRS. ADAMS: Of course he does. Why do you think . . .
NICK: Let him answer! (a moment of shocked silence) I'm sorry. Saturday will be fine, Dad.

Nick realizes that he cannot fight for his father because his father is already a defeated man. The next day the matter of Nick's viola practice comes up again. His mother reminds him that he has a lesson at four. But Nick is finished with it, and he defies her: "I don't want to play that damn box anymore!" By four o'clock he has run away to be out in the world on his own.

This confrontation and this running away are not in the Nick Adams stories themselves. Music lessons are never mentioned (though Harold Krebs plays clarinet). The character of the father is approximately what the stories suggest. So is the relationship between father and son, though the stories show them together when Nick is a much younger boy. The characterization of the mother is more extreme in the movie. She actually appears in only one story, "The Doctor and the Doctor's Wife." Also, she is remembered in a passage of "Now I Lay Me." This was the time she cleared out the clutter from the basement and destroyed Dr. Adams's collection of arrowheads. In the way she wants to keep her grown son a little boy, Mrs. Adams of the movie is like Mrs. Krebs of the story "Soldier's Home," which is not of the Nick Adams set.

If Ernest Hemingway begins where Nick Adams leaves off (as the movie slogan had said) the audience would assume that the screenplay is at least partly an adaptation of Hemingway's life. But when Hemingway was nineteen he did not run away from home. It is true that Hemingway adapted Dr. and Mrs. Adams (Mrs. Krebs also) from his memory of his own parents. The ways in which the characterizations are revealing projections of Hemingway's attitude toward his parents makes for hazardous interpretation.

Hotchner might have had his own interpretation from the way Hemingway recollected his parents in conversation with him. It also seems that Hotchner read Philip Young's book, which presents a psychological interpretation of the Hemingway family tensions exactly as dramatized in the movie. Hemingway took cello (not viola) lessons. This is Philip Young's interpretation of the symbols of the cello and gun in Hemingway's life:

> The conflicting interests of the parents evidently came into the open over the question of what the first son was to be like. . . . The boy's mother gave him a cello, and for many years made him practice it. But before Ernest was three his father had given him a fishing rod, and by the time he was ten he had a shotgun. . . . [The] masculine interests were to win out over the feminine ones.[12]

Hemingway gave up the cello; he probably did not play well anyway. If he had continued an interest in music, would it have meant that his masculine interests were compromised? Young's argument is too simplistic in its sexist typing to mean very much. On the other hand, in its very simplicity, it might have been an analysis the movie audience would comprehend—strong fathers should keep their sons from turning out to be sissies.

Movie reviewers believed it. The critic for *Time*, giving his article the credulous title "When Papa Was a Boy," thought that the movie was directly relevant to an understanding of Hemingway's character.

> The script pertinently explores the family conflict between Hemingway's mother, . . . a high-minded, iron-whimmed culture coach ("After you've practiced the viola, there'll be time enough for hunting"), and his father, . . . a gentle, out-doors-loving doctor who either ran away from or yielded to wifely pressures. This parental tug-of-war became part of the permanent tension of Hemingway's life and work, the he-man v. esthete contradiction in his personality.[13]

Of course Hemingway was not a simple personality, but complication is not the same as contradiction.

Pauline Kael thought that the movie was "a disgrace and a moral offense" for purporting to be "some sort of biographical film." But she, too, gave credence to the psychodrama about Hemingway's motivation towards art. "[It] didn't come out of all that All-American manly hunting and fishing with Papa—it probably had something to do with the cultural aspirations of that nagging, castrating mom, the villainess of the story."[14] The movie, she believed, was not wrong in its theory, but unfair in its failure to appreciate what the mother gave to her son.

Marcelline Hemingway Sanford, Hemingway's older sister, said in a letter to the *New York Times* that *Hemingway's Adventures of a Young Man* could only contribute to the "legends and distortions" about her brother. It was because she knew the movie was being made that she had given her publisher *At the Hemingways*—"the true story of our early years."[15]

The scenes from home life comprise only the first part of *Hemingway's Adventures of a Young Man*. The theme now changes to establish Nick's ambition to become a writer. The afternoon he leaves home, Nick goes to see his friend George to talk it all over, as in the story "Three-Day Blow." They get to talking about books.

GEORGE: When *you* gonna write a book, Nick?
NICK: I'll write a book. First, I'll get to New York and work on a paper. When I *know* enough, I'll write a book.
GEORGE: Write about fishing.
NICK: Sure.

The audience will hear the prophecy of those lines. This is Nick Adams who will write *The Old Man and the Sea*.

GEORGE: Just stay clear of all that mush. You're not going to write mush, are you?
NICK: Do I look like the kind of writer who'd write mush?

The audience would get that joke—the boy who will write *A Farewell to Arms* and *For Whom the Bell Tolls* believing he will never write "mush."

This passage of dialogue is Hotchner's composing. The story "Three-Day Blow" shows Nick only fond of books and admiring of writers. (As a set, the Nick Adams stories are not in an important way about the development of a writer.) In the screenplay it is not clear that Nick intends someday to write about father and home. It seems more clear that not until he gets away from home, on the road adventuring does he begin to collect the material for the stories he will write when he knows "enough."

He crosses the country, much of the time walking, also hitching rides from motorists and farmers, or hopping freights. He takes his hard knocks in adventures with a dangerously half-crazy wreck of a prize fighter ("The Battler") and with a raving, comic drunk who is the advance man for a burlesque show ("A Pursuit Race"). Finally he arrives in Manhattan. He starts making the rounds of the newspaper offices. He seems a kid with pluck, but he gets the same answer everywhere—that he has to have experience first.

Hemingway's father wrote the letter that landed him his job on the *Kansas City Star*. At first, young man Hemingway lived securely with relatives there, but the movie audience did not know that. If aware of anything about his early career, they would have known vaguely that he had once been a newspaperman. What actually happened in Hemingway's life was not quite an acceptable version for myth anyway. Myths follow patterns, which is to say that the same lines appear over and over again in what a culture believes to be true. Young men succeed best when they succeed on their own, although they will surely fail before they succeed. They have to leave home in order to succeed in a realm of experience larger than their families and towns. They grow up faster, stronger, and with more common sense going through the school of experience. Especially in the myth of how writers are made, it is acceptable that they should live rough lives for a while—without money, even associating with bums, drunks, and burlesque girls. Writers have to know all sides of life. As for the writing, that is not something they learn from a book or a college. That is something they get in blue pencil when they turn in reports to the City Desk. The movie redrew Hemingway's life so that it even more clearly followed the lines of the myth.

The audience might know that Hemingway served in World War I. The longest sequence of the movie shows how Nick Adams learned enough to write about war.

Broke in New York, Nick takes a job as a waiter and kitchen helper in an Italian restaurant. One night at a war rally there, an Italian countess calls for heroic young men to volunteer for the ambulance service. Nick enlists. In *A Farewell to Arms* Frederic Henry had had a difficult time explaining to Catherine why he joined the Italian ambulance service. "I don't know. . . . There isn't always an explanation for everything." The movie offers an explanation suitable for a romantic myth; he responds to a beautiful woman's impassioned plea.

Nick has to prove his sense of duty and his heroism before he is entitled to his own love (though in another sense, it is Frederic Henry's love that he steals). Like Frederic Henry, and Hemingway, Nick is wounded in the field. Though the operation on his legs is successful, Nick becomes deeply depressed, certain that he will never walk again. For weeks he refuses any visitors, his only companion being his frail and lovely nurse, Rosana. With endless patience Rosana (played by Susan Strasberg) draws Nick out of his self-pity, for she has fallen in love with him. In turn it is Nick's love for Rosana that gives him the courage to stand and walk again. They decide to marry. Nick visits Count Griffi to ask his consent. As he leaves the Griffi villa, he sees Austrian planes flying toward the city. Nick rushes back to find that the hospital has been bombed. Rosana has been gravely injured and evacuated to the cathedral with the other casualties. When Nick finds her, she is dying. A priest, who is their friend and knows they intend to marry, blesses their ring and begins the marriage ceremony. Before they can exchange vows, Rosana dies.

If movie audiences were still wondering about the original for Catherine Barkley, here she was in Rosana. The audience might believe that Nick Adams's love story, now finally revealed after Hemingway's death, was the source of the more famous fiction, and that Rosana was the character who "inspired the character of *Farewell's* Catherine," to cite one credulous movie review.[16]

It is a long while before Nick is recovered enough from his wounds and his grief to go back to his Michigan home. He has a silver medal to take with him, but he is not proud of that. He will only be happy to see his father, especially because it is the fall of the year, and the ducks are flying.

His mother is at the station platform to meet him, along with photographers, a welcoming committee, and the high school band. His father is absent. Did Nick not get the letter explaining? Nick's mother is sorry Nick has to learn it this way. "He's dead, Nick. Henry is dead. Your father killed himself."

In the Nick Adams stories there is only an oblique suggestion that Dr. Adams killed himself: "He died in a trap that he had helped only a little to set" ("Fathers and Sons"). Because Hemingway was a suicide himself, the line in the screenplay has a sudden significance, as if it must explain something, or everything, that the father killed himself, too.

The movie holds the audience's fascination with the death one scene longer. Nick's mother has left Dr. Adams's room exactly as it was the night she found him shot in the head. He had written a letter for Nick. Pained that he had not left a letter for her, Mrs. Adams had opened the envelope first. Now she gives the letter to

Nick. The movie mysteriously does not show its contents. (Perhaps it is like the legacy in the envelope that Uncle Bill gave to Gregory Peck.)

The script implies that Hemingway's impulse toward suicide could be traced back this far. The next two scenes in a preliminary script version show this. The coroner sends for Nick, thinking he would like to have the suicide weapon. (For this scene and the next, Hotchner has gone to *For Whom the Bell Tolls* and Jordan's remembrance of *his* father's suicide.) Nick accepts it, though not to keep. The next day he visits his father's grave near the lake, then rows out to deep water. The script notes that there is a possibility he intends to do as his father has done and commit suicide. In one of the preliminary versions of Hotchner's screenplay a voice-over is heard as Nick stares into the depths of the water. It is his father's voice in Nick's imagination. The water is eight hundred feet deep here, his father's voice tells him. The best fish live among the rocks at the bottom. This will be their secret place; they'll never tell. They can always come out here and have a fine time. It is a strong temptation for Nick, but then he decides not to do it, and he sinks the gun in the lake.

That quiet and frightening scene might have made an exceptionally dramatic and provocative ending for the movie. It was, however, too controversial a scene for Jerry Wald. (Wald, it will be remembered, changed the story "Indian Camp" so as to avoid a suicide.) To see Nick, a decent young man, considering suicide, was inappropriate in a movie for families. The scenes with the gun were not filmed.

The fact of Dr. Adams's suicide was left as it was in Hotchner's screenplay. That was a premise needed for the last scene, which is a painful resolution of the relationship between Nick and his mother. Like Mrs. Krebs in "Soldier's Home," she is worried that Nick has no sense of purpose. She is bitterly hurt, too, that Nick shows no affection for her. She wants him to stay with her and for theirs to be a happy house. She says she will help him as she helped his father. "And bury me as you buried him?" Nick accuses. She slaps his face very hard. In that moment they understand each other and can almost forgive. Nick explains that he does not mean to hurt her, but that he has changed very much, that he has to be alone and away from home. He wants to write about the real world in his books, Nick explains to his mother. They are not books that can be written at home. An editor at a New York newspaper told Nick that he should come back and ask for a job when he knew enough. (In a preliminary version of the script Hotchner made the biographical references to Kansas City and Toronto.) Nick thinks he knows enough now.

The movie ends with a shot of Nick leaving home, looking for a last time at the scenes of his childhood—the lake, the woods, and the house where he was born. There is no scene like this in the Nick Adams stories. At this point the movie seems more like an adaptation of Sherwood Anderson's *Winesburg, Ohio*, the ending when young George Willard, young newspaper man and aspiring author, leaves home. But in another sense, the movie *Hemingway's Adventures of a Young Man* is an adaptation of history into myth, as much as it is adaptation of story into movie. And the scene is very appropriate for the myth.

A voice is heard on the soundtrack, with the lines of an epilogue that Hemingway himself was to have read. The voice says that you're not running *from* something this time, you're going toward something now. A final version of the script shows at the very end a quotation from Hemingway's Introduction to *Men At War*. The voice was to say:

> *When you go to war as a boy, you have a great illusion of immortality. Other people get killed; not you. Then when you are wounded the first time, you lose that illusion and you have a bad time until you figure out that nothing could happen to you that had not happened to all men before you.* Whatever you had to do men had always done. If they had done it, then you could do it, too.

In the final editing of the film the passage was cut (the lines in italics) except the last two sentences. Hemingway's idea was about mortality and accepting the idea you would die, then knowing that you could do it. This was a very grim idea for an entertainment movie, especially if it seemed to refer to Hemingway's own suicide, as if to say that from the time he was a young man he had accepted the thought of his death, because it was something that had to be done. Of course when the lines about immortality and getting killed were cut away, the ending of the passage meant something completely different. In the context of the movie ending, the fragment of a quotation from Hemingway means that a young man has to leave home to search for the accomplishments of his future. Men had always done that. "If they had done it, then you could do it, too." This was an altogether happier idea for a movie.

Nick Adams—that is, Hemingway's Nick, not the Hollywood character—would not have wanted a movie made from his life. In a manuscript version of the story "Big Two-Hearted River" Nick has the thought, "The movies ruined everything. Like talking about something good."

Byron asked in *Don Juan*, "What is the end of fame?" He answered at the end of the stanza, "To have, when the original is dust, / a name, a wretched picture, and a worse bust" (CCXVIII). For years Hollywood has thought about making a Hemingway picture with a star so important that it could not turn out wretched. Among movie people and Hollywood columnists there has been talk that Rod Steiger, Anthony Quinn, and Richard Burton wanted the role. Sheila Graham once offered the rumor that Lee Marvin was Mrs. Mary Hemingway's choice.[17] Actually, at the time she did not intend that a movie biography should be made. That was her right, for any movie about the late years of Hemingway's life would have to include her as a character, and she could not be represented on the screen without her consent.

Then in May, 1977, Mrs. Hemingway announced that she had sold the movie rights to her autobiography *How It Was*. The movie would be called *Hemingway*, to be produced by Jay Weston for MGM. Again there was talk about who would play Hemingway: possibly George C. Scott, Robert Redford, Nick Nolte, or Robert DeNiro. Faye Dunaway, Jane Fonda, Diane Keaton, and Shirley MacLaine were mentioned as possible co-stars in the identities of the women who were married to him. Late in 1979 Weston announced that the leads for his movie would be taken by Jill Clayburgh, as Mary Hemingway, and Jon Voight.

Plans have been imagined for other Hemingway movies. For a

long time John Huston has intended to direct a script he adapted himself from *Across the River and into the Trees.* Word was that Richard Burton would play Colonel Cantwell and Marcello Mastroianni the "Gran Maestro." Soon after the release of his production of *Islands in the Stream,* Peter Bart began to consider a third movie version of *A Farewell to Arms.* Both pictures have been delayed indefinitely. It is not as simple to make a movie as when the original *Farewell to Arms* was in release only a year after the screen rights were sold. Today it might take longer than that to develop a script. And the financial backing might not be there, and contracts might expire. The Hemingway biographical movie could be long delayed like the others.

New books about Hemingway will come out, of course, but not just scholars and readers of scholars' books will want to know about the complexity of Hemingway's character, especially at the time of his death. People remember Hemingway's death and still want to know why. A Mrs. C. T. writes to the question-and-answer column of her local newspaper, "What's the *real* reason Ernest Hemingway committed suicide?" "Electric shock treatments," the "Since You Asked" editor tells her, and he goes on to explain something about Hemingway's depression and his failure to respond to treatment at the Mayo Clinic.[18] The chief of the paint crew is supervising his men as they set up the scaffold to replaster the walls of my classroom. He asks me, "What do you teach in this room?" I answer, "Mostly American Lit." The painters are taking drawings of American authors down from their hooks. The crew chief comments, "That's Hemingway's picture." Then, "Just tell me one thing and I'll let you get back to work. In the end did Hemingway let himself go? I mean his *mind.*"

Perhaps there would be a vast audience for a movie that confronts the despair of the last reel of Hemingway's life. In other cultures remote from us now, heroes' deaths were recited in sagas and epics. In our time, myths are for movies.

# Notes

## Notes to Chapter I: **Introduction**

1. Justin Kaplin, *Mr. Clemens and Mark Twain* (New York: Simon and Schuster, 1966), 358.

2. A full listing of movie stars pictured on the cover of *Parade* magazine: Jack Palance, Cyd Charisse, Clark Gable, Fred McMurray, Gary Cooper, Marlon Brando, John Wayne, Deborah Kerr, Bob Hope, Gary Cooper again, Dick Powell, Donald O'Connor, Charlton Heston, Zsa-Zsa Gabor, Dean Martin, May Britt, William Holden, Alan Ladd, Lucille Ball, David Niven, Brando again, Brigitte Bardot, Leslie Caron, Fred Astaire, Audrey Hepburn, Mitzi Gaynor, Rhonda Fleming, Betty Hutton, Katharine Hepburn, Natalie Wood, Elizabeth Taylor, Jerry Lewis, Tony Perkins, Doris Day, Lauren Bacall, Gregory Peck and wife, Jane Russell, Debra Paget, Jane Powell, Ava Gardner (with Darryl F. Zanuck), Gloria Howard, Sandra Dee, Mary Martin, Rita Hayworth, Bob Hope again, Grace Kelly, Jackie Gleason, Fabian, Martin and Lewis, Clark Gable and Sophia Loren, Shirley MacLaine, Nancy Kwan, Elvis Presley, Debbie Reynolds, Roy Rogers, Jimmy Stewart, Kim Novak, Rock Hudson, Ingrid Bergman, Pat Boone and his wife, Shirley Temple and her daughter, Orson Welles, Marilyn Monroe, Loretta Young, Dick Powell.

3. F. Scott Fitzgerald, *The Crack-Up* (New York: New Directions, 1956), 69.

4. "Hemingway Stories for Wald Picture Accents Writer," *Hollywood Reporter*, December 1, 1960, p. 1.

5. Lloyd Shearer, "Hollywood Goes Hemingway," *Parade*, July 28, 1957.

6. *Ibid.* A fourth Hemingway movie was also due to come out—a second remake of *To Have and Have Not* called *The Gun Runners*. Shearer might not have known about this movie, or he might not have thought it was worth mentioning with the others, since it was a cheap and minor production.

7. *Ibid.*

8. "Drama Mailbag," *New York Times*, March 17, 1968, Section D, p. 13.

9. Barbara Pearce Johnson and Dennis Bohenkamp, "Course File: Film and Literature," *AFI Education Newsletter* (March–April, 1979), 5.

10. Nelson Algren, *Notes From a Sea Diary: Hemingway All The Way* (New York: Putnam's Sons, 1965), 105–106.

## Notes to Chapter II: **Hemingway on Movies: *The Old Man and the Sea***

1. "Hemingway's Old Man and the Movie Epic," *Life*, XLI (October 6, 1956), 124.

2. Unless otherwise noted, all quotations from publicity materials are taken from the pressbooks. A "pressbook," sometimes called an exhibitor's campaign manual, is an illustrated catalogue of publicity material which the studio's advertising department or agency distributes to theater owners and managers ("exhibitors") in advance of a movie's release. From the pressbook the theater owner orders the posters, lobby cards, etc. that he intends to use in his local campaign. The pressbook also includes a wide assortment of press releases which the exhibitor may submit to his local paper. The newspaper prints these in the amusement section free of charge—an editor being likely to run more of this free publicity the more display advertising space that the exhibitor is buying. Among the articles in the pressbook are usually one or two "prepared reviews" written by studio staff in

praise of their movie. A small-town newspaper without its own movie critic could print the studio's review without telling readers its source.

3. "Hemingway and the Motion Picture," *Wisdom*, III (June, 1958), 10.

4. Shearer, "Hollywood Goes Hemingway," 9.

5. Hemingway to Charles T. Lanham, June 10, 1956.

6. Hemingway to Adriana Ivancich, December 16, 1952.

7. Hemingway to Charles T. Lanham, undated letter.

8. Hemingway had signed an unusual contract with Paramount before the book was published. Confident that the book would be a best-seller, Hemingway accepted a first payment of $110,000 with Paramount to pay him an additional ten cents for every copy of the novel sold, including Book of the Month Club copies, not to exceed $40,000. See Carlos Baker, *Ernest Hemingway: A Life Story* (New York: Scribner's, 1969), 354. Hemingway was very pleased with himself and for some time carried Paramount's check around in his wallet to show it off to friends. Leicester Hemingway, *My Brother, Ernest Hemingway* (Cleveland: World, 1961), 226.

Previously Hollywood had once or twice paid $100,000 for movie rights to a novel. A decade earlier, for example, RKO had paid that much for Edna Ferber's *Cimmaron*.

9. Hemingway to Hadley Mowrer, July 27, 1939. Calling $10,000 a derisory amount in this letter to his first wife was touching on a sensitive point. Hemingway had given her the royalties and rights to *The Sun Also Rises* in their divorce settlement, and she had sold the movie rights for $10,000. She sold too soon and too low. Subsequently the rights were bought and sold several times before Darryl F. Zanuck and Twentieth Century-Fox bought the novel for $125,000.

10. Neither Hemingway nor his estate was paid for permission to remake *A Farewell to Arms* in 1957 or *The Killers* in 1964. By the terms of Hemingway's contracts the studios retained movie rights for the duration of the copyright on the original story; thus the studio could make a new movie version at a later date without paying Hemingway again. From Hemingway's standpoint a leasing agreement would have been preferable. Then after a movie had been produced the rights would revert to Hemingway, who could renegotiate terms for any remake. But Hemingway had never been able to arrange such a contract. Talks with producer Jerry Wald about the rights to *Across the River and Into the Trees* came to an impasse on precisely this point. Hemingway claimed to have refused Wald's offer of a quarter of a million dollars because he could not get the terms of a lease. See Baker, *Ernest Hemingway*, 487–88.

11. Patrick Hemingway, "My Papa, Papa," *Playboy*, XV (December, 1968), 263. According to A. E. Hotchner, *Papa Hemingway: A Personal Memoir* (New York: Random House, 1966), 248, Hemingway sacrificed to his tax account all but $20,000 of the $125,000 that Jerry Wald paid for the set of Nick Adams stories used in the 1962 movie *Hemingway's Adventures of a Young Man*. According to Leicester Hemingway, *My Brother, Ernest Hemingway*, 268, Hemingway had once refused an offer of $50,000 for the rights to the story "Fifty Grand" because four-fifths of the sum would have been lost to taxes.

After the success of Mark Hellinger's 1946 production of *The Killers* Hemingway agreed to sell Hellinger four more stories for $75,000 each plus 10 percent of the profits over $1 million. From a tax consideration this was Hemingway's best deal, since the payments were to be in installments of $25,000 spread over twelve years. Hellinger died before the project could be begun. Hemingway had received an advance, which he returned to Hellinger's widow.

12. Hemingway to Adriana Ivancich, December 16, 1952.

13. Hemingway to Charles T. Lanham, August 2, 1953.

14. Lillian Ross, *Portrait of Hemingway* (New York: Avon Books, 1961), 67.

15. Hemingway to Lillian Ross, September, 1950, and July 3, 1950.

16. Ross, *Portrait of Hemingway*, 71.

17. Patrick Hemingway, "My Papa, Papa," 263.

18. Hemingway to Donald Friede, March 3, March 16, and April 12, 1942. Not all of Hemingway's suggestions were followed. Either Hemingway changed his mind about repudiating the movie or he had been bluffing a little.

19. Art Buchwald, "Zanuck vs. Hemingway," *Beverly Hills Citizen*, December 3, 1957, p. 2.

20. Hemingway to Charles T. Lanham, December 15, 1952.

21. Hemingway to Adriana Ivancich, October 1, 1952.

22. Hemingway to Lillian Ross, September, 1950.

23. Hotchner's version of "The Killers" was produced for the CBS Buick Electra Playhouse, November 19, 1959.

24. Hemingway to Adriana Ivancich, December 16, 1952, January 19, 1953.

25. Hemingway to Harvey Breit, April 4, 1953; Hemingway to Gianfranco Ivancich, April 15, 1953.

26. Hemingway to Gianfranco Ivancich, February 20, 1953.

27. Hemingway to Charles T. Lanham, April 17, 1953.

28. Hemingway exaggerated Hollywood's interest in the novel in a letter to Adriana Ivancich dated December 16, 1952.

29. Quoted in William Manchester, *The Glory and the Dream: A Narrative History of America, 1932–1972* (New York: Random House, 1975), 649.

30. Dwight MacDonald, *Against the American Grain* (New York: Random House, 1952), 40–43.

31. *Life*, September 2, 1952, 9.

32. Ibid., 20.

33. Shearer, "Hollywood Goes Hemingway," 7.

34. An MGM press release of June 8, 1953, announced that Hemingway would write the screenplay. Perhaps that had been the understanding with MGM, which Hemingway thought no longer applied now that Warner Brothers had the picture.

35. Quoted in Andrew Sarris (ed.), *Interviews With Film Directors* (New York: Bobbs-Merrill, 1967), 123.

36. For example, in a 1937 interview Faulkner said, "I don't like scenario writing because I don't know enough about it. I feel as though I can't do myself justice in that type of work." Quoted in James B. Meriwether and Michael Millgate (eds.), *Lion in the Garden: Interviews with William Faulkner, 1926–1962* (New York: Random House, 1968), 33–34. For a similar statement, see p. 241. See also Tom Dardis, *Some Time in the Sun* (New York: Scribner's, 1976), 115.

37. Hemingway to Ned Calmer, October 24, 1934.

38. Hemingway to Arnold Gingrich, April 3, 1953.

39. Hemingway to Thomas Shevlin, April 4, 1939.

40. "Hemingway To Script, Play Self in African Safari Filmization," *Variety*, September 2, 1954, p. 1.

41. Several good stories have been told about other times when Hemingway was in Hollywood, but attempts to confirm them suggest that they are just stories, not true. For example, Aaron Latham was told that for a time Hemingway was living at a beach house in Malibu while writing *For Whom the Bell Tolls*. One day Fitzgerald took Hemingway to the Metro-Goldwyn-Mayer studio, where Hemingway behaved so rudely that Louis B. Mayer had to call a security man to get Hemingway off the premises. See Aaron Latham, *Crazy Sundays: F. Scott Fitzgerald in Hollywood* (New York: Viking, 1971), 177–79.

Sheilah Graham in *College of One* sets a comic scene during a Hemingway visit to Hollywood. Two movie producers were trying to flatter him. One said that he admired *A Farewell to Arms,* then had to admit that he knew only the movie. The other producer did not even know the Hollywood version—but he had heard the song! See Sheilah Graham, *College of One* (New York: Viking, 1967), 179–80.

In 1941, one John Igual De Montijo sued Hemingway and Scribner's claiming that *For Whom the Bell Tolls* had been plagiarized from an unpublished screenplay. A big man called "Ernie," De Montijo claimed, had heard him read the screenplay at a Los Angeles party in February, 1939. Hemingway submitted a sworn statement to the court that he had been living in Cuba at the time. The case was dismissed. See Frank M. Laurence, "5000 Grand: The Plagiarism Suit Against Hemingway," in Matthew J. Bruccoli and C. E. Frazer Clark, Jr. (eds.), *Fitzgerald/Hemingway Annual 1974* (Englewood, Colorado: Microcard Editions, 1975), 193–199.

42. Hemingway to Lillian Ross, undated letter, c. 1950.

43. Hemingway to Adriana Ivancich, September 20, 1955.

44. Hemingway to Philip Percival, September 14, 1955.

45. Baker, *Ernest Hemingway*, 533.

46. Hemingway to Adriana Ivancich, September 20, 1955.

47. Hemingway to Philip Percival, September 4, 1955.

48. Ernest Hemingway, "A Visit With Hemingway: A Situation Report," in William White (ed.), *By-Line: Ernest Hemingway* (New York: Scribner's, 1967), 473.

49. Hemingway to Charles T. Lanham, August 2, 1953.

50. According to Hayward the picture was finally brought in for something in excess of $5 million. Until *Islands in the Stream*, it was the most expensive Hemingway production.

51. Quoted by Keiichi Harada, "The Marlin and the Shark: A Note on *The Old Man and the Sea*," in Carlos Baker (ed.), *Hemingway and His Critics: An International Anthology* (New York: Hill and Wang, 1961), 269.

52. "Two With Tracy," *Time*, October 2, 1958, 42.

53. Hemingway to Charles T. Lanham, June 10, 1956.

54. Hemingway to Harvey Breit, July 23, 1956.

55. Robert E. Ginna, "Life in the Afternoon," *Esquire*, LXVII (February, 1962), 106.

56. William Lewin, *Guide to the Discussion of the Leland Hayward Production of The Old Man and the Sea* (Summit, N.J.: Education and Recreational Guides, 1958).

57. Ernest Hemingway, "A Visit With Hemingway," 470.

58. Mrs. Hemingway used this passage to summarize her husband's attitude toward the movies. See Oriana Fallaci, "An Interview with Mary Hemingway: 'My Husband, Ernest Hemingway,'" *Look*, XXX (September 6, 1966), 65–66.

## Notes to Chapter III:
## **Screen Romance: *A Farewell to Arms***

1. Hemingway to Harvey Breit, June 6, 1957.

2. This was the first *movie* adaptation of a Hemingway work. Two years earlier, in 1930, Laurence Stallings had adapted *A Farewell to Arms* for the Broadway stage. Hemingway had heard disappointing accounts of the play. That might have been a warning to him that he would also be disappointed with the movie, for screenplay writers Benjamin Glazer and Oliver H. P. Garrett used Stallings's version as a preliminary treatment. Some of the movie publicity credited Stallings's work. This author's attempts to recover a Stallings script (which was never published) have been unsuccessful. See Paul R. Reynolds, *The Middle Man: Adventures of a Literary Agent* (New York: William Morrow, 1970), 36–39.

3. Lewis Jacobs, *The Rise of the American Film: A Critical History* (New York: Teachers College Press, 1968), 42.

4. "Hemingway Mad at Happy Ending of His War Picture," *New York Daily News*, December 6, 1932, p. 40.

5. "Inspired Genius Creates a Masterpiece!" *New York Sun*, December 6, 1932, p. 35.

6. "Hemingway Mad at Happy Ending of His War Picture," *New York Daily News*, December 6, 1932, p. 40.

7. *Ibid.*

8. *Variety*, December 13, 1932, p. 14.

9. Percy Hutchinson, "Love and War in the Pages of Mr. Hemingway," *New York Times*, September 29, 1929, p. 5.

10. Edwin Schallert, "Film Retains Somber Ending," *Los Angeles Times*, December 8, 1932, p. 11.

11. Thornton Delehanty, "Some Aspects of 'A Farewell to Arms' and 'The Sign of the Cross,'" *New York Evening Post*, December 15, 1932, p. 17.

12. Regina Crew, "Wartime Romance Colorfully Acted," *New York American*, December 9, 1932, p. 13.

13. Irene Thirer, "Farewell to Arms Poignant Picture," *New York Daily News*, December 9, 1932, p. 62.

14. See Paul Michael (ed.), *The American Movies Reference Book: The Sound Era* (Englewood Cliffs, New Jersey: Prentice-Hall, 1969), 10.

15. "Cannes Listens Attentively To Harlequin Romanticism in Age of Bouncing Beds," *Variety*, May 25, 1977, p. 7.

16. See Lester E. Asheim, "From Book to Film" (Ph.D. dissertation, University of Chicago, 1949), 92.

17. Hemingway to Harvey Breit, June 6, 1957.

18. *Ibid.*

19. Sales figures are no longer available for any of the three editions of *A Farewell to Arms* in print in 1933. But it is known, as a point of comparison, that the Selznick remake of *A Farewell to Arms* increased the sales of the Scribner's hardbound edition by a factor of three, from 1,500 copies sold during the last six months of 1957 to 4,500 copies sold during the first six months of 1958 (figures given by Charles Scribner, Jr.).

20. "To: Whom It May Concern, From: David O. Selznick, Subject: Making a Movie," *Life*, XLIV (March 17, 1958), 92; hereinafter cited as "Selznick Memo." There is some doubt that Hemingway ever received this telegram, since Selznick later picked up a rumor that Hemingway was sore about not being notified as soon as a new adaptation was being planned. See Rudy Behlmer (ed.), *Memo from David O. Selznick* (New York: Viking, 1972), 460.

21. "Selznick Memo."

22. Behlmer (ed.), *Memo*, 445, 448.

23. *Ibid.*, 444, 447.

24. S. H. Butcher (trans.), *Aristotle's Theory of Poetry and Fine Art* (New York: Dover Press, 1951), 29.

25. "Selznick Memo," 106.

26. *Ibid.*

27. Alfred Kazin, *Bright Book of Life* (New York: Little, Brown), 9.

28. Eugene Löhrke (ed.), *Armageddon: The World War in Literature* (New York: Jonathan Cape and Harrison Smith, 1930), 15, 19.

29. Jaroslav Hasek, *The Good Soldier Schweik* (New York: Signet, 1963), vi.

30. Behlmer (ed.), *Memo*, 449.

31. Bob Thomas, *Selznick* (Garden City, N.Y.: Doubleday, 1970), 282.

32. Behlmer (ed.), *Memo*, 450.
33. Hemingway to Harvey Breit, June 6, 1957.
34. "Selznick Memo," 99.
35. Hotchner, *Papa Hemingway*, 30.
36. Archer Winston, review of *A Farewell to Arms*, *New York Post*, December, 1957; "Oh, what they've done to HEMINGWAY!" *London Sunday Express*, c. March, 1958.
37. Thomas, *Selznick*, 287.
38. "Selznick Memo," 99.
39. Quoted in Margaret Farrand Thorpe, *America at the Movies* (New Haven: Yale University Press, 1939), 243.

## Notes to Chapter IV:
## **Action Adventure: *To Have and Have Not***

1. James Agee, "Films," *Nation*, CLIX (November 4, 1944), 569.
2. Robin Wood, *Howard Hawks* (New York: Doubleday, 1968), 25.
3. Andrew Sarris (ed.), *Interviews with Film Directors* (New York: Bobbs-Merrill, 1957), 193.
4. In a conversation with this writer, Hawks remembered it as a fishing trip.
5. Baker, *Ernest Hemingway*, 294, 287.
6. Sarris, (ed.), *Interviews*, 193.
7. Agee, "Films," 569.
8. Hawks in interview with Hollywood correspondent Frederic C. Othman, March, 1944.
9. Fred Stanley, "The Warners Revamp Hemingway Novel to Please Government," *New York Times*, April 2, 1944, p. X3.
10. Quoted in Lauren Bacall, *Lauren Bacall By Myself* (New York: Knopf, 1979), 107. Some reviewers noticed the similarities between the movies. James Agee said *To Have and Have Not* was "the kind of tinny romantic melodrama which millions of cinemaddicts have been waiting for ever since *Casablanca*." *Time*, October 23, 1944, p. 92. Robin Wood writes in *Howard Hawks*, "*To Have and Have Not* perhaps owes more to Michael Curtiz's *Casablanca* than to Ernest Hemingway" (p. 11).
11. *Casablanca* was adapted from a play by Murray Burnett and Joan Alison entitled "Everybody Comes to Rick's Place."
12. Joseph Blotner, *Faulkner: A Biography* (New York: Random House, 1974), 1157.
13. There is a scene in the novel in contrast to this. Albert's wife (it is Albert, not Wesley) comes down to the dock looking for her husband. When she sees the bodies of the Cubans she becomes hysterical. She falls in the water and in thrashing around loses her false teeth. Two Coast Guard men fish her out:

> No one in the crowd had made a move to aid her, and as she stood dripping on the stern, she looked up at them, shook both her fists at them and shouted, "Basards! Bishes!" Then as she looked into the cockpit she wailed "Alber. Whersh Alber?"
>
> "He's not on board, Mrs. Tracy," the sheriff said, taking up a blanket to put around her. "Try to be calm Mrs. Tracy. Try to be brave."
>
> "My plate," said Mrs. Tracy tragically. "Losht my plate."
>
> "We'll dive it up in the morning," the skipper of the Coast Guard cutter told her. "We'll get it all right."

It is a passage of grotesque comedy—very rare in Hemingway. Its function is to contrast with and balance the tough tragedy of Morgan's death. But the effect of such comedy would have been totally unfamiliar and confusing to a movie audience in 1950.

14. Bosley Crowther, "*Breaking Point*, Adapted from Hemingway Story," *New York Times*, October 7, 1950, p. 10.

15. Ernest Hemingway, "One Trip Across," *Cosmopolitan*, XCVI, (April, 1934), 20–23, 108–22.

16. "Hemingway Protests 'Gun' Script But Hasn't Read It, Greene says," *Variety*, February 24, 1958, pp. 1, 4. In a letter to this author Greene said that the remark was attributed to him by a studio press agent as part of a publicity gimmick.

17. Peter Bogdanovich, "Working Within the System: Interview with Donald Siegel," *Movie*, XV (Spring, 1968), 8.

18. Christopher Porterfield, "The Big One Gets Away Again," *Time*, March 21, 1977, p. 89.

## Notes to Chapter V: **Hemingway Entertainment in the Hollywood Style**

1. Quoted in *Gertrude Stein: If This You See Remember Me*, a documentary film for the PBS network in 1970, distributed by Corinth Films.

2. Frank Borzage, "Directing a Talking Picture," in Joe Bonica (ed.), *How Talkies Are Made* (Hollywood, 1930), reprinted in Richard Koszarski (ed.), *Hollywood Directors 1914–1940* (New York: Oxford University Press, 1976), 235.

3. Remark to Christopher Lucas, for the London *Sunday Express*, quoted in Art Buchwald, "Zanuck vs. Hemingway," *Beverly Hills Citizen*, December 3, 1957, p. 2.

4. F. Scott Fitzgerald, *The Crack-Up*, ed. by Edmund Wilson (New York: New Directions, 1945), 176.

5. Pauline Kael, *I Lost It at the Movies* (New York: Little, Brown, 1965), 234.

6. Lloyd R. Arnold, *High on the Wild with Hemingway* (Caldwell, Idaho: Caxton, 1968), 146.

7. But Hotchner would have known the biographical parallel. Though Hemingway was severely wounded in the legs, he carried the body of another wounded man through machinegun fire.

8. Studio press releases cited "A Very Short Story" as being the source for the love story of the picture.

9. Norman Sheldon Grebstein, *Hemingway's Craft* (Carbondale: University of Southern Illinois Press, 1973), 2.

10. *TV Guide*, May 5–11, 1973, p. A-4.

11. Casey Robinson, "Adapter's Views," *New York Times*, October 12, 1952, p. 4.

12. And he said that the 60 percent (*sic*) won. Hemingway to Adriana Ivancich, October 1, 1952.

## Notes to Chapter VI: **Hemingway Censored**

1. Baker, *Ernest Hemingway*, 180.

2. The code is printed as an appendix to Murry Schumach's book on Hollywood censorship, *The Face on the Cutting Room Floor* (New York: William Morrow,

1964), 278–92. The code in its original 1930 wording is appended to Olga J. Martin's *Hollywood's Movie Commandments: A Handbook for Motion Picture Writers and Reviewers* (New York: H. W. Wilson, 1937), 271–90.

3. Hollis Alpert, "Pass the Salt Please," *Saturday Review of Literature*, XL (September 7, 1957), 25.

4. For a review of Hemingway's worries with his editor and publisher about the morality and decency of *A Farewell to Arms* and also for a description of outrage from some quarters that greeted the book all the same, see Michael S. Reynolds, *Hemingway's First War: The Making of "A Farewell to Arms"* (Princeton, N.J.: Princeton University Press, 1976), especially the chapter on "Publication."

5. William K. Zinsser, "Hemingway Is Vulgarized," *New York Herald Tribune*, February 2, 1958, p. 38.

6. "Selznick Memo," 99.

7. Michael Reynolds says that Hemingway worried over there being a slim chance of his being sued by the Italian government for the description of Caporetto. It is difficult to think how a foreign government would have been able to sue an American citizen. See Reynolds, *Hemingway's First War*, 80.

8. "Selznick Memo," 97.

9. Thomas Brady, "Hollywood Strikes a New 'Bell,'" *New York Times*, August 24, 1941, sec. 9, p. 3.

10. Lewis Jacobs, *The Rise of the American Film: A Critical History* (New York: Teachers College Press, 1968), 529.

11. Baker, *Ernest Hemingway*, 246.

12. Hemingway to Donald Friede, March 3, 16, 1942.

13. "On Film," *The Nation*, CLVII (July 24, 1943), 108.

14. Quoted in "For Whom?" *Time*, August 2, 1943, p. 60.

15. "'For Whom the Bell Tolls' Strikes Screen; Talk Seethes," *Milwaukee Journal*, July 17, 1943, "Green Sheet," p. 1.

16. Baker, *Ernest Hemingway*, 383.

17. *Ibid.*, 351.

18. Brady, "Hollywood Strikes a New 'Bell,'" 3x.

19. Arnold, *High on the Wild with Hemingway*, 186.

20. Eileen Creelman, "Sam Wood Here for Premiere, Talks of Directing 'For Whom the Bell Tolls,'" *New York Sun*, July 15, 1943, p. 20.

21. Philip Young, *Ernest Hemingway: A Reconsideration* (University Park, Pa.: Pennsylvania State University Press, 1966), 32.

22. Philip K. Scheuer, "Hotchner Reveals Hemingway 'Inside,'" *Los Angeles Times*, February 13, 1962, p. 21.

23. Schumach, *Face on the Cutting Room Floor*, 92.

## Notes to Chapter VII:
## **Story, Movie, Film: "The Killers"**

1. Blotner, *Faulkner*, 1164.

2. "Overkill," *Newsweek*, August 3, 1964, p. 72.

3. Louis Chapin, "'Killers'—But Hemingway's?" *Christian Science Monitor*, July 25, 1964, p. 4.

4. Eugene Archer, "'Killers' Remade," *New York Times*, July 18, 1964, p. 10.

5. James Agee, review of *The Killers*, *The Nation*, CLXIII (September 14, 1946), 305.

6. John McNulty, review of *The Killers*, *New Yorker*, XXII (September 7, 1946), 52.

7. Arnold, *High In the Wild with Hemingway*, 163.

8. Oriana Fallaci, "An Interview with Mary Hemingway: 'My Husband, Ernest Hemingway,'" *Look*, XXX (September 6, 1966), 65.

9. Jim Bishop, *The Mark Hellinger Story* (New York: Appleton-Century-Crofts, 1952), 315.

10. Hotchner, *Papa Hemingway*, 18. Mrs. Mary Hemingway does not remember this.

11. *Ellery Queen's Mystery Magazine*, XLIII (June, 1947), 54.

12. In *The Bad Guys: An Illustrated History of the Movie Villain* (New York: Citadel, 1964), 70, 72, William K. Everson suggests that, in some of the tough talk of Al and Max, Hemingway could have been imitating the gangster picture *Walking Back*. But *Walking Back* was not released until 1928.

13. Cleanth Brooks and Robert Penn Warren, *Understanding Fiction* (New York: Appleton-Century-Crofts, 1959), 305.

14. *Ibid.*, 306.

15. For a description of "Cinema Noir" or "Film Noir" one may see James Monaco's *How To Read a Film* (New York: Oxford University Press, 1977), 244–45, 251–52.

16. Andrew Sarris, *The American Cinema Directors and Directions 1929–1968* (New York: E. P. Dutton, 1968), 138.

17. But not a radio play, or a ballet.

## Notes to Chapter VIII:
## **Hemingway's Cinematic Style**

1. Louella Parsons, "Hemingway's Magic Touch," *Cosmopolitan*, CXXXIII (October, 1952), 15.

2. "Hemingway Stories for Wald Picture; Accents Writer," *Hollywood Reporter*, December 1, 1960, p. 1.

3. Hemingway to Lillian Ross, undated letter, c. 1950.

4. W. M. Frohock, "Violence and Discipline," in John K. McCaffery (ed.), *Ernest Hemingway: The Man and His Work*, (New York: World, 1950), 272–73.

5. Carlos Baker, *Hemingway: The Writer As Artist* (Princeton: Princeton University Press, 1963), 249.

6. Frohock, "Violence and Discipline," 273–74.

7. Introduction to *A Farewell to Arms* (New York: Modern Library, 1932), ix.

8. Marshall McLuhan, *Understanding Media: The Extensions of Man* (New York: McGraw-Hill Paperbacks, 1965), 8.

9. *Ibid.*, 286.

10. Frank D. McConnell, *The Spoken Seen: Film and the Romantic Imagination* (Baltimore: Johns Hopkins University Press, 1975), 27–28.

11. Robbe-Grillet is the author of *The Erasers* and other fiction and the director and writer of *Last Year at Marienbad*. His short story "The Secret Room" (in *Snapshots*) is a very deliberate experiment in composition like film, each paragraph a separate shot, described by a narrator who seems to be watching a strangely edited film of a melodramatically erotic crime.

12. *Writers at Work: The Paris Review Interviews, Second Series* (New York: Viking, 1963), 227–28.

13. Edward Murray, *The Cinematic Imagination: Writers and the Motion Pictures* (New York: Frederic Ungar, 1972), 218.

14. *Ibid.*, 221.

15. *Writers at Work*, 228.

16. Murray, *Cinematic Imagination*, 227.

17. Harry Levin, "Observations on the Style of Ernest Hemingway," in Robert P. Weeks (ed.), *Hemingway: A Collection of Critical Essays* (Englewood Cliffs, New Jersey: Prentice-Hall, 1962), 79–80.

18. *Ibid.*, 80.

19. Gertrude Stein, *Lectures in America* (Boston: Beacon Press, 1957), 176–77.

## Notes to Chapter IX:
## **The Hemingway Hero as Hollywood Star**

1. Hemingway to Donald Friede, March 16, 1942.

2. See, for example, Frohock, "Violence and Discipline," 73: "I believe he was working on *For Whom The Bell Tolls* with Hollywood production and even possibly a specific Hollywood actor in mind."

3. "Ernest Hemingway Meets Ingrid Bergman," *Life*, X (February 24, 1941), 48.

4. John Rosenfield, "Why It Takes Time to Make a Big Movie," *Dallas Morning News*, June 15, 1943, p. 14. Of course the novel would have been sold without Cooper's influence. Donald Friede, for the Myron Selznick Agency, was distributing prepublication copies in Hollywood. Twentieth Century-Fox was another studio very anxious to buy it. See Baker, *Ernest Hemingway*, 353–54, and Arnold, *High on the Wild with Hemingway*, 102.

5. Arnold, *High on the Wild with Hemingway*, 130.

6. See, for example, "Just a Suggestion," *New York Times*, December 1, 1940, p. 4x.

7. Thornton Delehanty, "The Public Is Casting 'For Whom Bell Tolls,'" *New York Herald Tribune*, February 8, 1941.

8. "Ernest Hemingway Meets Ingrid Bergman," p. 48.

9. Gregory Hemingway, *Papa: A Personal Memoir* (New York: Houghton Mifflin, 1976), 45–46.

10. [Sam Wood], "Director Sam Wood's Location Diary," *Screenland*, February, 1943, p. 90.

11. Rosenfield, "Why It Takes Time to Make a Big Movie," 14.

12. Delehanty, "The Public Is Casting 'For Whom Bell Tolls.'"

13. T.S., "The Screen" [review of *I Was an Adventuress*], *New York Times*, May 2, 1940, p. 13.

14. Bosley Crowther, "The Screen in Review" [review of *Louisiana Purchase*], *New York Times*, January 1, 1942, p. 37.

15. Producers made enormous sums of money for hiring out the stars they had under contract. In 1943 alone, the year after Bergman starred in *For Whom the Bell Tolls*, David O. Selznick made $425,000 from loaning her to other producers. According to Selznick's biographer, Selznick had never been reluctant to loan Bergman to Paramount for *For Whom the Bell Tolls*; in fact, he had wanted her to play the part. His original asking price for her services had been $90,000. Later, when Paramount decided they needed Ingrid Bergman right away, Selznick raised his price to $120,000. See Thomas, *Selznick*, 198–99.

16. Hemingway to Donald Friede, August 13, 1943.

17. Jane Corby, "Ingrid Bergman's Costume . . . Gave Hollywood a Headache," *Brooklyn Daily Eagle*, January 19, 1944, p. 11.

18. *Ibid.*

19. Eileen Creelman, "Sam Wood, Here for the Premier . . .," *New York Sun*, July 13, 1943, p. 20.

20. Alton Cook, "Views of *For Whom the Bell Tolls* Conflict," *New York World Telegram*, July 17, 1943, p. 5.

21. Hemingway to Donald Friede, March 3, 1942.

22. Rose Pelswick, "For Whom Bell Tolls' Opens . . .," *New York Journal American*, July 15, 1943, p. 10.

23. Kate Cameron, "Tale of Spanish War and Love at Rivoli," *New York Daily News*, July 15, 1943, p. 40.

24. William Whitebait, "The Movies" [review of *For Whom the Bell Tolls*], *The New Statesman and Nation*, XXVI (November 13, 1943), 316.

25. Alfred Kazin, *On Native Ground* (New York: Harcourt, Brace, 1942), 338.

26. Maxwell Geismar, *Writers in Crisis: The American Novel Between Two Wars* (Boston: Houghton Mifflin, 1942), 80; Maxwell Geismar, *American Moderns* (New York: Hill and Wang, 1958), 165.

27. Edward Sackville-West, "Books in General "[review of *For Whom the Bell Tolls*], *New Statesman and Nation*, XXI (May 10, 1941), 488.

28. Malcom Cowley, "Nightmare and Ritual in Hemingway," in Weeks (ed.), *Hemingway: A Collection of Critical Essays*, 46.

29. Edmund Wilson, "Hemingway: Gauge of Morale," in McCaffery (ed.), *Ernest Hemingway: The Man and His Work* (New York: World, 1950), 257, 254.

30. "A Transatlantic Interview, 1946," in Robert Bartlett Haas (ed.), *A Primer for the Gradual Understanding of Gertrude Stein* (Los Angeles: Black Sparrow Press, 1971), 21–22.

31. "Selznick Memo," 97–107, *passim*.

32. Thomas, *Selznick*, 286. Note that here Hemingway says that Catherine is twenty-four.

33. Hollis Alpert, "A Second Farewell," *Saturday Review*, XLI (February 1, 1958), 27.

34. Agnes Von Kurowsky was almost this much older than Hemingway when they had their romance.

35. Thomas, *Selznick*, 276–77.

36. "Selznick Memo," 105.

37. *Ibid.*, 98.

38. *Ibid.*, 106.

39. Behlmer (ed.), *Memo*, 443, 461.

40. Hotchner, *Papa Hemingway*, 183.

41. Hemingway to Harvey Breit, October 17, 1954.

42. Mel Gussow, *Don't Say Yes Until I Finish Talking: A Biography of Darryl F. Zanuck* (New York: Pocket Books, 1972), 176.

43. See various descriptions of Duff Twysden in Bertram D. Sarason, *Hemingway and the Sun Set* (Washington, D.C.: Microcard Editions, 1972).

44. Hemingway to Harvey Breit, June 16, 1957.

45. Stanley Kauffmann, *A World On Film* (New York: Harper & Row, 1966), 73, 89.

46. Frederic Hunter, *Hemingway Play*, PBS Hollywood Television Theatre, March, 1976.

47. Richard Schickel, "Marinade," *Time*, April 19, 1976, p. 82.

48. A. E. Hotchner, "The Guns of Hemingway," *True* (September 1971), 48–54.

49. Hemingway to Lillian Ross, August 24, 1950.

50. Jack Kroll, "Poor Papa," *Newsweek*, March 14, 1977, p. 96.

## Notes to Chapter X:
## **The Ernest Hemingway Story**

1. Kurt Singer, *Hemingway: Life and Death of a Giant* (Los Angeles: Holloway House, 1961).

2. Irwin R. Blacker, *Standing On a Drum* (New York: Putnam, 1969).
3. Michael Reynolds, *Hemingway's First War*, 16.
4. Baker, 235.
5. Michael Reynolds, *Hemingway's First War*, pp. 181–219 *passim*.
6. Baker, *Ernest Hemingway*, 289.
7. *U.S. Congressional Record*, CVIII (May 29, 1962), 9456.
8. A. E. Hotchner, "One Thing After Another—The Adaptation," *The Eighth Art* (New York: Holt, Rinehart, Winston, 1962), 86.
9. Philip Young, *Ernest Hemingway* (New York: Rinehart, 1952).
10. Quoted in "Nick Adams Grows Up," *Newsweek*, November 20, 1961, p. 107.
11. "Hemingway Stories For Wald Picture Accents Writer," *Hollywood Reporter*, December 1, 1960, p. 6.
12. Young, *Ernest Hemingway*, 135.
13. "When Papa Was a Boy," *Time*, July 27, 1962, p. 69.
14. Kael, *I Lost It at the Movies*, 223.
15. Marcelline Hemingway Sanford, letter to the *New York Times*, August 12, 1962, p. II, 7. See Marcelline Hemingway Sanford, *At the Hemingway's: A Family Portrait* (Boston: Little, Brown, 1962).
16. "When Papa Was a Boy," 69.
17. *Philadelphia Evening Bulletin*, March 24, 1969, p. 31.
18. Hy Garner, "Hemingway Death Blamed on Shocks," *Memphis Commercial Appeal*, June 23, 1973, p. 23.

APPENDIX A

# Production Credits and Cast Lists for the Hemingway Movies

These production credits and cast lists are copied from the pressbooks for the various Hemingway movies. The studios might offer these lists in different formats and with different headings—"Players" instead of "Cast," for example. The lists have been adapted to the same format for this appendix, but they are given here complete and in the original order.

Pressbooks for three of these movies—*To Have and Have Not, Under My Skin,* and *The Breaking Point*—were not available when this appendix was compiled. The lists for these movies are taken instead from the papers filed by the studios with the Library of Congress at the time the copyright was registered.

Phrases such as "Based on the story by" or "From the novel by" match the original wording. Sometimes Hemingway's name did not appear in the Production Credits. It would have to appear then in the official billing, which is the studio's legal notice of how names must be ordered and arranged, in what relative percentage of letter form size, on advertisements, promotions, theater marquees, and the like.

## A FAREWELL TO ARMS
**Paramount**
**Release Date: December, 1932**
**Running Time: 78 Minutes**

PRODUCTION CREDITS

| | |
|---|---|
| *Produced and Directed by* | Frank Borzage |
| *Screenplay by* | Benjamin Glazer and Oliver H. P. Garrett |
| *From the novel by* | Ernest Hemingway |
| *Photographed by* | Charles Lang |
| | Passed by the National Board of Review |
| | Western Electric Recording System |

CAST

| | |
|---|---|
| *Catherine Barkley* | Helen Hayes |
| *Lieut. Frederic Henry* | Gary Cooper |
| *Major Rinaldi* | Adolphe Menjou |
| *Helen Ferguson* | Mary Philips |
| *The Priest* | Jack LaRue |
| *Head Nurse* | Blanche Friderici |
| *Bonello* | Henry Armetta |
| *Piani* | George Humbert |
| *Manera* | Fred Malatesta |
| *Miss Van Campen* | Mary Forbes |
| *Count Greffi* | Tom Ricketts |
| *Gordoni* | Robert Cauterio |
| *British Major* | Gilbert Emery |

**FOR WHOM THE BELL TOLLS**
**Paramount**
**Release Date: July, 1943**
**Running Time: 170 Minutes**

PRODUCTION CREDITS

| | |
|---|---|
| *Executive Producer* | B. G. DeSylva |
| *Produced and directed by* | Sam Wood |
| *Screenplay by* | Dudley Nichols |
| *From the celebrated novel by* | Ernest Hemingway |
| *Director of Photography* | Ray Rennahan, A.S.C. |
| *Music score by* | Victor Young |
| *Technicolor Color Director* | Natalie Kalmus |
| *Associate* | Morgan Padelford |
| *Special photographic effects* | Gordon Jennings, A.S.C. |
| *Process photography* | Farciot Edouart, A.S.C. |
| *Art Direction* | Hans Dreier and Haldane Douglas |
| *Edited by* | Sherman Todd and John Link |
| *Make up Artist* | Wally Westmore |
| *Sound Recording* | Harold Lewis and Don Johnson |
| *Set Direction* | Bert Granger |
| *Production designed by* | William Cameron Menzies |
| | Western Electric Microphonic Recording |

CAST

| | |
|---|---|
| *Robert Jordan* | Gary Cooper |
| *Maria* | Ingrid Bergman |
| *Pablo* | Akim Tamiroff |
| *Agustin* | Arturo De Cordova |
| *El Sordo* | Joseph Calleia |
| *Pilar* | Katina Paxinou |
| *Anselmo* | Vladimir Sokoloff |
| *Rafael* | Mikhail Rasumny |
| *Fernando* | Fortunio Bonanova |
| *Andres* | Eric Feldary |
| *Primitivo* | Victor Varconi |
| *Joaquin* | Lilo Yarson |
| *Paco* | Alexander Granach |
| *Gustavo* | Adia Kuznetzoff |
| *Ignacio* | Leonid Snegoff |
| *General Golz* | Leo Bulgakov |
| *Lieut. Berrendo* | Duncan Renaldo |
| *Andre Massart* | George Coulouris |
| *Captain Gomez* | Frank Puglia |
| *Colonel Miranda* | Pedro Cordoba |
| *Staff Officer* | Michael Visaroff |
| *Karkov* | Konstantin Shayne |
| *Captain Mora* | Martin Garralaga |
| *The Sniper* | Jean Del Val |
| *Colonel Duval* | Jack Mylong |
| *Kashkin* | Feodor Chaliapin |

**TO HAVE AND HAVE NOT**
**Warner Brothers—First National**
**Release Date: October, 1944**
**Running Time: 100 Minutes**

PRODUCTION CREDITS

| | |
|---|---|
| *Executive Producer* | Jack Warner |
| *Produced and directed by* | Howard Hawks |
| *Screenplay by* | Jules Furthman and William Faulkner |
| *From the novel by* | Ernest Hemingway |
| *Photographed by* | Sid Hickox, A.S.C. |
| *Art Director* | Charles Novi |
| *Sound by* | Oliver S. Garretson |
| *Film Editor* | Christian Nyby |

| | |
|---|---|
| *Special Effects by* | Roy Davidson |
| [*Special Effects*] *Director* | Rex Wimpy, A.S.C. |
| *Set Decorations* | Casey Roberts |
| *Gowns by* | Milo Anderson |
| *Technical Advisor* | Louie Comien |
| *Makeup artist* | Perc Westmore |
| *"How Little We Know":* | |
| *Music by* | Hoagy Carmichael |
| *Lyrics by* | Johnny Mercer |
| *Musical Director* | Leo F. Forbstein |
| *Assistant Director* | Jack Sullivan |
| *Unit Manager* | Chuck Hansen |
| *Unit Publicist* | Bill Rice |

CAST

| | |
|---|---|
| *Morgan* | Humphrey Bogart |
| *Eddie (The Rummy)* | Walter Brennan |
| *Marie* | Lauren Bacall |
| *Helene De Bursac* | Dolores Moran |
| *Cricket* | Hoagy Carmichael |
| *Paul De Bursca* | Walter Molnar |
| *Lieut. Coyo* | Sheldon Leonard |
| *Gerard* | Marcel Dalio |
| *Johnson* | Walter Sande |
| *Capt. Renard* | Dan Seymour |
| *Capt. Renard's Bodyguard* | Aldo Nadi |
| *Beauclerc* | Paul Marion |
| *Mrs. Beauclerc* | Patricia Shay |
| *Bartender* | Pat West |
| *Emil* | Emmet Smith |
| *Horatio* | Sir Lancelot |

## THE KILLERS

**Universal**

**Release Date: August, 1946**

**Running Time: 105 Minutes**

PRODUCTION CREDITS

| | |
|---|---|
| *Directed by* | Robert Siodmak |
| *Produced by* | Mark Hellinger |
| *Screenplay by* | Anthony Veiller |
| *From the story by* | Ernest Hemingway |
| *Director of Photography* | Woody Bredell, A.S.C. |

| | |
|---|---|
| *Assistant to the Producer* | Jules Buck |
| *Film Editor* | Arthur Hilton |
| *Art Direction* | Jack Otterson and Martin Obzina |
| *Director of Sound* | Bernard B. Brown |
| *Technician* | William Hedgcock |
| *Set Decorations* | Russell A. Gausman and E. R. Robinson |
| *Gown supervision* | Vera West |
| *Hair Stylist* | Carmen Dirigo |
| *Director of Make-up* | Jack P. Pierce |
| *Assistant Director* | Melville Shyer |
| *Special Photography* | D. S. Horsley, A.S.C. |
| *Music* | Miklos Rozsa |
| *"The More I Know of Love":* | |
| *Sung by* | Ava Gardner |
| *Lyrics by* | Jack Brooks |
| *Music by* | Miklos Rozsa |

CAST

| | |
|---|---|
| *Swede* | Burt Lancaster |
| *Kitty Collins* | Ava Gardner |
| *Riordan* | Edmond O'Brien |
| *Colfax* | Albert Dekker |
| *Lubinsky* | Sam Levene |
| *Packy* | Charles D. Brown |
| *Kenyon* | Donald McBride |
| *Nick* | Phil Brown |
| *Jake* | John Miljan |
| *Queenie* | Queenie Smith |
| *Joe* | Garry Owen |
| *George* | Harry Hayden |
| *Sam* | Bill Walker |
| *Charleston* | Vince Barnett |
| *Dum Dum* | Jack Lambert |
| *Blinky* | Jeff Corey |
| *Charlie* | Wally Scott |
| *Lilly* | Virginia Christine |
| *Ginny* | Gabrielle Windsor |
| *Man* | Rex Dale |
| The Killers { *Al* | Charles McGraw |
| The Killers { *Max* | William Conrad |

**THE MACOMBER AFFAIR**
**United Artists**
**Release Date: April, 1947**
**Running Time: 89 Minutes**

PRODUCTION CREDITS*

| | |
|---|---|
| *Produced by* | Benedict Bogeaus and Casey Robinson |
| *Directed by* | Zoltan Korda |
| *Screenplay by* | Casey Robinson and Seymour Bennett |
| *Adaptation* | Seymour Bennett and Frank Arnold |
| *Music* | Miklos Rozsa |
| *Photography* | Karl Struss, A.S.C. |
| *Art Director* | Erno Metzner |
| *Make-up* | Otis Malcolm |
| *Sound Technician* | William Lynch |
| *Film Editor* | George Feld and Jack Wheller |
| *Assistant Director* | Joseph Depew |

*Hemingway's name appeared in the official billing:

| | |
|---|---|
| Ernest Hemingway's | 50% |
| "THE MACOMBER AFFAIR" | 100% |

CAST

| | |
|---|---|
| *Robert Wilson* | Gregory Peck |
| *Margaret Macomber* | Joan Bennett |
| *Francis Macomber* | Robert Preston |
| *Captain Smollet* | Reginald Denny |
| *Aimee* | Jean Gillie |

**UNDER MY SKIN**
**Twentieth Century-Fox**
**Release Date: March, 1950**
**Running Time: 86 Minutes**

PRODUCTION CREDITS

| | |
|---|---|
| *Producer* | Casey Robinson |
| *Director* | Jean Negulesco |
| *Screenplay by* | Casey Robinson |
| *From a story by* | Ernest Hemingway |
| *Music* | Daniele Amfitheatrof |

| | |
|---|---|
| *Photography* | Joseph La Shelle |
| *Art* | Lyle Wheeler and Maurice Ransford |
| *Sets* | Thomas Little and Walter M. Scott |
| *Editor* | Dorothy Spencer |
| *Orchestration* | Maurice de Packh and Earle Hagen |
| *Sound* | George Leverett and Harry M. Leonard |
| *Songs* | Alfred Newman Mack Gordon, and Jacques Surmagne |
| *Special effects* | Fred Sersen |

CAST

| | |
|---|---|
| *Dan Butler* | John Garfield |
| *Paule Manet* | Micheline Prelle |
| *Louis Bork* | Luther Adler |
| *Joe* | Orley Lindgren |
| *George Gardner* | Noel Drayton |
| *Maurice* | A. A. Merola |
| *Rico* | Ott George |
| *Max* | Paul Bryar |
| *Henriette* | Ann Codee |
| *Bartender* | Steve Geray |
| *Rigoli* | Joseph Warfield |
| *Doctor* | Eugene Borden |
| *Nurse* | Loulette Sablon |
| *Detective* | Alphonse Martell |
| *Hotel Clerk* | Ernesto Morelli |
| *Express Man* | Jean Del Val |
| *Attendant* | Hans Herbert |
| *Flower Woman* | Esther Zeitlin |
| *Doorman* | Maurice Brierre |
| *Barman* | Gordon Clark |
| *Official* | Frank Arnold |
| *American Mother* | Elizabeth Flournoy |
| *Italian Officer* | Mario Siletti |
| *Porter* | Guy Zanette |
| *Gendarme* | Andre Charise |
| *Drake* | Harry Martin |

## THE BREAKING POINT

**Warner Brothers—First National**
**Release Date: October, 1950**
**Running Time: 97 Minutes**

PRODUCTION CREDITS

| | |
|---|---|
| *Produced by* | Jerry Wald |
| *Directed by* | Michael Curtiz |
| *Screenplay by* | Ranald MacDougall |
| *Based on a story by* | Ernest Hemingway |
| *Photography by* | Ted McCord, A.S.C. |
| *Art Director* | Edward Carrere |
| *Film Editor* | Alan Crosland, Jr. |
| *Sound by* | Leslie G. Hewitt |
| *Dialogue Director* | Norman Stuart |
| *Set Director* | George James Hopkins |
| *Musical Direction* | Ray Heindorf |
| *Second Unit Director* | David C. Gardner |
| *Wardrobe by* | Leah Rhodes |
| *Assistant Director* | Sherry Shourds |

CAST

| | |
|---|---|
| *Harry Morgan* | John Garfield |
| *Leona Charles* | Patricia Neal |
| *Lucy Morgan* | Phyllis Thaxter |
| *Duncan* | Wallace Ford |
| *Wesley Park* | Juano Hernandez |
| *Rogers* | Edmon Ryan |
| *Hannagan* | Ralph Dumke |
| *Danny* | Guy Thomajan |
| *Concho* | William Campbell |
| *Amelia* | Sherry Jackson |
| *Connie* | Donna Jo Boyce |
| *Mr. Sing* | Victor Sen Yung |
| *Macho* | Peter Brocco |
| *Gotch* | John Doucette |
| *Charlie* | James Griffith |

## THE SNOWS OF KILIMANJARO
**Twentieth Century-Fox**
**Release Date: September, 1952**
**Running Time: 117 Minutes**

PRODUCTION CREDITS*

| | |
|---|---|
| *Produced by* | Darryl F. Zanuck |
| *Directed by* | Henry King |
| *Screenplay by* | Casey Robinson |
| *Color by* | Technicolor |
| *Technicolor Color Consultant* | Leonard Doss |
| *Music* | Bernard Herrmann |
| *Director of Photography* | Leon Shamroy, A.S.C. |
| *Art Direction* | Lyle Wheeler and John De Cuir |
| *Set decorations* | Thomas Little and Paul S. Fox |
| *Film Editor* | Barbara McLean, A.C.E. |
| *Wardrobe direction* | Charles Le Maire |
| *Choreography by* | Antonio Triana |
| *Make-up Artist* | Ben Nye |
| *Special photographic effects* | Ray Kellogg |
| *Sound* | Bernard Freericks and Roger Heman |

*Hemingway's name appeared in the billing:

| | |
|---|---|
| Ernest Hemingway's | 50% |
| "THE SNOWS OF KILIMANJARO" | 100% |

CAST

| | |
|---|---|
| *Harry* | Gregory Peck |
| *Helen* | Susan Hayward |
| *Cynthia* | Ava Gardner |
| *Countess Liz* | Hildegarde Neff |
| *Uncle Bill* | Leo G. Carroll |
| *Johnson* | Torin Thatcher |
| *Beatrice* | Ava Norring |
| *Connie* | Helene Stanley |
| *Emile* | Marcel Dalio |
| *Guitarist* | Vincente Gomez |
| *Spanish Dancer* | Richard Allan |
| *Dr. Simmons* | Leonard Carey |
| *Witch Doctor* | Paul Thompson |
| *Molo* | Emmett Smith |
| *Charles* | Victor Wood |
| *American Soldier* | Bert Freed |

| | |
|---|---|
| *Margot* | Agnes Laury |
| *Georgette* | Monique Chantal |
| *Annette* | Janine Grandel |
| *Compton* | John Dodsworth |
| *Harry (age 17)* | Charles Bates |
| *Venduse* | Lisa Ferraday |
| *Princesse* | Maya Van Horn |
| *Marquis* | Ivan Lebedeff |

## THE SUN ALSO RISES
**Twentieth Century-Fox**
**Release Date: August, 1957**
**Running Time: 129 Minutes**

PRODUCTION CREDITS

| | |
|---|---|
| *Produced by* | Darryl F. Zanuck |
| *Directed by* | Henry King |
| *Screenplay by* | Peter Viertel |
| *Based on the novel by* | Ernest Hemingway |
| *Ava Gardner's Wardrobe by* | Fontana Sisters, Rome |
| *Music* | Hugo Friedhofer |
| *Conducted by* | Lionel Newman |
| *Director of Photography* | Leo Tover, A.S.C. |
| *Art Direction* | Lyle R. Wheeler and Mark-Lee Kirk |
| *Set Decorations* | Walter M. Scott, Paul S. Fox, and Jack Stubbs |
| *Film Editor* | William Mace |
| *Executive Wardrobe Designer* | Charles LeMaire |
| *Assistant Director* | Stanley Hough |
| *Make-up by* | Jack Obringer |
| *Hair Styles by* | Gladys Rasmussen, C.H.S. |
| *Sound* | Bernard Freericks and Frank Moran |
| *Orchestration* | Edward B. Powell |
| *Cinemascope lenses by* | Bausch & Lomb |
| *Color by* | Deluxe |
| *Color Consultant* | Leonard Doss |

CAST

| | |
|---|---|
| *Jake Barnes* | Tyrone Power |
| *Lady Brett Ashley* | Ava Gardner |
| *Robert Cohn* | Mel Ferrer |

| | |
|---|---|
| *Mike Campbell* | Errol Flynn |
| *Bill Gorton* | Eddie Albert |
| *Count Mippipopolous* | Gregory Ratoff |
| *Georgette* | Juliette Greco |
| *Zizi* | Marcel Dalio |
| *Doctor* | Henry Daniell |
| *Harris* | Bob Cunningham |
| *The Girl* | Danik Patisson |
| *Romero* | Robert Evans |
| *Mr. Braddock* | Eduardo Noriega |
| *Mrs. Braddock* | Jacqueline Evans |
| *Montoya* | Carlos Muzquiz |
| *Frances* | Rebecca Iturbi |
| *Mgr. Romero* | Carlos David Ortigos |

## A FAREWELL TO ARMS
**The Selznick Studio/Twentieth Century-Fox**
**Release Date: January, 1958**
**Running Time: 150 Minutes**

PRODUCTION CREDITS*

| | |
|---|---|
| *Produced by* | David O. Selznick |
| *Directed by* | Charles Vidor |
| *Screenplay by* | Ben Hecht |
| *Photographed by* | Piero Portalupi, A.I.C., and Oswald Morris, B.S.C. |
| *Music by* | Mario Nascimbene |
| *Conducted by* | Franco Ferrara |
| *Production Designer* | Alfred Junge |
| *Associate* | Gastone Medin |
| *Art Director* | Mario Garbuglia |
| *Costumes and Set Decoration* | Veniero Colasanti and John Moore |
| *Supervising Film Editor* | James E. Newcom, A.C.E. |
| *Film Editors* | Gerard J. Wilson and John M. Foley, A.C.E. |
| *Camera Operators* | Arthur Ibbetson and Idelmo Simonelli |
| *Sound Recording* | Charles Knott |
| *Re-Recording Supervisor* | Murray Spivack |

*Hemingway's name appeared in the billing:
Ernest Hemingway's
"A FAREWELL TO ARMS"

| | |
|---|---|
| *Music Editor* | Audray Granville |
| *Hairstylist* | Larry Germain, C.H.S. |
| *Master Grip* | Morris Rosen |
| *Scenario Assistant* | Lydia Schiller |
| *Executive Production Associates* | Douglas F. Brunger<br>Arthur Fellows<br>Guy Luongo<br>Giorgio Adriani, and<br>J. Walter Daniels |
| *First Assistant Director* | Carlo Lastricati |
| *Script Supervisor* | Eva Monley |
| *Production Assistants* | Alexander Whitelaw and<br>L. Jeffrey Selznick |
| *Casting Director* | Guidarino Guidi |
| *Make-up Artists* | Alberto De Rossi and<br>Gaspare Carboni |
| *Special Effects* | Costel Grozea and<br>Willis Cook |
| *Sound Effects Editors* | Harold McGhan<br>Karl Brandon, and<br>Milton C. Burrow |
| *Property Master* | R. Dudley Holmes |
| *Technical Advisors* | Luigi Barzini, Jr.<br>Prof. Guilio Ferrari, and<br>Lt. Col. Alessandro Paoletti |
| *The producer also wishes gratefully to acknowledge the services of* | Andrew Marton<br>Stephen Grimes, and<br>Peter Newbrook |

CAST

| | |
|---|---|
| *Lt. Frederic Henry* | Rock Hudson |
| *Nurse Catherine Barkley* | Jennifer Jones |
| *Major Alessandro Rinaldi* | Vittorio De Sica |
| *Father Galli* | Alberto Sordi |
| *Bonello* | Kurt Kasznar |
| *Miss Van Campen* | Mercedes McCambridge |
| *Doctor Emerich* | Oscar Homolka |
| *Helen Ferguson* | Elaine Stritch |
| *Passini* | Leopoldo Trieste |
| *Aymo* | Franco Interlenghi |
| *Major Stampi* | Jose Nieto |
| *Captain Bassi* | Georges Brehat |

| | |
|---|---|
| *Nino, the Porter* | Memmo Carotenuto |
| *Boy Scout* | Guido Martufi |
| *Barber* | Umberto Spadaro |
| *Ambulance Driver* | Umberto Sacripanti |
| *Colonel Valentini* | Victor Francen |
| *Red-Headed Nurse* | Joan Shawlee |
| *Officer of The Carabinieri* | Enzo Fiermonte |
| *Arrested Officer* | Alberto D'Amario |
| *1st Carabiniere* | Giacomo Rossi Stuart |
| *2nd Carabiniere* | Carlos Pedersoli |
| *Officer of The Carabiniere* | Alex Revides |
| *The Major (the accuser)* | Peter Meersman |
| *The Captain (the defendant)* | Stephen Garret |
| *Captain at Outpost* | Franco Mancinelli |
| *Medical Lieutenant* | Patrick Crean |
| *Esmeralda* | Ina Centrone |
| *Civilian Doctor* | Guidarino Guidi |
| *Hospital Receptionist* | Diana King |
| *Hairdresser* | Clelia Metania |
| *Lt. Zimmerman* | Eduard Linkers |
| *Mrs. Zimmerman* | Johanna Hofer |
| *Court Martial Colonel* | Luigi Barzini |
| *Race Track Announcer* | Carlo Licari |
| *Woman with Pekingese* | Gemma Bolognesi |
| *Firing Squad Commander* | Angiolo Galassi |
| *First Diner* | Carlo Hintermann |
| *Second Diner* | Tiberio Mitri |
| *Delivery Room Nurse* | Eva Kotthaus |
| *The Anesthetist* | Antonio La Raina |
| *Nurses in Operating Room Gallery* | Michela Ciustiniani<br>Margherita Horowitz |
| *Nurse in Catherine's Room* | Gisella Mathews |
| *Hotel Proprietor* | Vittorio Jannitti |
| *Milan Hotel Clerk* | Peter Illing |
| *Swiss Sergeant* | Sam Levine |

## THE GUN RUNNERS
**Seven Arts/United Artists**
**Release Date: September, 1958**
**Running Time: 83 Minutes**

PRODUCTION CREDITS

| | |
|---|---|
| *Producer* | Clarence Greene |
| *Director* | Don Siegel |
| *Cameraman* | Hal Mohr |
| *Art Director* | Howard Richmond |
| *Sound Recorder* | Harry Alphin |
| *Film Editor* | Chester Schaeffer |
| *Based on a story by* | Ernest Hemingway |
| *Screenplay by* | Daniel Mainwaring and Paul Monash |
| *Composed and Scored by* | Leith Stevens |
| *Songs by* | Joe Lubin |

CAST

| | |
|---|---|
| *Sam Martin* | Audie Murphy |
| *Hanagan* | Eddie Albert |
| *Lucy Martin* | Patricia Owens |
| *Harvey* | Everett Sloane |
| *Eva* | Gita Hall |
| *Buzurki* | Richard Jaeckel |
| *Sy Phillips* | Paul Birch |
| *Arnold* | Jack Elam |

## THE OLD MAN AND THE SEA
**Warner Brothers**
**Release Date: October, 1958**
**Running Time: 89 Minutes**

PRODUCTION CREDITS*

| | |
|---|---|
| *Produced by* | Leland Hayward |
| *Directed by* | John Sturges |
| *Screenplay by* | Peter Viertel |

*Hemingway's name appears in the billing

| | |
|---|---|
| SPENCER TRACY | 100% |
| in | |
| ERNEST HEMINGWAY'S | 100% |
| Pulitzer and Nobel | |
| Prize-Winning Story | 75% |
| "THE OLD MAN AND THE SEA" | 100% |

| | |
|---|---|
| *Director of Photography* | James Wong Howe, A.S.C. |
| *Additional photography by* | Floyd Crosby, A.S.C. and Tom Tutwiler, A.S.C. |
| *Underwater photography by* | Lamar Boren |
| *Film Editor* | Arthur P. Schmidt, A.C.E. |
| *Art Directors* | Art Loel and Edward Carrere |
| *Sound by* | M. A. Merrick |
| *Music composed and directed by* | Dimitri Tiomkin |
| *Set Decorator* | Ralph Hurst |
| *Special effects by* | Arthur S. Rhoads |
| *Make-up Supervisor* | Gordon Bau, S.M.A. |
| *Assistant Director* | Russ Llewellyn |
| *Production Manager* | Gene Bryant |

CAST

| | |
|---|---|
| *The Old Man* | Spencer Tracy |
| *The Boy* | Felipe Pazos |
| *Martin* | Harry Bellaver |

## HEMINGWAY'S ADVENTURES OF A YOUNG MAN

**Twentieth Century-Fox**
**Release Date: July, 1962**
**Running Time: 145 Minutes**

PRODUCTION CREDITS

| | |
|---|---|
| *Produced by* | Jerry Wald |
| *Directed by* | Martin Ritt |
| *Associate Producer* | Peter Nelson |
| *Screenplay by* | A. E. Hotchner |
| *Based on stories by* | Ernest Hemingway |
| *Music composed and conducted by* | Franz Waxman |
| *Director of Photography* | Lee Garmes, A.S.C. |
| *Art Direction* | Jack Martin Smith and Paul Groesse |
| *Set Decorations* | Walter M. Scott and Robert Priestly |
| *Special Photographic Effects* | L. B. Abbott, A.S.C. and Emil Kosa, Jr. |
| *Assistant Director* | Eli Dunn |
| *Film Editor* | Hugh S. Fowler, A.C.E. |
| *Costumes Designed by* | Don Feld |
| *Make-up by* | Ben Nye |

| | |
|---|---|
| *Hair styles by* | Helen Turpin, C.H.S. |
| *Sound* | E. Clayton Ward and Warren B. Delaplain |
| *Italian sequences serviced by* | International Film Service, Rome |
| *Orchestration* | Leonid Raab |
| *Color by* | De Luxe |

CAST

| | |
|---|---|
| *Nick Adams* | Richard Beymer |
| *Carolyn* | Diane Baker |
| *Contessa* | Corinne Calvet |
| *Mr. Turner* | Fred Clark |
| *Billy Campbell* | Dan Dailey |
| *Telegrapher* | James Dunn |
| *Bugs* | Juano Hernandez |
| *Dr. Adams* | Arthur Kennedy |
| *Major Padula* | Ricardo Montalban |
| *Rosana* | Susan Strasberg |
| *Mrs. Adams* | Jessica Tandy |
| *John* | Eli Wallach |
| *Brakeman* | Edward Binns |
| *Ludstrum* | Whit Bissell |
| *Montecito* | Philip Bourneuf |
| *Sig. Griffi* | Tullio Carminati |
| *Eddy Bolton* | Marc Cavell |
| *Mayor* | Charles Fredericks |
| *Joe Boulton* | Simon Oakland |
| *George* | Michael Pollard |
| *The Battler* | Paul Newman |

## THE KILLERS
**Universal**
**Release Date: July, 1964**
**Running Time: 95 Minutes**

PRODUCTION CREDITS*

| | |
|---|---|
| *Produced and Directed by* | Donald Siegel |
| *Screenplay by* | Gene L. Coon |
| *Director of Photography* | Richard L. Rawlings |

*Hemingway's name appeared in the billing:

| | |
|---|---|
| Ernest Hemingway's | 50% |
| "THE KILLERS" | 100% |

| | |
|---|---|
| *Art Directors* | Frank Arrigo and George Chan |
| *Set decorations* | John McCarthy and James S. Redd |
| *Sound* | David H. Moriarty |
| *Technical Advisor* | Hal Brock |
| *Assistant Director* | Milton Feldman |
| *Music* | Johnny Williams |
| *Music supervision* | Stanley Wilson |
| *Costumes by* | Helen Colvig |
| *Film Editor* | Richard Belding |
| *Editorial Department Head* | David J. O'Connell |
| *Make-up* | Bud Westmore |
| *Hair Stylist* | Larry Germain |
| *"Too Little Time":* | |
| *Music by* | Henry Mancini |
| *Lyrics by* | Don Raye |
| *Sung by* | Nancy Wilson |

CAST

| | |
|---|---|
| *Charlie* | Lee Marvin |
| *Shelia Farr* | Angie Dickinson |
| *Johnny North* | John Cassavetes |
| *Lee* | Clu Gulager |
| *Earl Sylvester* | Claude Akins |
| *Mickey* | Norman Fell |
| *Browning* | Ronald Reagan |
| *Miss Watson* | Virginia Christine |
| *Mail Truck Driver* | Don Haggerty |
| *George* | Robert Phillips |
| *Receptionist* | Kathleen O'Malley |
| *Gym Assistant* | Ted Jacques |
| *Mail Truck Guard* | Irvin Mosley |
| *Salesman* | Jimmy Joyce |
| *Maitre D'* | Davis Roberts |
| *Race Marshall* | Hall Brock |
| *Elderly Man* | Burt Mustin |
| *Instructor* | Peter Hobbs |
| *Porter* | John Copage |
| *Steward* | Tyler McVey |
| *Postal Clerk* | Seymour Cassel |
| *Hotel Clerk* | Scott Hale |

**ISLANDS IN THE STREAM**
**Paramount**
**Release Date: March, 1977**
**Running Time: 105 Minutes**

PRODUCTION CREDITS

| | |
|---|---|
| *Directed by* | Franklin J. Schaffner |
| *Produced by* | Peter Bart and Max Palevsky |
| *Screenplay by* | Denne Bart Petitclerc |
| *Based upon the novel by* | Ernest Hemingway |
| *Director of Photography* | Fred J. Koenekamp, A.S.C. |
| *Music* | Jerry Goldsmith |
| *Associate Producer* | Ken Wales |
| *Production designed by* | William J. Creber |
| *Film Editor* | Robert Swink, A.C.E. |
| *Casting by* | Mike Fenton and Jane Feinberg |
| *Unit Production Manager* | Francisco Day |
| *Assistant Director* | Kurt Neumann |
| *Second Assistant Director* | Lorin B. Salob |
| *Set Decorator* | Raphael Bretton |
| *Special effects* | Alex Weldon |
| *Construction Coordinator* | Don Nobles |
| *Camera Operator* | Tom Laughridge |
| *Sound Mixer* | Darin Knight |
| *Re-Recording Mixer* | John K. Wilkinson |
| *Script Supervisor* | Marshall Schlom |
| *Make-up* | Del Acevedo and Rick Sharp |
| *Wardrobe* | Tony Scarano |
| *Gaffer* | Gene Stout |
| *Key Grip* | John Murray |
| *Hair Stylist* | Lola Skip McNalley |
| *Property Master* | Ernie Sawyers, Sr. |
| *Sound effects editor* | Howard Beals |
| *Music Editor* | June Edgerton |
| *Orchestrations* | Arthur Morton |
| *Services by* | Connaught Productions |
| *SEA camera stabilization by* | Tyler Camera Systems Gyro Platform |
| *Filmed in* | Panavision |
| *Color by* | Metrocolor |

CAST

| | |
|---|---|
| *Thomas Husdon* | George C. Scott |
| *Eddy* | David Hemmings |
| *Captain Ralph* | Gilbert Roland |
| *Lil* | Susan Tyrrell |
| *Willy* | Richard Evans |
| *Audrey* | Claire Bloom |
| *Joseph* | Julius Harris |
| *Tom* | Hart Bochner |
| *Andrew* | Brad Savage |
| *David* | Michael-James Wixted |
| *Helga Ziegner* | Hildy Brooks |
| *Andrea* | Jessica Rains |
| *Herr Ziegner* | Walter Friedel |
| *Constable* | Charles Lampkin |

APPENDIX B

## Hemingway Movie Scripts

The following is a partial list of scripts, in various states, which were used in the preparation of this book.

1. A FAREWELL TO ARMS, Paramount, 1932.
   Screenplay by Benjamin Glazer and Oliver H. P. Garrett
   A. First Script, June 22, 1932, [211 pp.].
   B. Release Dialogue Script [with Alternate Ending], December 7, 1932, 105 pp.
2. FOR WHOM THE BELL TOLLS, Paramount, 1943.
   Screenplay by Dudley Nichols
   A. [First] Screenplay by Louis Bromfield, October 10, 1941, 188 pp.
   B. Revised Final, July 20, 1942, 202 pp.
   C. [Release Dialogue, 1943, 166 pp.]
3. TO HAVE AND HAVE NOT, Warner Brothers—First National, 1944.
   Screenplay by Jules Furthman and William Faulkner
   A. Second Revised Final, February 26, 1944, with revisions dated March 3, 13, 27, April 22. 141 pp.
4. THE KILLERS, Universal, 1946.
   Screenplay by Anthony Veiller
   A. [Release Dialogue and Continuity], April 3, 1946, 135 pp.
5. UNDER MY SKIN, Twentieth Century-Fox, 1950.
   Screenplay by Casey Robinson
   A. "The Big Fall" [original title], Shooting Final, September 2, 1949, 157 pp. with interleaved revisions.
6. THE BREAKING POINT, Warner Brothers—First National, 1950.
   Screenplay by Ranald MacDougall
   A. Second Revised Final, March 25, 1950, with revisions dated April 10, 17, 18, 29, and May 1, 129 pp. with interleaved revisions.
7. THE SNOWS OF KILIMANJARO, Twentieth Century-Fox, 1952.
   Screenplay by Casey Robinson
   A. Third Revised Shooting Final, January 17, 1952, 131 pp. with interleaved revisions.
8. THE SUN ALSO RISES, Twentieth Century-Fox, 1957.
   Screenplay by Peter Viertel
   A. Final Script, February 20, 1957, 142 pp. with interleaved revisions.
9. A FAREWELL TO ARMS, The Selznick Studio—Twentieth Century-Fox, 1958. Screenplay by Ben Hecht
   A. [Undated Release Dialogue, 1958], 173 pp.
10. THE GUN RUNNERS, Seven Arts/United Artists, 1958.
    Screenplay by Daniel Mainwaring

A. Final Revised Script, January 24, 1958, 97 pp.

11. THE OLD MAN AND THE SEA, Warner Brothers, 1958.
Screenplay by Peter Viertel
A. Final Continuity, August 28, 1957, 98 pp.

12. HEMINGWAY'S ADVENTURES OF A YOUNG MAN, Twentieth Century-Fox, 1962.
Screenplay by A.E. Hotchner
A. Final, September 5, 1961, 171 pp.
B. Revised Final, October 17, 1961, completed October 23, 1961, 167 pp. with interleaved revisions.

13. THE KILLERS, Universal, 1964.
Screenplay by Gene L. Coon
A. Continuity and Dialogue, April 13, 1964, 104 pp.

14. ISLANDS IN THE STREAM, Paramount, 1977.
Screenplay by Denne Bart Petitclerc
A. [Undated Release Dialogue], 126 pp.

# Index